Drugs, Sport and the Law

by

Antonio (Tony) BUTI

BPE (Hons), Dip Ed, MIR (W Aust), LLB (Hons) (ANU)
Senior Lecturer in Law, Murdoch University
JLV/Louis St John Johnson Fellow in Aboriginal Legal Issues and
Public Policy and the Director of the Asia-Pacific Centre for Human Rights and the
Prevention of Ethnic Conflict at the School of Law, Murdoch University
Barrister and Solicitor of the Supreme Court of Western Australia
and the High Court of Australia
Director of Club Athlete (Professional Sports Management).

and

Saul FRIDMAN

LLB (Western Ont), BCL (Oxon)
Senior Lecturer in Law, University of Sydney
Barrister and Solicitor, ACT and Ontario
Solicitor, England and Wales.

Saul dedicates the book to Ellis Blaskey (Saul's grandpa, great Sheffield Wednesday supporter, athlete and human being).

Tony dedicates the book to Mandy, his beautiful wife and fantastic mother to Alkira, Paris and Tennessee.

SCRIBBLERS PUBLISHING

Published by:
Scribblers Publishing
PO Box 501, Mudgeeraba
Queensland 4213
Australia

National Library of Australia
Cataloguing-in-Publication entry

Fridman, Saul, 1960-
Drugs, Sport and the Law

Includes Index
ISBN 0 9586727 8 4

1. Sports - Law and legislation - Australia. 2. Athletes - Drug use - Australia.
3. Drugs - Law and legislation - Australia. I. Buti, Antonio.

344.94099

© *Saul Fridman and Antonio Buti* 2001

This publication is copyright. Subject to the terms of the Copyright Act, no part of this publication may be reproduced or stored in a retrieval system or copied or transmitted in any way or used or adapted for film or other media without prior written permission of the copyright holders.

Purchases: Copies of this book can be purchased for Aust $28.50 each (plus $5 postage) from *Scribblers Publishing,* PO Box 501, Mudgeeraba, Qld, Australia 4213. Fax/Phone: +61 7 55 25 2528

Printed and bound in Adelaide by Hyde Park Press
Typeset by Jennifer Corkery and Elaine Maloney

CONTENTS

Chapter 1
Introduction 9

Chapter 2
Organisation of Sporting Activity 9
    Problem One: Jurisdiction 9
    The Legal Framework 11
    Olympic sports: the IOC and affiliated organisations 11
    International Organisation of Sports: Prominence of the IOC 13
    Non-Olympic Sports 17
    Organisation of Sports in Australia 18
    Federal Controls 18
    The Increasing Dominance of Drug Testing by ASDA 22
    The Impact of State and Territory Organisations 23
    Conclusion 23
    Professional Sporting Activity in Australia 24

Chapter 3
History of Doping and Doping Control 27
    Introduction 27
    Development of Drug Testing 30
    Olympic International Committee: Medical Code and
        Accreditation for Laboratories 37
    Australian Developments 39

Chapter 4
Doping Policy 45
    The Policy Debate: What Drugs Should Be Included? 47
    The Ethical Basis of Sport 50
    Sports Ethics 52
    Health and Safety of the Athlete and the Public 57
    Public Image and Confidence 60
    Discouraging Illegal Activity Generally 60
    Conclusions 61

Chapter 5
The Testing Authorities 65
    Introduction 65
    The ASDA Legislation 65
    Athletes and "Technicalities" 66
    Other Rules and Regulations 74
    Inconsistent Policies 75
    The International Position 75
    The Australian Position 82
    The Athletes' Legal Position in Australia 83

Chapter 6
Dispute Resolution in Sports: Appeals and Arbitration 85
    Litigation and Alternative Dispute Resolution 88
    Litigation: the Traditional Way of Resolving Disputes 88
    Alternatives to Litigation: Alternative Dispute Resolution (ADR) 89
    Mediation 96
    The Court of Arbitration for Sport 97
    The National Sports Dispute Centre 100

Chapter 7
Legal Challenges to Drug Testing 103
    Introduction 103
    Failure to Follow Appropriate Testing Protocol 103
    Lack of Procedural Fairness 107
    Defects with the Evidence 110
    Absence of Intent: The "Inadvertency" Defence 113
    Restraint of Trade 125
    Possible Criminal Penalties 135

Chapter 8
The Future 145
    The Banned Substances 145
    The CAS and the IFs 146
    The Inadvertent Breach 148
    WADA, the IOC and Sponsors 148
    Sanctions and Restraint of Trade 149
    Consent to Drug Testing 150

List of Abbreviations 151
Index 153

ACKNOWLEDGEMENTS

Funding:

McCredie Trust
UNSW Law Foundation
ANUTECH
Sydney University Law School
ARC
ASDA (particularly Natalie Howson, Steve Richards, Kerry Knowler)
School of Law, Murdoch University.

Individual contributions:

Nikki Cable, Andrew Berger, Josh Brian, Emma Yarrow, Kimberley Moldaver, Carolyn Vivian, Kate Eastoe, Hayden Opie, Jim Parry, Chris Holt (The Federation Press) for his counsel and patience, Bernard Gross QC, Franklin Gaffeney, Arran Gerrard, Weeliem Seah, Hon Michael Beloff QC, Mandy Buti for her support and holding the fort together while I have been in Sydney, Rod Austin (from the AFL), Elouise Dellit for assisting with the index and table of contents.

Dean, Teresa and Erzo Capobianco for their time, information and supply of documentation re: Capobianco case.

Firms:

Ebsworth & Ebsworth (Eugenie Buckley)
Browne and Co
Doyle and Co.

FOREWORD

The newly elected President of the International Committee ("IOC") Jacques Rogge said in his first public statement, *"The priority for the Olympic movement is the fight against doping"*. The complexities of the strategy involved in such a battle are vividly exposed in this newest contribution to the expanding literature on drugs and sport. Although Sydney was for a brief, glorious and unforgettable moment, the focus of attention of a world sporting community ranging from the most golden of champions to the telewatching couch potato, it is the particular Australian perspective which gives novelty and bite to the book. Australia has provided one of the two non-Swiss outposts of the Court of Arbitration for Sport ("CASS") and this has generated a volume of case law arising out of antipodean disputes. Moreover, Robert Ellicott QC, former Attorney-General, is one of a sextet of judges of the tribunal of the International Athletic Federation ("IAAF"), and his determinations also provide one of the many threads of this analysis.

The mention of two international tribunals illustrates the proposition that the battle against substance abuse takes place on a minefield. Which bodies have jurisdiction, over what, and with what priority presents to the sports lawyer issues as complex as any in international commercial litigation. The authors properly grapple with this issue at the outset.

There are two other prime subjects for consideration. The first is a question of fact - how large is the problem? Some reputable observers of the sports scene cynically – or, depending on one's point of view, realistically - believe that the pure athlete is a figment of imagination or a fifties retread; others that a small handful of malefactors is unfairly giving world sports a bad name. The second is a question of judgment - what is the solution to the problem, whatever its dimension may be? Should resources be concentrated on pursuing disciplinary sanctions against alleged rule breakers, in the light of the time and expense involved, the difficulties of obtaining convictions, the uncertain jurisprudence as to the compatibility of strict liability offences with modern concepts of fair trials and human rights (not to speak of questions as to its inherent equity), or should the laws against the taking of performance enhanced substances be abandoned, leaving it to the market and morality to decide down which route athletes choose to travel? This book may not supply definitive answers to these and other questions, but it pithily, yet prudently, supplies the material from which readers can make their own judgments with a wealth of cogently considered case law and ample reference to the public and published literature. No serious sports lawyer or administrator could regard the book as other than a good investment.

Blackstone Chambers THE HONOURABLE MICHAEL J BELOFF QC
Blackstone House   Master of the Bench of Gray's Inn
Temple   Member of the Court of Arbitration for Sport
London EC4Y 9BW   Judge of the Court of Appeal of Jersey and
                            Guernsey

CHAPTER 1

INTRODUCTION

Like it or not, lawyers have become an integral part of most activity, including sport. The reasons for this have more to do with the commercialism of sport and the introduction of complicated rules and policies than the avarice of the legal profession, though given the huge commercial stakes involved in many cases, avarice must surely motivate some. Needless to say, the suits of the legal profession have now clearly taken their place alongside the athletes. Properly understood, the role of the legal profession should be to clarify the formulation and application of policy, rather than to obfuscate and undermine the same policy through use of "technicalities". Of course, just as one man's terrorist is another's freedom fighter, so a technicality to one is a vital point of legal or moral principle to another.

One of the most frequently misquoted literary references of all time must surely be the line: "The first thing we do let's kill all the lawyers..."[1]. The reference is not, as most mistakenly believe, based on hatred of the legal profession, but rather, if you like, a kind of basic respect. Shakespeare's character was referring to the important role lawyers play in preserving the status quo, as the elimination of lawyers was an instinctive first step towards dictatorial rule.

When it comes to drugs in sport, the legal profession has a similarly important role to play. Many decry the use of drugs by our athletes. There are, as we

---

1 2 Henry IV, Act 4, Scene 1.

explore in Chapter Four of this book, numerous arguments underpinning the policy of proscribing "drug" use. However, it is important to separate the "emotive" argument, so as to arrive at a policy that is capable of being implemented in a consistent and equitable manner. A major complication is the international scope of sporting activity and the multitude of organisations with jurisdiction over the athletes and sporting administrators (see Chapter Two).

As we were writing this book, we learned of the tragic death of former American sprinter, Florence Griffith Joyner. The coroner confirmed her death from heart failure, raising the connection between her untimely death and possible steroid use.[2] The ensuing debate led to further calls for increased efforts to control drug use in sport. This book is about those efforts and the legal problems they must overcome, as well as the need to ensure that these efforts are based on a sound and defensible policy.

Drugs are not new to sports. For centuries, athletes have been making use of any advantage available to achieve their goals. However, what has definitely changed is the environment within which sporting activity takes place.

The industrial revolution in the first half of the nineteenth century resulted in the advent of labour saving machinery which provided working people with the opportunity to seek leisure time activities. There was a standardisation of leisure time and activities. We can trace the origins of many sporting organisations and codes to this period.

The last half of the twentieth century has seen another transformation in the world of sport. Sport is no longer simply a leisure time activity. It is an industry: or if you prefer, a business. We could argue that sport has always been a business but the rate of commercialism of sport increased significantly after 1980.

This increased commercialisation and the availability of substantial rewards (in both financial and non-financial terms) to athletes have certainly led to an increased incentive to succeed. Furthermore, success is measured in terms of gold medals, world records and win/lose statistics. Merely participating, even at a high level, is not sufficient for most.

---

2 "Drug cloud hangs over death of golden girl", *The West Australian,* 23 September 1998 at 9.

INTRODUCTION

With these incentives, it is hardly surprising that athletes seek to use whatever means they can to make the grade. At the elite level, it is safe to assume that most athletes are gifted, well-trained and well-equipped. The margin between first and 10th in many competitions is minute. It is rare to find one athlete or team which, at the elite level, is head and shoulders above the rest. Therefore, it should not come as a surprise that there is a ready market for substances which promise an edge to the athlete.

So much for the athletes. Clearly athletes and those who support, coach, guide and derive their income from them are similarly motivated. But why is there this concern about drug use?

There are many reasons, which we shall explore in this book, but one worth focusing on is the interests of the spectating public. It seems clear that there is a general public distaste for those who cheat. And drug use is considered cheating. The public thirsts for athletic success. Athletic success, particularly at the international level, captures the imagination and interest, not to mention income, of the public. Hundreds of thousands cheered Australia's successful Olympic athletes in parades around the country in 2000. Similar celebrations occur whenever a team or individual celebrates a great victory. Sporting prowess has become a source of national pride. However, it seems that, despite the public demand for success, there is no support for success achieved by "illegitimate" methods. Drug use is particularly scorned, perhaps as a result of the never ending "war on drugs" conducted by many western governments. The public wants "clean" sport. Sport must, it is assumed, exemplify the traditional values of fair play, honesty and mateship. Drug use threatens this.

Australia's National Rugby League (NRL) has been rocked by numerous positive drug tests. This has led to expressions of concern by League officials that such drug tests not only leave fans disillusioned, but also have a debilitating effect on the game's supporter base. In the words of the chief executive of the NRL: "We want the mums and dads to be able to see that in our game success is built on hard work and commitment".[3] To some, the best response to the doping scandals in the NRL would be for the League to stop testing, thus ensuring that the "mums and dads" won't get disillusioned! And steroid use does not eliminate the need for hard work and commitment by the athlete.

---

3 "Drug Scandal Fails Fans' Big Test", *The Australian* 29 June 1998 at 30.

3

Sporting administrators appear to have concluded there is broad public support for drug testing. For example, the NRL official quoted above added: "We've got the policy in place to handle this and we're obviously taking a very strong stance against drugs".[4]

Instituting a strong anti-drug policy may be one thing, but ensuring that it works within the limits of a given legal system is another. If a substantial reason for the institution of a drug policy is the protection of the image of the sport, then to ensure that public perception of the sport improves in the wake of revelations of positive drug tests, correct and appropriate penalties must be handed out once the positive test is confirmed. Of course, a policy of drug testing creates the doping scandals. There would be no "public" scandal if athletes were not tested.

Potential damage to a sport is even greater where there is fear that doping is systematic or even state-controlled. In recent years the sporting world has had to deal with allegations of systematic doping instituted by the Chinese swimmers and United States' track and field athletes. Fallout from the collapse of the German Democratic Republic has included revelations of systematic doping of representative athletes and has led to criminal prosecution of those involved. Although western countries deplored the systematic doping of eastern bloc countries, they were not hesitant in hiring coaches from the former communist regimes. Who can forget the "Arbeit affair?" Athletics Australia rescinded its agreement to employ Ekkart Arbeit (a former East German coach) after it was revealed that Arbeit was involved in the doping of athletes. Yes, doping of athletes is not restricted to the former communist eastern bloc countries or China. The revelations of organised doping by a number of the top teams during the 1998 Tour de France demonstrates that.

This strong desire to maintain a sport's clean image ensures that mandatory drug testing of athletes is acceptable to most. More importantly, the belief by sporting administrators that the public demands clean sport ensures that organisers and administrators have an incentive to co-operate with government in this area. Of course, there are exceptions. In some cases a particular sport's activity may be outside the reach of government or the many international organisations governing sport. Here, those who govern the particular sport are free to make decisions concerning their sport's drug policy

---

4 Ibid.

with their own sport's interest in mind. An example is Australian Rules Football. This sport is not an Olympic sport. The premier professional league is self-funded, with very little (if any) reliance on funds provided by either federal or state government. Therefore, the League (AFL) is free to adopt whatever doping policy it wishes, without being subject to significant pressure from international governing authorities or domestic politicians. Notwithstanding this, however, an AFL player who tested positive to steroid use, Justin Charles, was called to appear before a drugs tribunal by the Australian Olympic Committee. This was despite the fact that Australian Rules Football is not an Olympic sport. Charles had previously had some involvement in baseball, which is an Olympic sport. Compounding the problem, and the confusion generated by the athlete having to confront two separate disciplinary proceedings, was the fact that the AFL and the Australian Olympic Committee applied different penalties for the same offence.

Arguably, the motivating force behind the doping policies of the AFL is a desire to maintain public interest in the sport. Presumably, if AFL supporters began to believe that the sport was rife with drug use, then attendance figures would decline. Interest in general would also decline and the sport would suffer.

It is difficult to provide empirical evidence to substantiate such an analysis. A case in point is the NRL. Attendances at NRL games declined in 1998. Given the stated views of the NRL chief executive, one might well conclude that this decline was due to the public's concern over drug use. However, this surely was not the case. Concerns over doping may have had marginal effect, but the decline in attendances was the result of the destabilising effect that two years of litigation and reorganisation has had on the league, following the attempt by Rupert Murdoch to establish a parallel league (Superleague).

What this all adds up to is that sporting organisations have adopted doping policies, there is substantial government money being expended on sport, and there are numerous government agencies with an interest in ensuring that sporting organisations adopt and apply fair doping policies. This concern is of importance to the Australian Sports Commission and the Australian Olympic Committee, whose roles are discussed in Chapter Two of this book. Another agency of importance in Australia is the Australian Sports Drug Agency, whose task it is to conduct drug testing on athletes. This organisation is also discussed in both Chapters Two and Five.

Needless to say, the advent of mandatory drug testing in sport has raised a number of important legal and political questions. The last several years have seen a number of very highly publicised disputes following positive drug tests of elite athletes. These disputes have revealed a number of concerns and difficulties.

1. Athletes are often unaware of their obligations. This has led to confusion surrounding the appropriateness of imposing penalties, as evidenced by the positive drug test of Australian swimmer Samantha Riley, as well as the numerous instances of athletes worldwide testing positive to clembuterol[5] or other stimulants commonly prescribed for asthmatics.[6]

2. Athletes and their advisors may also be unaware of their rights in relation to drug testing.

3. Administrators sometimes do not appreciate the importance of procedure and fairness when administering doping policies. Even during the Olympic Games, this presents such a problem that a team of professional arbitrators is on call to resolve disputes. Such was the case when, at the 1998 Winter Olympic Games, Canadian snowboarder, Ross Rebagliati was initially disqualified, having won a gold medal, for testing positive to cannibis. The Court of Arbitration for Sport eventually overruled the decision of the IOC to strip Rebagliati of his medal, following an appeal by the Canadian Olympic Association. The reasons for this decision centred on the absence of any agreement between the IOC and the International Ski Federation that marijuana should be treated as a banned substance.[7]

---

5 Two British weightlifters, Andrew Saxton and Andrew Davies were sent home from the 1992 Barcelona Olympics for testing positive to this substance. Both later averred that they were using the substance for medical reasons associated with asthma and their bans were later overturned. Unfortunately, the appeal came too late to prevent their being excluded from the Barcelona Summer Olympic Games. E Grayson, "Drugs, Sport and the Olympics" (1992) 142 *New Law Journal* 1171.

6 Canadian rower Silken Laumann was ultimately reinstated to international competion (though her medals were not returned to her) after initially failing a doping test following her use of "Benadryl", which contained the banned stimulant pseudoephedrine. Laumann had failed a drug test at the 1995 Pan American Games after having won the gold medal in the quadruple sculls. "Laumann cleared in 'fairy tale ending'", *Toronto Star*, 8 April 1995, E1.

7 Marijuana is, however, a "restricted" substance, according to the IOC Medical Code. In this class of substances, IOC officials may test for the substance, but ultimately the imposition of sanctions depends on agreement with the relevant international sports federation. The IOC rules are discussed further in Chapter 7.

4. There is inconsistency in penalties for drug use, leading to confusion amongst both athletes and the general public about the appropriate sanction to be applied. This also leads to the argument that a penalty may be unreasonable and therefore in restraint of trade (discussed in Chapter 7). This argument has been accepted by one Australian Court.[8]

5. There is disagreement about the extent to which drug use needs to be intentional in order to attract a penalty. Underlying disagreement about whether "inadvertent" doping ought to be penalised undoubtedly leads to inconsistent results: one athlete escapes penalty on the basis that she took a tablet given to her by her coach; another is stripped of her gold medals for essentially the same offence. This problem is discussed in Chapter Seven.

These are only a few of the issues that we explore in this book. We intend to describe accurately the manner in which doping policies are implemented in Australia and, to some extent, worldwide. In so doing, we find it necessary to provide background about the nature and extent of doping activity and about the manner in which sporting activity is organised (Chapters 2 and 3). We will then analyse many of the doping cases to provide the reader with a clear view of the nature of the problems often encountered in drug testing.

As procedural issues arise with great frequency, and as there is expressed concern about the need to avoid protracted legal disputes, it is equally important to consider the means provided by the international sporting community for the processing of these disputes. Accordingly, we discuss the system in place for the arbitration of sporting disputes in Chapter Six.

We hope that this book will serve as a useful reference for those whose lives are taken up with sporting activity, as well as for those seeking a concise explanation of what amounts to a very complex web of rules. The book should be of use to athletes, administrators, coaches and those involved in policy formation in this area. We hope lawyers, too, will find much that is of both interest and use in these pages.

---

8 Cyclist Bill Robertson argued successfully that the national federation's two year ban was in restraint of trade as it was greater than that imposed by the relevant international federation: see *Robertson v Australian Professional Cycling Council Inc,* unreported, Supreme Court of New South Wales, 10 September, 1992.

Finally, we intend to ask questions about those rules and the policies which they seek to implement (Chapter Four).

The law in this area is subject to rapid and frequent change. The task of writing this book has been arduous, often delayed by the desire to ensure that it is both up-to-date as well as enduring. Unfortunately, this is a problem shared by all who attempt to write legal treatises, even more so where the law involved is a combination of statutes, decided cases and policies promulgated by non-government organisations. Accordingly, we endeavour to state the law as it was on 1 July, 2001.

Antonio (Tony) Buti
Saul Fridman

Dominion Day, 2001

CHAPTER 2

ORGANISATION OF SPORTING ACTIVITY

There is no comprehensive organisation with overall control of sport in Australia. Rather, there are several distinct areas of sporting activity, each with varied links to different institutions.

In a book concerned with drug testing, it is important to outline the organisational framework of sport. Issues often arise concerning which rules apply and which organisation or tribunal has jurisdiction over an athlete.

Problem One: Jurisdiction

The first key problem is the jurisdiction of the organisation, namely, its capacity to impose and enforce its rules on athletes.

> **O'DAVIS**
>
> When Newcastle Knights rugby league player Robbie O'Davis tested positive to recombinant erythropoietin (rEPO), it was discovered that the newly constituted National Rugby League lacked the jurisdiction to impose any sanction as it had not properly bound players to abide by its rules and follow directions of its disciplinary tribunal.

Technical though this may be to the average non-lawyer, to the athlete and the sporting organisation, this "technical" issue is crucial. It is essential that the organisation ensure that it has the agreement of athletes to follow a certain set of rules and abide by decisions of a particular body.

Problem Two: Inconsistency

The second problem created by the irregular organisational framework is inconsistency of rules and policies. Determining the appropriate rules to apply can be crucial. An example of this is in cases of "therapeutic use".

> **LYNCH**
>
> Alistair Lynch, an Australian Football League (AFL) player with the Brisbane Lions, was the subject of a disciplinary hearing in respect of his use of DHEA, a banned anabolic steroid. Lynch was ultimately cleared of any wrongdoing on account of his reliance on advice provided by the Australian Sports Drug Agency (ASDA). However, his attempt to obtain AFL approval for the therapeutic use of a banned anabolic steroid was ultimately rejected. Lynch argued that the purpose for which he administered the substance in question was therapeutic (he claimed to be suffering from chronic fatigue syndrome). Had he been subject to the doping policy of the Australian Sports Commission (ASC), he might have been exempted from the definition of a doping offence.[1] However, the AFL does not follow the ASC Doping Policy and therefore administers its own rules.

---

1 According to the then football manager of the Australian Football League (AFL), Ian Collins, the use of an anabolic steroid is prohibited, even when for therapeutic purposes: see "Lynch cleared but may quit", *The Australian,* 26 May 1998. Presumably, Collins was referring to the AFL's policy. The ASC Doping Policy does contain a provision dealing with therapeutic use. Detection of a prohibited substance will not constitute a doping offence if the athlete's use of the substance is for a "therapeutic" purpose (para 3.1). A "therapeutic purpose" is defined (para 3.4) as follows: "A person uses a prohibited substance for a therapeutic purpose if:
(a) the person had written approval prior to the testing from a recognised medical authority for the therapeutic use of the prohibited substance;
(b) the level of the prohibited substance in the sample is consistent with the approved therapeutic use; and
(c) the therapeutic use of the prohibited substance is not inconsistent with the [relevant International Federation] rules.
The policy does not define "recognised medical authority". Lynch claimed to have been advised by the Australian Sports Drug Agency that the substance he was using (dehydroepiandrosterone or DHEA) was not specifically banned under the IOC *Medical Code.* Lynch was refused an

Such differences in rules can have a significant impact on the severity of penalties imposed on athletes for breaches. What at first appears to the uninitiated to be inconsistent application of the law is usually explained by the fact that different organisations often apply different rules. For example, suspended Newcastle Knights NRL players received suspensions of 22 weeks for steroid use. Had the ASC Doping Policy been applied, those individuals would have been subject to a two year suspension.

The Legal Framework

As a general rule, the organisational aspects of sporting activity can be divided up into Olympic sports, which come under the umbrella of the IOC and its affiliated organisations and non-Olympic sports, which are organised locally, nationally and internationally.

No single regulatory model applies. Likewise, there is no single set of rules (other than those rules derived from the Olympic Charter) applying across the board. This is one reason for the sometimes confusing inconsistency in decision making in doping cases. Even where two sports are both part of the Olympic movement, it is still possible for inconsistency to arise.

Olympic sports: the IOC and Affiliated Organisations

REBAGLIATI

When Ross Rebagliati, a Canadian Olympic snowboarder, tested positive to marijuana use at the 1998 Nagano Winter Olympics, it

---

exemption from any prohibition against use of this substance by the AFL authorities. He maintains that without such exemption and a consequent ability to use DHEA to combat Chronic Fatigue Syndrome his athletic career will end. Although Lynch continues to play, the matter of his eligibility for an exemption has still not been finally resolved. However, had Lynch been subject to the ASC Doping Policy, he might have been able to continue to use DHEA, confident of an ability to escape the umbrella of a "doping offence" on account of therapeutic use.
Interestingly enough, under the Disability Discrimination Act 1996 (Cth), sufferers of Chronic Fatigue Syndrome would clearly qualify as persons with a disability. Lynch might be able to argue that he is the subject of indirect discrimination on account of the differential effect that the prohibition (even for therapeutic use) has on him.
This case (discussed further below in Chapter 7) highlights the need to standardise the rules of the various organisations governing sport.
Since this controversial episode, the AFL has changed its doping policy to provide a means by which players can seek prior approval for therapeutic use of prohibited substances.

was unclear what sanction should or would be imposed. First of all, marijuana was not listed as a prohibited substance under the IOC Medical Code.[2]

Secondly, while the FIS (International Skiing Federation), which governs snowboarding, provides under its rules that concentrations of marijuana above a certain level (15 nanograms per millilitre) can lead to imposition of sanctions, opinions were expressed that snowboarding did not fall within the jurisdiction of the FIS. Indeed, within Canada, snowboarding is governed by the Canadian Snowboarding Federation and not the Canadian Skiing Federation. The IOC's original decision to disqualify Rebagliati was based on the absence of any agreement between the FIS and the IOC to permit the use of marijuana.

In the final analysis, Rebagliati's medal was restored and the IOC's initial decision was overturned by the CAS "ad hoc panel" which attends every Olympic Games (see Chapter 6). A compelling argument seemed to be that the Drug Formulary Guide, distributed

---

2 At 31 January 1998 the IOC *Medical Code* provided that marijuana was a class of drug "subject to certain restrictions". The specific entry in the Code for marijuana provided: "In agreement with the International Sports Federations and the responsible authorities, tests may be conducted for cannabinoids (eg Marijuana, Hashish). The results may lead to sanctions."
In practice, what this means is that where the rules of the relevant International Federation (IF) provide for imposition of sanctions for use of marijuana, then sanctions will be imposed where appropriate under the relevant rules. This leads to some degree of uncertainty.
In May 1998, the IOC indicated informally that the status of marijuana as a prohibited substance was under review. A conference under the auspices of the IOC was conducted early in 1999 to discuss, amongst other things, reform of the IOC *Medical Code* and the establishing of an independent IOC drug testing regime. This conference was substantially the result of concern expressed over remarks attributed to Jan Antonio Samaranch, President of the IOC, suggesting that restrictions against drug use should be eased. Samaranch was quoted as saying that the number of banned drugs should be drastically reduced so as to permit the use of performance enhancing drugs where they did not damage an athlete's health. It is unclear what effect such a policy, if adopted, would have on testing for marijuana: see "Games Drugs Row Boils Over", *The Sydney Morning Herald,* 29 July 1998 at 20. The IOC has since added marijuana to the list of banned substances.
The Australian Olympic Committee's (AOC) response was to present a "10 point plan" to reinvigorate IOC leadership against doping in sport at an international drugs summit in Lausanne on 20 August 1998, which operated as a prelude to the 1999 conference: see "Fine the Cheats, Say Australian Olympic Chiefs", *The Sydney Morning Herald,* 7 August 1998 at 38. The World Anti-Doping Authority (WADA) is the outcome of the conference.

by the Nagano Organising Committee, did not list marijuana as a prohibited substance, but as a "substance to be used cautiously".[3]

The IOC is presently working to establish a uniform regime for doping in sport. This effort commenced in 1994 and the World Conference on Doping in Sport took place in February 1999 in Lausanne.[4] The aim of the Conference was

> to discuss and adopt concrete measures... and to examine the possibility of creating a uniform structure in the form of an Olympic Movement anti-doping agency to support the establishment and implementation of measures in the fight against doping.[5]

At the conference support was expressed for the establishment of the World Anti-Doping Agency (WADA) which would consider:

> expanding out of competition testing, co-ordinating research, promoting preventative and educational actions and harmonising scientific and technical standards and procedures for analyses and equipment.[6]

Whilst establishment of WADA appears to be a positive step towards some kind of uniformity of doping control rules and procedures, the existing problems stemming from lack of jurisdiction and the plethora of other sporting organisations may remain insurmountable.

International Organisation of Sports: Prominence of the IOC

Sporting activity at the international level is governed by a plethora of organisations. There are the International Olympic Committee (IOC),

---

3 See "Ross Wows Em, Shows His Medal", *The Province,* 13 February 1998 at A62. The text of the CAS decision is reported at CAS, *Nagano 002,* 12 February 1998.
4 A Ljungqvist, "United International Efforts in the Fight Against Doping in Sport" (1994) 40 *Olympic Message* 43. Ljungvist notes that a working group was established within the IOC in 1994 to supervise the harmonisation of doping rules and anti-doping activities amongst the International Olympic Federations. We note that there is, however, often conflict between the various national Olympic Federations and national sporting bodies (see footnote 1 above). There may also be conflict between IOC and national Olympic Federation rules and those of the relevant International Federation.
5 World Conference on Doping in Sport website at
< http://www.nodoping.org/confmond_day1_e.htm>
6 Lausanne Declaration on Doping in Sport.

international sports federations, national sports bodies (some Olympic and some non-Olympic), National Olympic Committees, regional organisations and national and local governments.[7] However, through its influence and a system of divested authority, the IOC has ensured that it plays a key role in determining the international legal norms which govern sport.

These organisations (excepting national sports bodies) are a part of the international legal system and operate generally within the framework of the United Nations Charter. In particular, there are agencies of the United Nations which play an active role in sports. The IOC has established working groups with the World Health Organisation (WHO) and United Nations Education Scientific and Cultural Organisation (UNESCO). It has co-operated with the International Narcotics Board in efforts to combat doping.[8] In this way, the Olympic Movement (constituted by the IOC, International Federations, National Olympic Committees, organising committees for each games and Olympic Congress) is able to assert an important autonomy in the area of establishing international legal norms in sport.

Internationally, the most influential sporting organisation is the IOC. The legal status of the IOC is not clear, but it appears to be essentially what lawyers refer to as an "NGO" or non-government organisation. It is recognised as a legal entity, although it is not incorporated in the usual sense of that word. The IOC was "born" on 23 June 1894 at the International Athletic Congress of Paris, where the modern Olympic Games were launched. The IOC owns the rights to the Olympic Games and is, according to its Charter, "the final authority on all questions concerning the Olympic Games and the Olympic Movement."[9]

According to Rule 19 of the Olympic Charter:

The IOC is an international non-governmental non-profit organisation, of unlimited duration, in the form of an association with the status of a legal person, recognised by decree of the Swiss Federal Council of September 17th, 1981.

---

7 See J Nafziger, *International Sports Law* (New York, Transnational, 1988).
8 Ibid at 25.
9 See IOC, *Olympic Charter,* Rule 1.1 (IOC is the supreme authority of the Olympic Movement), Rule 9.2 (The authority of last resort on any question concerning the Olympic Games rests with the IOC), Rule 11 (Olympic Games are the exclusive property of the IOC). Some limited scope is given for arbitral determinations by CAS in Rule 19.4.

ORGANISATION OF SPORTING ACTIVITY

> The IOC is resident in Lausanne, Switzerland and operates under the "authority" of the Swiss government. Essentially, then, the IOC is an international organisation with legal personality, given recognition world-wide.

The importance of the IOC derives from the universal appeal of the Olympic Games, resurrected in 1896 by Baron Pierre de Coubertin. As the quadrennial celebration of sport (although only two years separates the summer from the winter games) held in various locations around the world, the Olympic Games has become the premier international sporting carnival. In addition, recently there has been intense bidding and lobbying of the IOC for the right to host the Olympic Games, whether for reasons of assumed prestige or for perceived financial advantages flowing from the Games. The financial success of the Olympic Games and the associated Olympic Movement means the IOC is in a position to establish itself as a governing authority over international sports. The scandal surrounding the determination of host city may have tarnished the IOC's moral position.

The IOC establishes rules governing eligibility to participate in the Olympic Games as well as, indirectly, rules governing each Olympic sport. The Olympic Charter recognises various international federations as having authority to oversee and regulate various sports. Each international federation enforces rules concerning its particular sport. The Olympic Charter provides (in Rule 30) that the international federations are to:

> 30.1.1 establish and enforce the rules concerning the practice of their respective sports and to ensure their application.

For example, the IOC recognises the International Federation of Association Football (FIFA) as the international federation governing the sport of association football (or soccer, as it is known in some parts of the world such as Australia and North America).

However, the international federations must operate within norms established by the IOC. Rule 29 of the Olympic Charter provides:

[the international federation's] statutes, practice and activities must be in conformity with the Olympic Charter.

Each international federation is made up of constituent national federations in the relevant sport. Five national federations in a particular country can make up a National Olympic Committee. The role of the National Olympic Committees is to "develop and protect the Olympic Movement in their respective countries, in accordance with the Olympic Charter" (Charter Rule 31). The workings of a National Olympic Committee are independent of the government of the country in question. This explains how it is that there can be disputes between National Olympic Committees (NOC) and state agencies regarding questions of doping policy.[10] In fact, the Australian Olympic Committee contains a constituent commission dealing exclusively with doping matters and which has, under the auspices of the AOC, promulgated its own doping policy.

The ability of the IOC to perform its overall supervisory function is a direct result of its control of the Olympic Games and all associated intellectual property. The world-wide following of the Olympic Games has led to the IOC becoming recognised as the accepted authority. Only voluntary submission to its rules obliges particular sports to apply IOC standards. The consequence for a particular sport of not following the IOC's rules would presumably be withdrawal of its recognition by the IOC, as well as loss of ability to offer athletes participating under its rules the opportunity to participate in the Olympic Games. In other words, there would presumably be nothing to prevent a particular sport from choosing to establish its own international federation. Indeed, all Olympic sports do have IFs (International Federations) which conform to IOC standard policies. Even wealthy and powerful IFs such as FIFA continue to play an important role within the IOC movement, despite being in disagreement with aspects of IOC doping policy.[11] However, unless that federation were recognised by the IOC (which would involve compliance with the IOC Charter), then athletes competing under its rules would not be able to compete in the Olympic Games.

Thus, from an international perspective, we start with the IOC and, for each Olympic Sport, we can locate a recognised IF which establishes rules of competition and eligibility. The international federations, in turn, recognise different national federations in their sports. Therefore, in the sport of soccer, FIFA (the relevant IF) recognises Soccer Australia as the governing body for

---

10 Hence a senior Australian official chose to resign from the Australian Sports Commission (ASC), a government agency, over differences between the ASC's doping policy and that promulgated by the Australian Olympic Committee (AOC), of which he is president: see "Split Over Drugs Policy", *The Age,* 7 April 1998 at C 1.

11 At the 1999 Doping Conference, FIFA was one of two IFs objecting to the concept of standard minimum doping penalties. See <http://nodoping.org/confmond_day2_e.htm>.

Australian soccer. One can therefore see how the rules established by the IOC find their expression at all levels of sport, even in events that are not officially part of the Olympic Games (for example, the Australian National Soccer League competition). Although whether FIFA considers itself subordinate to the IOC is not clear, at the 1999 Conference the IOC and FIFA were at odds over doping penalties.[12] Athletes wishing to participate in the sport in question must also be members of the relevant federation. Becoming a member of the relevant federation generally obliges the athlete to comply with that federation's rules, including rules concerning drug use.

Therefore, in the context of a doping incident, one of the first questions we must ask is whether the athlete in question is a member of any particular sporting federation. If so, the answer to the question of "what happens?" is found by reading the doping policy and rules of that federation. If the sport in question is an Olympic sport, the relevant rules will follow the prescribed IOC model.

Non-Olympic Sports

In non-Olympic sports, there is no obligation to follow rules promulgated by the IOC. Thus in the sport of rugby league, the relevant rules are established by the NRL. Presumably, if the NRL wished to establish rugby league as an Olympic sport, it would ensure that its rules were consistent with IOC rules and policy. It would also need to ensure that it was a constituent member of an international federation which, in turn, was recognised by the IOC.

However, there is no obligation for a national sporting association's rules to conform to any Olympic norm at present, so long as the relevant association is not linked to the Olympic movement by membership in a recognised international federation. Insofar as international ramifications are concerned, a national sporting association's action in suspending a player for drug use may or may not affect the individual player's ability to participate in the same sport in another country. Questions of eligibility in these cases would be determined by the relevant national sporting organisation. In the case of rugby league, for example, individual players are bound by the NRL rules by

---

12 IOC wants four years for a first offence, FIFA only two.

virtue of a term in the standard player contract which obliges the player to abide by NRL rules.[13]

Organisation of Sports in Australia

Sporting activity in Australia involves a complex web of government departments and statutory authorities. Each of these has a different role and impact upon sporting activity.

Federal Controls

At the federal level, sporting activity generally comes within the jurisdiction of the Department of the Environment, Sport and Territories. It is only in the last 20 to 30 years that governments around the globe have recognised the importance of developing national policy in sport.[14] The reasons for this are complex and varied, ranging from the desire to achieve international status by sporting success (hence the development of national "institutes" of sport in various countries) to the desire to fund and oversee the development of sports facilities to encourage greater physical fitness in citizens. (Governments demand success, thus contributing to the "win-at-all cost" mentality.) Drug use in sport is one issue that merits particular attention, and is, as we shall see, a problem that has led to the establishment of a particular statutory authority in Australia, the Australia Sports Drug Agency (ASDA).

There are other government departments with an interest in sporting activity. Some of these are responsible for initiatives, which have an impact on drug testing and drug policy in sport. At the federal level, there is the Department

---

[13] As a matter of law, this indirect means of binding a player to the league rules raises interesting contractual questions, which are further explored in Chapter 7 below. Suffice to say that normally a person is only bound by contract to terms which they have agreed. Further, only parties to the contract are normally in a position to enforce its terms. In rugby league the player agrees to be bound by the NRL rules and accept the jurisdiction of its disciplinary tribunal by virtue of a term in his contract with his team which incorporates those rules by reference. Presumably, a breach of the NRL rules, places the player in breach of the player contract with his club. Furthermore, it is in the team's best interest to abide by disciplinary determinations, for the NRL is in a position, by virtue of its own legal composition (as a corporation limited by guarantee, with each of the teams as members, bound by its constitution) to enforce its rules against the teams.

[14] For a good review see J Barnes, *Sports and the Law in Canada* (3rd ed Toronto Butterworths 1996).

of Foreign Affairs and Trade, which is responsible for the negotiation of international agreements to which Australia is party. There are a number of these international agreements which specifically concern doping in sport. The Council of Europe adopted an Anti-Doping Convention in 1989, to which Australia is a party. In addition, Australia is a member of the Monitoring Committee, established under the Anti-Doping Convention. The purpose of the Convention is to establish rules to harmonise anti-doping regulations. It also contains a reference list of banned substances.

Australia also signed the November 1989 Multilateral Agreement in the Unification of Actions in the Struggle Against Doping in Sport. Under this agreement a number of governments such as the governments of Australia, Canada and the UK entered into a multilateral anti-doping arrangement, evidenced by a Memorandum of Association, containing agreement on the reciprocal development and enforcement of measures against doping in sport. Pursuant to this arrangement, the signatories agreed to reciprocal testing of each other's athletes. This further agreement is of importance to Australia when one considers one of the most widely known successful challenges to a positive drug test.

VINNICOMBE

This challenge concerns Martin Vinnicombe, an Australian cyclist, who was tested while in the United States prior to taking part in a competition. Although the direction to conduct a test emanated from the Australian Sports Drug Agency, the actual test was conducted by the Canadian Anti-Doping Authority under Australian law. After testing positive to stanozolol, a banned anabolic agent, Vinnicombe challenged the recording of a positive test result on the grounds that the Canadian authority was not authorised and did not follow appropriate Australian protocol. The challenge was eventually dealt with by arbitration. According to the arbitrator, Robert Ellicott, QC:

> ASDA should not have taken Vinnicombe to have recorded a positive test result because the Australian sample collection procedures were not strictly complied with...[the Canadian authority] had not complied with what were mandatory testing steps under the Australian Sports Drug Agency Act 1991.[15]

---

15 *Martin Vinnicombe v The Australian Professional Cycling Council (APCC) and the Australian Cycling Federation (ACF) and the Australian Sports Commission (ASC)* (Unreported Arbitration 24 April 1992). Following this decision the Australian Sports Drug Agency Act was amended in 1992 by adding what became ss 16, 17 and 18. The amendments provided that test results would be valid so long as the testing authority "substantially complied" with ASDA protocol.

These international agreements are not only between States. Recently ASDA entered into a trilateral anti-doping agreement with the Canadian Centre for Ethics in Sport and the United States Olympic Committee to promote and work in concert toward a drug free sporting environment world-wide. The agreement provides for co-operation in areas of research, education and testing and allows for reciprocal testing of each country's athletes training or competing in Australia, Canada and the United States.[16]

There are other Australian federal departments whose activities affect the sporting environment. The Department of Employment Education Training and Youth Affairs is responsible for initiatives in the areas of training and employment, as well as policies concerning youth that have a clear connection with sporting activity.

The Attorney-General's Department and the Department of Justice are also influential in administration of aspects of the criminal law which apply to trafficking in banned substances. Indeed, the Australian Olympic Committee is urging the Prime Minister and all State and Territory Governments to make offences involving performance-enhancing drugs carry penalties equivalent to those applicable to trafficking in narcotics and amphetamines.[17]

Finally, the Department of Health is the author of numerous initiatives affecting the formulation and implementation of drug policy, including policy impacting on drug use in sport. One example of this is the National Drug Strategic Plan, a joint initiative by the Commonwealth, State and Territory governments through their respective Ministries of Health.

There are also several important Commonwealth statutory authorities. Most important in relation to drugs in sport are the Australian Sports Commission and the Australian Sports Drug Agency (each established as a corporate body by legislation: Australian Sports Commission Act 1989 (Cth) and Australian Sports Drug Agency Act 1990 (Cth)).

ASC was established to oversee the delivery of services to sport in Australia. It is a corporate body and its activities are supervised by the Commonwealth Minister responsible for the Environment Sports and Territories. The general mandate of the ASC is to encourage and provide for participation and

---

16 ASDA – Drugs in Sport, <http://www.ausport.gov.au/asda/drugsin.html>
17 "Jail Drug Cheats: Olympics Chief", *The West Australian*, 25 August 1998 at 1.

achievement by Australians in Sport. To this end, the Commonwealth Government provides substantial funding. The government appropriation for the ASC for the 1999-2000 financial year was $109 million.[18]

Probably the most visible aspect of the ASC's activities for the public at large is the establishment of the Australian Institute of Sport (AIS) and efforts to use the Sydney 2000 Olympics to increase sports participation and sports-related activities. The AIS, which was established to promote the achievements of elite level athletes, operates as a part of ASC. The AIS also undertakes research and development related to sports science and sports medicine, both activities which play a significant role in the development of policies on drugs in sport.

More importantly, from the perspective of the athlete, is the Commission's role in distributing funds to sporting organisations and the imposition of policy. ACS imposes sanctions against persons and organisations found to have participated in a doping practice. This aspect of the ASC's regulatory activities has profound importance for athletes, as the sanctions include:

- Loss of eligibility to represent Australia in international competition;
- Banning from competition in events and competitions conducted under the auspices of sporting organisations;
- Withdrawal of awards and records;
- Loss of eligibility to receive funding or assistance from the ASC or other sports organisations;
- Refunding money received.

Therefore, the ASC is in a position to impose its policy in any case involving athletes who seek to represent the nation or are in any way dependent on the ASC for recognition or assistance. The same applies to sporting organisations.

To this end, the ASC has published its Anti-Doping Policy, which contains a definition of what constitutes a doping offence as well as prescribes procedures for the investigation of doping offences and the imposition of recommended sanctions.[19]

---

[18] ASC, *Annual Report* 1999-2000. Available online at <http://www.ausport.gov.au>.
[19] ASC, *Anti-Doping Policy* (April 1998).

The Increasing Dominance of Drug Testing by ASDA

Perhaps the single most important statutory body involved in this area is ASDA. Although interest at Commonwealth level in the development of policy for drug-free sport has been visible for about 20 years, it was not until 1989 that the Commonwealth Government established ASDA.[20]

The essential functions of ASDA are the conduct of drug testing and the sponsorship of drug education programmes. ASDA's role complements that of the ASC and sporting organisations. The ASC recognises ASDA as the primary authority to conduct drug tests on athletes in Australia. This means that any athlete with any connection to Australian national representation or in receipt of Commonwealth assistance is liable to be tested by ASDA. However, in recent years, ASDA's activities have broadened to include State competitors (by virtue of legislation in force in some states[21]) and also professional athletes (by virtue of the rules drafted by the sporting organisations: eg, the NRL designates ASDA as having exclusive authority to conduct drug tests on its behalf).

There are other ways in which an Australian athlete may be required to submit to an ASDA-conducted drug test. Some national sporting organisations endorse and apply the ASC's doping policy and designate ASDA as the appropriate authority for the conduct of tests, or, simply oblige athletes who are members to submit to testing as a condition of eligibility, whether or not the organisation has adopted the ASC doping policy.

Thus, increasingly, ASDA is becoming the single, exclusive agency for the conduct of drug tests on athletes in Australia, regardless of what sport or whether they are international competitors or state-based.

We will discuss the particular workings of ASDA in the next chapter.

These are only the Commonwealth Departments whose activities may be relevant. In each State and Territory of Australia, there are also Departments and Agencies which have an impact on sporting activity.

---

20 ASDA was formally established as a Commonwealth statutory authority by the Australian Sports Drug Agency Act 1991 (Cth).
21 See, for example, Sports Drug Testing Act 1995 (NSW) and Sports Drug Testing Act 1995 (Vic).

The Impact of State and Territory Organisations

Every State and Territory in Australia has its own government department responsible for sport and recreation. The activities of these State departments have been somewhat controversial, as it is unclear what their objectives are. Initially, these departments were focussed on increasing local participation in sporting activity. More recently, the State governments have established state-based Institutes of Sport, designed to foster the participation of athletes at the elite level. Thus, to use Victoria as an example, the State Government established a department responsible for sport and recreation (Sport and Recreation Victoria), which in turn established the Victorian Institute of Sport.[22] Like the federal government, the state and territorial governments also demand sporting success in return for government funding of sport.

Conclusion

As far as drug testing of athletes is concerned, the key point is that State-based athletes are now liable to be tested by ASDA. The question of applicable sanction will be determined by the application of the rules established by the relevant national federation, which may or may not follow either the ASC or AOC model policy.

The web of government departments, regulatory agencies and statutory authorities is complex. The competing athlete is likely to be subject to rules promulgated by ASC, ASDA, AOC, National Federation, International Federation and possibly even State agencies.

This complex structure means the imposition of sanctions against an athlete who tests positive to a particular substance is a complicated matter. First of all, you need to be aware of which substances are within the various applicable rules and policies. Further, you must understand the protocols established by each regulatory actor.

ROBERTSON

In a celebrated case, cyclist Bill Robertson tested positive to nandrolone (a banned anabolic steroid). He was initially suspended

---

22 The other states and territories also have their own institutes of sport.

> by the Australian Professional Cycling Council for two years. Robertson challenged this sanction on the basis that it was inconsistent with the rules established by the relevant international federation, UCI, whose rules prescribed a three month sanction for a similar offence. Robertson's challenge was successful.[23]

Ross Rebagliati successful challenge of his disqualification illustrates the same problem.

One must not forget the involvement of local government which, according to the 1989 First Report of an Inquiry into Sports Funding and Administration, is responsible for 73% of total government expenditure on sport and recreation. However, local government activity is mainly concentrated on the provision of facilities and facilitation of recreational activity.[24]

Professional Sporting Activity in Australia

Finally, we consider the professional sporting leagues. Prior to the advent of the professional league, it was the national sporting organisation, or national federation, which was responsible for the administration of sporting activity in a particular sport. In those sports where there is a professional league, both national federation and the league itself may exert organisational control.

In Australia, separate organisations now control some of the national leagues (for example, the AFL, NBL, ABL, NRL and NWBL). National federations still represent some of these sports at international level.

Thus, for example, the NBL (made up of several corporate sports teams) organises and manages the professional basketball competition in Australia and Basketball Australia is the national federation. The NBL organises and manages the professional league but relies on Basketball Australia's capacity to supply new talent from the amateur leagues it organises. In this sense, the two work together, as Basketball Australia relies on the professional competition to "sell" the sport. Ultimately, each organisation is capable of

---

[23] See *Robertson v Australian Professional Cycling Council Inc,* Waddell CJ (Unreported Decision, NSW Supreme Court, 10 September 1992). This case is discussed in more detail in Chapter 7 below.

[24] See H Westerbeek, "The Australian Sports System: Its History and an Organisational Overview" (1995) 2 *European Journal for Sport Management* 42.

formulating its own rules concerning drug testing and applicable sanctions. In the interests of the sport, the two policies ought be identical. If this is the case, then, given that basketball is an Olympic sport, the policy would follow the AOC and IOC Medical Code model. However, eligibility for the professional competition would be a matter for the NBL to determine.

In the case of a non-Olympic sport with a professional league, the tendency is for the league's doping policy to differ from the IOC/AOC and ASC model. Thus, players testing positive for anabolic steroids in both the AFL and the NRL were subjected to a 22 week ban under the applicable league policy, rather than the two year ban prescribed by both the ASC and AOC.

The questions arising relating to the application of sanctions will be discussed in Chapter 7.

CHAPTER 3

HISTORY OF DOPING AND DOPING CONTROL

Introduction

Ever since athletic competition began, athletes have used a variety of methods to gain the upper hand on their opponents. So, modern developments should come as no surprise. Centuries ago, athletes engaged in training combined with drinking special elixirs or eating a special diet. The Greek physician, Galen, is reputed to have prescribed "the rear hooves of an Abyssinian ass, ground up, boiled in oil, and flavoured with rose hips and rose petals" to improve performance.[1] There have always been herbal concoctions available which promise to enhance performance.

Then, as now, it seems that the rewards consequent on athletic success provided a significant incentive to seek the winning edge. The society which spawned the Olympic Games, Greece, incorporated sport into its lifestyle in significant ways. Athletic festivals were common and athletic training was considered a useful adjunct to military training. The marathon has origins in ancient Greek times (5th century BC), when a military message bearer - thought to be called Pheidippides - ran from Marathon to Athens bringing news of victory over the Persians. The distance (approximately 26 miles) covered by the running soldier became the inspiration for the modern

---

[1] United States Olympic Committee, *Olympic Gold: a 100 Year History of the Summer Olympic Games* (Colorado, SEA Multimedia 1995).

marathon.[2] Sporting prowess was highly valued in Greek society, and the availability of handsome prizes for successful athletes resulted in the emergence of a class of professional sports people. Furthermore, the Greek citizen had sufficient leisure time to indulge in spectating at sporting events.

Then, as now, professionalism and commercialism led to the desire to seek any means to achieve success. The market for what we now know as doping emerged. According to many, one of the reasons for the dissolution of the ancient Olympic Games was the use of drugs.[3]

Doping was also recorded in the Roman era, mainly consisting of feeding substances to horses to make them run faster in chariot races and feeding substances to gladiators to make their fights more spectacular. Little seems to have changed!

Sporting activity designed to appeal to spectators died off with the advent of the Christian era. In 396 AD, the Emperor Theodosius called for an end to these spectacles, condemning them as "pagan". Spectator and professional sports as we now know them did not re-emerge in any significant way until the nineteenth century.

Cricket, horse racing and prize-fighting were organised professionally in the nineteenth century. However organisation and growth of professional sport and spectator sports, as we know them today accelerated in the twentieth century. The combination of people moving to the cities, developments in technology and communication and increase leisure time coincided with the period of development of the modern sports. Many sporting clubs trace their histories to this period and the rules of many team sports were developed then.

Old rural "sports" such as animal baiting and cockfighting lost their popularity (they were legally suppressed). Newer sports such as rugby union, association football, soccer and tennis emerged.

Over the twentieth century, continual technological advances have led to improvements in equipment, development of new sports, and development

---

2 The modern measure, 26 miles 385 yards was established formally at the 1948 Summer Olympiad in London, England, being the distance from Windsor Castle to Wembley Stadium.
3 These tended to be naturally available pharmacological agents, such as mushrooms and plant seeds: see ASDA – Drugs in Sport, <http://www.ausport.gov.au/asda/drugsin.html> [2].

of facilities and stadiums to support the growth of commercial and professional sports.

In recent years, there have been many who, decrying what they see as a decline in moral standards, have seen parallels between modern society and the fall of Rome. The modern obsession with spectator sports and the "spectacle" is argued to be similar in many respects to the Roman obsession with gladiatorial combat. Indeed, when it comes to drug use in sport, some draw parallels between the modern professional athlete and the ancient gladiator, sacrificing health and wellbeing for commercial success and popularity.

According to a 1998 survey conducted by *Inside Sport* magazine, 60 percent of Australian teenagers have responded that they would not rule out using performance-enhancing drugs in sport if they were "undetectable and safe". Forty percent would not rule out using performance-enhancing drugs regardless of whether or not they were "safe" according to the survey.[4] Although one might quibble with the accuracy of the survey results, they clearly show some evidence of a trend to accept doing whatever it takes to achieve sporting success. All this contributes to an environment where there is an almost irresistible temptation to make use of whatever advantage might be available to grasp Olympic gold. "Drug" use, or doping, if we use the modern term, is hardly a novel phenomenon.

The use of special training regimes and special diets, even when combined with either natural or "unnatural" herbal concoctions appears to have escaped much notice until the last half of this century. Modern chemistry changed doping practices significantly. Even though the Germans developed steroids in the 1930s, until relatively recently the performance enhancement choices for most athletes were pretty much limited to using potions, lotions, tinctures, herbal extracts and other substances that were ingested or rubbed on the body. Probably the first artificially produced performance enhancing substances were amphetamines, which began to surface in cycling and soccer circles in the 1950s. There was reputedly evidence of drug taking amongst cyclists at the 1956 Melbourne Summer Olympic Games. The Americans developed sports steroids after the 1956 Games to combat eastern bloc success. Still, there was little or no public attention and virtually no official scrutiny, although the International Cycling Union (UCI) introduced drug testing programs in the 1950s and the

---

4 "Teenagers say yes to sport drugs", *The Sun-Herald*, 4 October 1998 at 13.

French Association Nationale d'Education Physique formed a Doping Commission in 1959.[5] So what triggered the change in attitudes that led to increased scrutiny over the training methods and pharmacological practices of our athletes?

Development of Drug Testing

The death of the Danish cyclist, Knut Jensen, at the 1960 Rome Olympic Games, raised concern about the use of drugs in sport.[6] Since then, the international sporting community has taken a serious interest in questions relating to the use of substances to improve performance. Whether that concern is based primarily on a desire to maintain fairness or a desire to protect the health and safety of athletes, or both, is a matter for conjecture.[7]

---

5 S Rofe and C Ordway, "Anti-Doping Policies", unpublished paper, Browne & Co Solicitors, 26 June 1998.

6 Jensen's was not the first recorded death due to doping. Two cyclists died in the late nineteenth century. A Dutch cyclist died in 1886 after taking heroin and cocaine and a Welsh cyclist, Arthur Linton, died in 1896 after taking strychnine. Refer to GM Kelly, *Sport and the Law* (Sydney, Law Book Company 1987) at 398.

7 The moral arguments in favour of drug control and drug testing are well explored in S Mugford, "The Value of Sport, Ethics, and the Control of Performance Enhancing Drugs: A Study in the Australian Sports Community", A Report Commissioned by ASDA (December 1993). Mugford specifically refers to the argument that drug control is justified on grounds of concern for the health and safety of the athlete. He writes (at 105):

"To oppose performance enhancing drugs (PED) on the grounds of health/danger is to raise a wide variety of questions. First, is it the case that PED use is dangerous and health risking? What if we could offer regimes of use under medical supervision to make (say) steroid use (reasonably) safe? Would our objection then collapse? And anyway, is it not the case that much of what athletes do is somewhat risky? What, for example, of a young woman I know who trained so hard as a potential Olympic cyclist that she dropped her body fat content very low, as a consequence ceased having menstrual periods, and now in her early thirties is diagnosed as having early signs of osteoporosis? Is that not a result of "danger" or "health risk"? What of running many kilometres a week, training while not fully recovered or taking a pain killer to play with an injury? And so on.

Second, by what moral mandate do we ban people from taking risks, as long as they know they take them? We do not ban hang-gliding or caving, we do not ban alcohol nor even tobacco use as such (we ban it only where it may cause health damage to others, where it is a fire risk, or where the user is too young to know better). With some 500 people a week dying in Australia from un-banned tobacco use, our mandate for banning steroids on paternalistic health grounds would be weak." The policy dimensions of doping control are more fully explored in Chapter 4.

Following the death of Knut Jensen, a major international conference on doping was held in Brussels and Ghent in Belgium in May 1964.[8] During this period of intense debate, both the French and Belgian legislatures took the first tentative steps towards prohibiting doping in sport by enacting laws in 1963 and 1964 respectively, in an attempt to curb the supply of drugs in the sporting arena.[9] The IOC became aware of the tarnished reputation that doping would have on the sporting community. The IOC took steps to introduce a rudimentary form of testing for stimulates, such as amphetamines, in cycling events at the following Summer Olympic Games in Tokyo in 1964. The IOC's intention was to safeguard the health of all athletes and to ensure respect for the ethical concepts of fair play, the Olympic spirit and medical practice.

Unfortunately, the increased efforts and measures to deter drug-taking failed in the case of British cyclist Tommy Simpson, who collapsed and died during the 1967 Tour de France (which was not under the control of the IOC). Simpson was later found to have been heavily dosed with stimulants. The televised death of Tommy Simpson greatly increased the pressure to introduce more wide-ranging testing for drug use. Consequently, the IOC's Medical Commission was spurred into action. They began developing a wide-ranging drug-testing program whose main focus was to deter athletes from resorting to drug use. This drug-testing program had two elements. First, the authorities began to conduct drug tests on athletes. Second, efforts were made to educate athletes about the potential health risks associated with performance-enhancing drugs.

At the 1968 Olympic Games in Mexico City, preliminary drug-testing for stimulants was conducted in all events. These Games saw the first disqualification of an athlete for drug use. Hans-Gunnar Liljenvall, a modern pentathlete, had his medal withdrawn after tests revealed a blood alcohol level over the allowable limit. He had drunk a few beers prior to the competition to steady his nerves.

In 1971, the IOC Medical Commission published the first list of banned substances, including both stimulants and narcotic analgesics[10]. By the time the 1972 Munich Olympic Games were held, the IOC had implemented its

---

8 H Opie, "Legal Regimes for the control of performance-enhancing drugs in sport" (1990) 12 *Adelaide Law Review* 335.
9 Ibid.
10 Senate Standing Committee on Environment, Recreation and the Arts, *Drugs in Sport: An Interim Report* (Canberra, Australian Government Publishing Service 1989) at 82.

first comprehensive testing at international competition level. All athletes were tested. Anabolic steroids were banned in 1974, when the technology to detect these substances was developed. During the 1976 Montreal Olympic Games testing procedures had expanded to include testing for anabolic steroids.[11] During the 1976 Games, 11 athletes were disqualified for drug use, eight of those for steroid use.

At the 1982 Brisbane Commonwealth Games, a test was introduced to detect the use of testosterone to enhance performance. By 1985, beta-blockers[12] were included on the list of banned substances. In 1987, the IOC Medical Commission included diuretics[13] on the list of banned substances. In 1988, blood doping[14] was also added to the IOC's list of banned substances and practices.

Of course, as the regulations concerning drugs grew along with the introduction of testing, those wishing to continue to use these substances developed methods designed to defeat the testers. Athletes using banned substances attempted to substitute urine samples and also timed their use of the substance in question to allow sufficient time for the drug to clear their system prior to testing, which was predictably undertaken during competitions.

During the late 1980's, the Medical Commission of the IOC maintained its vigilance against performance-enhancing substances. It banned practices which alter the integrity and validity of urine samples. It developed testing protocols and specimen-handling procedures to ensure the reliability of its policy. It implemented an accreditation program to ensure that all laboratories which conducted drug tests for its purposes met rigid criteria for quality and accuracy in their testing procedures.[15]

---

11 Ibid.
12 These include substances used to control heart rate and blood pressure. While normally one might think such effects would decrease athletic performance, they are regarded as performance enhancing in events such as shooting and archery where control is more important than activity.
13 These substances assist in the process of rapid weight loss required to compete in a particular weight division and have also been used to help dilute the concentration of banned substances in urine, thus making detection more difficult.
14 The most common method of blood doping involves the withdrawal of an athlete's blood sample some weeks prior to an event and storing it until required. Then, shortly before the required event, the infusion of blood into the athlete takes place. The aim is to increase the ration of red blood corpuscles in the blood stream. The process assists the body with the delivery of oxygen to the muscles.
15 E Zemper, "Drug Testing In Athletics" in R H Coombs and L J West (eds), *Drug Testing: Issues and Options* (New York, Oxford University Press, 1991) at 114.

1980 saw the drafting by the IOC of requirements for the accreditation of drug-testing laboratories. The standards are stringent so far as technical and professional competence are concerned. There are presently approximately 20 accredited laboratories world-wide, including the Australian Government Analytical Laboratory (AGAL) at Pymble, NSW. In 1996, AGAL established the Australian Sports Drug Testing Laboratory (ASDTL) for the specific purpose of conducting drug testing in sport.

The IOC protocols are complicated. Accredited laboratories are forbidden to conduct tests on samples unless they are submitted from a bona fide sports program. This is to prevent athletes from using these laboratories to determine whether they are able to evade detection. Accreditation is granted on the basis of a number of varied criteria. These include the ability to detect doping agents to a specified measure as well as capacity and speed of turnover of samples. The volume of testing required during a major sporting event, such as a Summer Olympic Games, is significant. During the 1972 Munich Olympic Games, more than 2000 samples were analysed during the 14 days of the event, while the Atlanta Summer Games of 1996 saw 1850 samples processed.[16]

Technology has also not been idle. Perhaps the most important development in this area was the introduction of gas chromatography and mass spectrometry in 1983, which allowed accurate results to be obtained consistently. The introduction of this new technology at the 1983 Pan-American Games in Caracas led to the embarrassing result of numerous athletes testing positive to prohibited drugs and many others deciding to withdraw from competition rather than risk a positive test result.[17] Nineteen athletes were disqualified, two of whom were Canadian weightlifters. These Canadian disqualifications triggered the first Sport Canada policy on doping.[18]

Of course, there are arguments that, despite the increasing use of drug testing and the development of accurate and reliable methods of detection, the IOC drug testing program is ineffective.

Perhaps the biggest controversy to affect a modern Summer Olympic Games was the disqualification of Ben Johnson after his world record, gold medal-

---

16 C Yesalis and V Cowart, *The Steroids Game: An Expert's Inside Look at Anabolic Steroid Use in Sports* (Champaign, Human Kinetics, 1998) at 76.
17 ASDA-Drugs in Sport, <http://www.ausport.gov.au/asda/drugsin.html>[5].
18 J Barnes, *Sports and the Law in Canada* (3rd ed, Toronto, Butterworths 1996) at 88-89.

winning performance in the 100 metre sprint at Seoul in 1988. Johnson's disqualification led to the Government of Canada establishing a Commission of Inquiry into the use of Drugs and Banned Practices Intended to Increase Athletic Performance in 1988. The Commission was headed by Justice Charles Dubin, who questioned the effectiveness of the IOC testing programme. Dubin said:

> Despite knowing the fallacy of in-competition testing, as they have for many years, the medical commissions of sports organisations such as the IAAF and the IOC have taken no steps to make the fallacy more widely known. They have given the impression that their competitions are fair and that the laboratories cannot be fooled.[19]

Others have opined that the IOC has an interest in maintaining an image that is not tainted by drug use. Certainly, some of the remarks attributed to IOC President, Juan Antonio Samaranch, concerning alleged drug use by Chinese swimmers suggest an alarming naivete.[20] Whatever the truth is about the interests of the IOC or the various international federations, it is certainly true that economic and political conditions vary in the different countries where the IOC-accredited labs are located. Evidence heard by the German authorities has established that the IOC-accredited laboratory in what was East Germany played a major role in assisting its athletes in circumventing drug tests.[21] One might speculate whether the Chinese laboratory has acted similarly.[22]

The IOC continually reviews and amends its list of banned substances and practices. Any new techniques or performance-enhancing substances will be added to the IOC list of banned substances and practices.

---

19 The Honourable Charles L Dubin, *Commission of Inquiry into the Use of Drugs and Banned Practices Intended to Increase Athletic Performance* (Ottawa, Minister of Supply and Services Canada, 1990) at 397.

20 Samaranch is reported to have said that "Chinese sport is very clean", according to Andrew Jennings, whose work is extremely critical of the working of the IOC, particularly in the area of doping policy. Jennings alleges that post-competition analysis of samples routinely reveals an alarming level of drug use. Further, Jennings tells an interesting story of how IOC officials conspire to conceal positive drug tests so as to preserve the image of the sport. See A Jennings, *The New Lords of the Rings* (London, Simon & Schuster 1996) at 232-249.

21 C Yesalis and V Cowart, *The Steroids Game: An Expert's Inside Look at Anabolic Steroid Use in Sports* (Champaign, Human Kinetics, 1998) at 76.

22 Perhaps as a result of this concern, during 1994-1995, ASDA established an anti-doping agreement with the Chinese Olympic Committee's Anti-Doping Commission. This includes an agreement on the part of ASDA to assist China in establishing an anti-doping agency with increased emphasis in out-of-competition testing, exchange of information and encouragement of national federations to conduct out-of-competition testing.

Presently there are over 150 banned substances which fall into seven broad doping classes: psychomotor stimulates (eg, amphetamines and cocaine); sympathomimitic amines (eg, chlorprenaline and ephedrine); central nervous system stimulants (eg, amiphenzole); anabolic steroids (eg, stanozolol and testosterone), beta-blockers; narcotic analgesics; and diuretics.[23] Accompanying these prohibited classes of substances are the two prohibited doping methods of blood doping and pharmacological, chemical or physical manipulation of urine. The IOC Medical Commission has also included a class of drugs which do not necessarily enhance performance per se. These include alcohol, local anaesthetics, corticosteroids and human chorionic gonadotropin. Athletes who test positive for these substances will not necessarily face the same sanctions as those who test positive for substances listed in the doping classes.[24]

The major reason for classifying these substances into different classes is the difficulty of establishing a precise, universal definition of doping. Furthermore, as performance-enhancing techniques and substances become more sophisticated, the detection of these substances becomes harder to achieve. This is particularly the case where the human body produces a number of substances that are found on the banned list (ie testosterone and rEPO). An additional and more basic problem is that there seems to be no consensus on a unifying, underlying principle supporting prohibition (see Chapter 4).

The principal method of detection is chemical analysis of a urine sample provided by the athlete. This process is known as urinalysis. While all IOC accredited laboratories use gas chromatography combined with mass spectrometry (GC/MS) as the primary analytical technique to test for banned substances, some laboratories have developed more sophisticated techniques such as high performance GC/MS tests.[25] This can lead to the possibility of the same urine sample providing two different sets of results.

Furthermore, not all the banned substances can be detected by GC/MS or high GC/MS analysis. In the case of corticoids, high performance liquid chromatography (HPLC) is used in conjunction with a mass spectrometer

---

[23] For a comprehensive analysis on the side-effects of the use of banned drugs see H Opie, "Legal Regimes for the control of performance-enhancing drugs in sport" (1990) 12 *Adelaide Law Review* at 336 – 339. The issue of health and drug taking is discussed in Chapter 4.
[24] IOC Medical Commission, *Medical Code* (1994) at Chapter II.
[25] IOC Medical Commission, *Requirements for accreditation and good laboratory practice* (1988).

and particle beam interface. One substance that has been notoriously difficult to detect is rEPO (recombinant erythropoietin), a substance which operates to stimulate the production of red blood cells within bone marrow. Use of this substance has been rife within the cycling industry, where it is claimed that a significant number of cyclists who have died of heart failure may have been affected by the use of this substance. Owing to the difficulty of detection, reliable data relating to rEPO use is not available. At the Sydney Olympic Games testing for rEPO was performed by a combination of blood and urine testing. The international cycling federation has also announced that it will be freezing urine samples collected during the recent Tour de France with a view to subjecting them to reliable testing methods, once they become available.

The correlation and testing of urine samples will not conclusively determine whether a particular test result is determinative. The IOC Medical Commission has also developed a very precise and detailed protocol for collecting, identifying, handling, and transporting of the samples, from the time they are given by the athlete to the time the tests have been carried out.[26] Furthermore, all personnel involved in the testing procedure must possess the necessary qualifications and authorisation.[27] If these procedures are not complied with, the validity of the tests results cannot be assured.

CAPOBIANCO

Australian sprinter Dean Capobianco underwent routine testing at an athletics meet in the Netherlands in May 1996. About a month later the athlete was advised that the sample collected contained stanozolol, a banned anabolic steroid. In accordance with the applicable protocol, the sample originally collected from Capobianco had been divided into "A" and "B" samples. The athlete was invited to attend the unsealing of the "B" sample, which also tested positive. Subsequently, at a hearing of the Athletics Australia Doping Control Tribunal, Capobianco disputed the validity of the test results on the basis that the sample had not been dealt with in accordance with the applicable IAAF Doping Control procedures. Of particular concern to Robert Ellicott QC, the Chairman of the Doping Control Tribunal, was a

---

26 IOC Medical Commission, *Medical Code* (1994).
27 IOC Medical Commission, *Requirements for accreditation and good laboratory practice* (1988) at clause 3.2.

failure on the IAAF to account for the treatment of the samples between the date they were collected in the Netherlands and the date they were tested, some one month later, in Germany. IAAF doping procedures specifically required storage of the samples in a suitable tamper-proof container as well as transportation by a courier, who was to be identified. The doping rules also required details to be recorded as to the method of transport, the treatment of the samples in the hands of the courier and evidence that the samples arrived at the testing facility with the seals intact. As a consequence of the lack of evidence of proper compliance with doping control procedures, Mr Ellicott dismissed the case against Capobianco.

IAAF rules, uniquely, provided at the time for further appeal to an IAAF Appeal Panel. Despite the finding of Mr Ellicott at the Athletics Australia Tribunal, the IAAF Panel concluded that there was "no real doubt" as to whether proper procedure had been followed. As a consequence, Capobianco was found to have tested positive for stanozolol and was banned for four years (later reduced to two).

Olympic International Committee: Medical Code and Accreditation for Laboratories

The Olympic Charter empowers the IOC to prohibit doping, establish lists of prohibited classes of substances and prohibited methods, provide for the obligation of athletes to submit themselves to medical controls and examination and make provision for sanctions to be applied in the event of a violation of the *Medical Code*.[28] Consequently, on 13 January 1994, the IOC in collaboration with the International Federations and the Olympic Committees, drew up the IOC *Medical Code* (the Code).[29] The Code was established to ensure that the spirit of fair play prevails in sport, to lead the fight against doping in sport and take such measures to prevent endangering the health of athletes.[30] The IOC Medical Commission is charged with the responsibility of administering the Code. The Commission operates through several sub-commissions. The sub-commission on "doping and biochemistry of sport" is responsible for defining the rules and procedures pertaining to:

---

28 IOC, *Olympic Charter*, Rule 48.
29 IOC Medical Commission, *Medical Code* (1994).
30 Ibid at 2.

- the classes of prohibited substances;
- the collection of samples;
- the selection of accredited laboratories;
- the procedures for testing;
- the preparation of education programs on the implications of drug misuse among athletes; and
- co-ordination with national sporting bodies.[31]

Under Chapter One, Article II of the Code, doping prohibition applies to all athletes, coaches, trainers, officials and medical and para-medical personnel working with or treating athletes participating in or preparing for sports competitions of the Olympic games, and all other competitions conducted within the framework of the Olympic movement.[32] Furthermore, the Code places the responsibility upon the athlete to ensure that they do not ingest any prohibited substance or engage in any prohibited method.[33]

Each year the Medical Commission makes recommendations with respect to prohibited classes of substances and prohibited methods. These recommendations can be in terms of laboratory practice or procedures, or for the inclusion of new substances or methods onto the prohibited list. The IOC then issues a revised list of prohibited substances which is published and distributed to all International Federations. Any new substances contained on the banned list will come into effect as of 1 February of that year.[34]

Furthermore, the IOC Medical Commission is responsible for determining the necessary prerequisites required for laboratories to be accredited by the IOC. The Medical Commission also establishes the practices and procedures that accredited laboratories must follow. Before accreditation is granted, the laboratories must analyse three sets of 10 samples successfully over a period which can vary from six to 12 months. These control samples will contain substances which are examples of prohibited substances. In order to be successful, the laboratories must correctly identify the dope agents and their relevant metabolites within a period of three days. The Medical Commission

---

[31] Senate Standing Committee on Environment, Recreation and the Arts, *The Circumstances Surrounding the Positive Drug Test on Mr Alex Watson* (Canberra, Australian Government Publishing Service 1992) at 15.
[32] IOC Medical Commission, *Medical Code* (1994) at 3.
[33] Ibid.
[34] Ibid at 4.

will then make a determination as to whether the laboratory should be accredited. After accreditation, laboratories will be challenged with one set of up to 4 samples, periodically, in order that their practices and procedures maintain the highest quality standards.[35]

The laboratories must also agree to abide by the IOC Medical Commission's *Code of Ethics*. The Commission is strongly opposed to laboratories testing athletes solely during training or just prior to a particular sporting event. Testing limited to these periods permits athletes engaging in doping practices to regulate their intake of the prohibited substances so as to avoid detection. In conjunction with the requirements for accreditation of good laboratory practices, the *Code of Ethics* establishes procedures to be followed for competition and out-of-competition testing. The laboratories should only accept and analyse samples originating from known sources within competitions organised by national and international sporting governing bodies.[36]

Since February 1999, the IOC has been working to establish a World Anti-Doping Authority (WADA). It is hoped that this Authority will eventually result in standardised testing and sanction protocols, as well as increase the confidence of the public and the athletic community in the independence and reliability of testing authorities. WADA and its implications for the future of doping control will be addressed in Chapter 8.

Australian Developments

As early as 1978, the Commonwealth Government provided funds to the Australian Sports Medicine Federation to undertake surveys of drug use in Australian sport. The survey revealed that athletes were indeed using a variety of substances to enhance their performance. This led to the establishment of a National Programme of Drugs in Sport, administered by ASC. The Commonwealth Government created AIS in 1980 to provide Australian athletes with "a very high level of coaching with intensive training in conjunction with complementary educational opportunities".[37] From January 1982, all AIS scholarship holders were required to abide by the AIS "Code of Ethics". This included the agreement to undertake a random

---

35 Ibid at Chapter V & Appendix "B".
36 Ibid at Appendix "B".
37 Australian Institute of Sport, *First Annual Report* (1981) at 10.

drug test and not to "take or use drugs or stimulants nor participate in other practices prohibited by the Institute".[38] However, no tests were required by the AIS until June 1986. Over the period of six months, 23 random tests were carried out, and all were recorded as negative.[39]

In 1987 agreement was reached for AOC and ASC to adopt anti-doping policies along similar lines. The following year, the AOC policy was put to the test when Australian pentathlete Alex Watson tested positive at the Seoul Olympics for an excessive quantity of caffeine. Watson was disqualified from the Games and later suspended by the AOC.[40]

By the late 1980s, community perceptions about the use of performance enhancing drugs and techniques led to calls for a Senate inquiry into the issue of drugs in sport. Community fears about drug-taking were given more credence in a November 1987 ABC "Four Corners" program, during which allegations concerning drug use in track and field at the AIS were made. On 19 May 1988, the Senate resolved that the matter be referred to the Standing Committee on Environment, Recreation and the Arts. The Committee was charged with the responsibility to look into "the use by Australian sportsmen and sportswomen of performance enhancing drugs and the role played by Commonwealth agencies".[41]

The Committee handed down its interim report in May 1988 and its final report in 1990. It recommended that the Commonwealth Government establish an independent Australian Sports Drug Commission to carry out all sports drug testing is Australia.[42] The Commission would be responsible "for developing sports drug policies, conducting relevant research, selecting sportspeople for drug testing, collecting samples, dispatching samples to an IOC accredited laboratory, receiving results, conducting necessary investigations and carrying out the necessary liaison activities with law enforcement agencies, customs officials and health departments". The Committee said that for a drug policy to be an effective deterrent to sportspeople, the Commission should carry out a

---

38 ASDA – Drugs in Sport, <http://www.ausport.gov.au/asda/drugsin.html>.
39 Ibid.
40 Watson's disqualification led to the establishment of yet another Parliamentary inquiry, this one leading to the publication of the previously cited report: Senate Standing Committee on Environment, Recreation and the Arts, *The Circumstances Surrounding the Positive Drug Test on Mr Alex Watson* (Canberra, Australian Government Publishing Service, 1992).
41 *Drugs in Sport: An Interim Report of the Senate Standing Committee on Environment, Recreation and the Arts* (Canberra, AGPS, 1989) at xvii.
42 Ibid at Recommendation 4.

minimum of 2000 tests a year. Of these 2000 tests, 350 of Australia's best athletes should be tested four times per year using targeted, random and competition testing.[43]

The Commonwealth Government responded with the establishment of ASDA in 1991,[44] although an interim agency had been in operation since August 1989. ASDA was charged with the responsibility to collect samples from athletes and arrange for the testing of those samples to detect the use of substances and practices included in the IOC's List of Doping Classes and Methods. The Agency would also implement education programs to make the sporting and general community aware of the dangers of using such drugs and doping methods. The Agency was also responsible to encourage State and Territory governments, and national, State and Territory sporting organisations, to adopt uniform drug sampling and testing procedures at least to the level espoused by the IOC.[45] In her Second Reading Speech of the Bill, the then Minister for the Arts, Sport, the Environment, Tourism and Territories, Ms Ros Kelly, stated that the establishment of the Agency was an integral part of the government's commitment to achieve drug free sport in Australia and to contribute to the global "clean-up" of sport.

Following the establishment of ASDA, ASC revised its doping policy in September 1992. The ASC Doping Policy aims to deter doping practices in sport by requiring sporting organisations to endorse the Policy, or to establish a doping policy which is consistent with the ASC policy and supporting the drug testing program and education initiatives of ASDA.[46] If organisations refused to comply with the Policy, their funding arrangements could be terminated. The ASC has recently revised its doping policy and adopted a new "anti-doping policy" in April 1998. At the same time, the ASC produced a model anti-doping policy for national sporting organisations. At the time of writing, the ASC and the AOC are discussing means of ensuring consistency between their respective anti-doping policies, the AOC having adopted its most recent policy in December 1997. We discuss the contents of these policies in Chapter 7.

---

43 Ibid.
44 Australian Sports Drug Agency Act 1991 (Cth).
45 Ibid s 8.
46 ASC, *Drugs in Sport: Revised Doping Policy September 1992* (Reprinted November 1994) at 1.

The IOC Medical Commission's list of banned substances and drug testing protocol are incorporated into the drug policy of the ASC and ASDA. The regulations which control the administration of these agencies contain detailed provisions dealing with the method of selection of athletes for testing as well as procedures for the collection of samples, requirements for a chain of custody with respect to those samples, standards to be met in respect of the analysis of any urine samples are also prescribed procedures for the notification of results. ASDA has the power to test Australian athletes within or outside Australia. Furthermore, ASDA can arrange for overseas testing of Australian athletes by "approved" foreign anti-doping agencies.

Where an athlete refuses to comply with a request to provide a sample, and ASDA decides that the individual concerned does not have a reasonable cause to refuse, he or she is deemed to have committed an offence and will be placed on the Register of Notifiable Events (the register). Equally, if a positive test is returned, the name of the athlete will also be entered on the register. In either case, by virtue of s 13(6) of the ASDA Act, an athlete may appeal to the Commonwealth's Administrative Appeals Tribunal (AAT) for review of the decision. If the application for review is successful, the result would be removal of the athlete's name from the register.

Where an athlete's name is entered on the register, or remains so entered following an unsuccessful review by AAT, ASDA is required to provide similar notice to the relevant sporting organisation and, where the athlete is in receipt of Commonwealth support, to ASC.

The consequences for an athlete who has his or her name placed on the register are dependant on the sport concerned. If the athlete receives Commonwealth funding, such funding will be terminated for the duration of any sanction imposed. Again, the period of sanction will vary, depending on which sporting organisation is involved. The ASC doping policy states in clause 6.1(b) that there should be a minimum suspension of two years for the first breach and a life ban for any subsequent breach. Lower penalties may apply where the banned substances may have been administered for therapeutic purposes or if the athlete is "out-of-competition".

Under ASC policy, an athlete is to be given a hearing to determine whether a breach of the ASC doping policy has occurred and, if so, to determine what sanction should be applied. Pursuant to ASC policy, the ASC executive director is to set up a three-person committee to conduct the hearing, but with the right to cross-examine and legal representation.

In practice, sporting organisations conduct their own hearings and, for those sports under the aegis of the ASC, the Commission will have one nominee on the disciplinary committee. It is for the ASC to determine if the procedure adopted by the sporting organisation for its disciplinary proceeding is consistent with its own policy. Professional leagues, such as the AFL for example, are afforded more flexibility to depart from ASC policy. There is no requirement for them to have an ASC nominee on their disciplinary tribunals.

CHAPTER 4

DOPING POLICY

The Sydney Games were, by all accounts, a huge success. The world was captivated by an Olympic Games that were supremely well-organised and held in one of the world's most attractive cities. However, the Games were not free of doping with over 60 doping cases arising during the two weeks of competition. Nonetheless, some believe that the steps that were taken to reform anti-doping policy and practice in the years leading up to the Games can be regarded as successful. Without the reforms, some believe doping would have been more widespread during the 2000 Games.

However, how do we judge that success? Do we look at the low number of positive test results, the number or tests overall, the rate of positive test results as a proportion of tests taken? Sydney may have been spared some controversy by the late withdrawal of a number of Chinese athletes. Press reports intimated that the true motivation of the late withdrawals was fear of being caught by the new combination blood and urine tests for recombinant erythropoietin (rEPO). Professor Barrie Houlihan sums up the problem well.

> Overall, the development of reliable performance measures for the assessment of the success of current anti-doping policy remains elusive and generally a low priority. A key problem is the reliability of the data currently collected. The number of positive results will be affected by various factors and the balance between in-competition and out-of-competition tests. Further, not all positive test results are deemed to be doping infractions. A second difficulty with the interpretation of doping records is that the decline in the number of positives for one type of drug might indicate success in anti-doping

policy implementation but might, more plausibly, indicate an evolution in the drug culture, for example, away from amphetamines to steroids and, more recently, from steroids to testosterone, or greater sophistication among users in avoiding detection or, indeed, a shift to other less easily detected drugs. Finally, it remains difficult to identify reliable time series indicators of progress due to the rapidity with which the nature of the problem evolves. Not only do the range of available and preferred drugs continue to expand, but so too do the range of, and application of, testing procedures. As a result it is not possible to draw firm conclusions about the current level of policy success. Consequently, the repeated claims to be "winning the war on doping in sport" will continue to prompt scepticism rather than congratulations until a set of agreed benchmarks is established. Ironically, probably the best indicator of success is the decline in performance in some events at recent Olympic games. For example, there was a marked decline in performance in women's javelin, discus and shot-put following the introduction of out-of-competition testing in 1989. Not only did the best performance of the year decline but so too did the average performance of the ten best athletes. In the shot, for example, the best performance in 1987 was over 22.5 metres, but between 1989 and 1993 no female athlete put the shot further than 22 metres and in 1996 no athlete exceeded 21 metres. A similar pattern is found in the javelin where no one has got within 4 metres of the 1988 world record and in 1996 the best throw was some 10.5 metres short of the record.[1]

In view of the ethical controversies surrounding the IOC in the wake of the Salt Lake City scandal, the IOC was keen to resuscitate its declining image. Therefore, one of the successes of the Sydney Games was the restoration of the Olympic Image. Clearly the Sydney Games presented the world with numerous positive images. However, one way of evaluating the effectiveness of an image-based campaign is to measure public reaction. Probably as a result of the 15 hour time difference between Sydney and the East coast of the United States, and the strange decision of NBC, the US broadcaster, to televise delayed coverage of most events, television ratings for these Games were the lowest in 20 years. However, one further possible explanation for lower ratings might be the relatively low number of world records set in Sydney. Might it be that there is some correlation between drug use and performance levels, and that the relative "cleanliness" of the Sydney Games resulted in fewer records?

---

1 B Houlihan, *Beyond Sport: Doping in Sport and the Development of Anti-Doping Policy* (Strasbourg, Council of Europe Publishing, 1999) at 104.

Much of this is pure speculation. However, interesting policy questions arise. Below we list the usual justifications for regulating use of performance enhancing drugs:

- Protection of the health and safety of the athletes and spectators
- Preservation of the "ethics" of sport
- Protection of the image of sport
- Ensuring a "level playing field"
- Ensuring that contests are true contests between athletes and not between chemists.

There are other arguments to be sure, but these are the most commonly used.

The problem with creating uniform doping policy is that the various interested parties use different justifications to explain their preferred policies.

The Policy Debate: What Drugs Should be Included?

A good example of how disagreement on underlying policy aims translates into difficulties with the actual rules is the very public disagreement in 1998 between Juan Antonio Samaranch and General Barry McCaffrey, the US "Drug Czar". During a routine, pre-Olympic inspection visit to Sydney, Samaranch remarked that perhaps there should be a drastic cut in the number of banned drugs and an easing of restrictions on which drugs can be used by athletes.[2]

Samaranch had been quoted as saying that athletes should be able to use "harmless" drugs that improve their performance provided these drugs did not damage their health. Many banned pharmaceuticals are harmless and do not improve performances. Samaranch's remarks provoked a barrage of criticism, particularly from General McCaffrey.

Aside from the obvious policy question raised by this debate, whether the purpose of the drug bans is to protect (albeit paternalistically) the health of participating athletes, the American response raised a further question of whether it is appropriate to treat sports drug policy as an arm of a broader "anti-drug offensive".

---

2 M Moore, "Olympic Chief's Stunning Call: Relax Ban on Drugs", *Sydney Morning Herald*, 28 July 1998 at 1.

Most are well familiar with mainly American efforts to prohibit illicit drug use. The American policy of prohibition is attracting a growing number of critics worldwide, and it is safe to say that there is by no means a consensus view that the American approach is successful. This approach in the fight to clean up sports may be no more successful. One might speculate that Samaranch was thinking laterally, and trying to find a way to protect the interest of the IOC in attracting public interest by continually smashing world records, while at the same time taking a lead role in the move to eradicate inappropriate drug use. Some of the more cynical observers pointed out that statements such as this were good evidence of why it would be inappropriate to entrust the IOC with the task of policing the doping rules.[3]

Unfortunately for Samaranch, the virtually unanimous condemnation of his remarks ensured that the list of banned substances would not be reduced.[4] In

---

[3] Those subscribing to this viewpoint often refer to the fact that the IOC has been accused of concealing positive test results obtained during past Olympic Games: see A Jennings, *The New Lords of the Rings* (London, Simon & Schuster 1996) at 232-249. In fairly bombastic style, Jennings accuses the IOC of deliberately misleading the public in order to preserve the image of its spectacle: for example (at 237):

"...the 1984 Olympics must appear 'pure', without too many embarrassing dope results. Sports lovers, athletes, TV networks and sponsors were misled by Samaranch and his IOC leadership; as they publicly proclaimed victory in their 'war' against doping, they ought to have known the figures they published about the Los Angeles Games were false. The inside story of doping control at the 1984 Olympics is at odds with the published facts.

At the end of the Games the IOC could have revealed that many more athletes had tested positive than the twelve it admitted to. Vital documents identifying the cheats were mysteriously shredded. Why, if the IOC is so keen on good clean sport, didn't they tell us? Could it, by any chance be because they didn't want to spoil the salesmen's pitch?"

By contrast, note the IOC's own statement (taken from its website: <hppt://www.olympic.org>). In a document entitled "Policy Commitment", the following is stated:

"There is no organisation in the world that has done more to fight against doping in sport than the IOC. The Olympic Movement is the only movement that has developed an ethical platform as the basis of the practice of sport..."

[4] See "Alarm, anger over backflip on cheats", *The Sydney Morning Herald* 29 July 1998 at 4. The staff writers quoted a variety of individuals regarding their response to Samaranch's remarks:

"...fellow IOC member Phil Coles said Mr Samaranch was being "realistic". "If an athlete can take a handful of vitamin E tablets, it might help his performance but it won't harm his or her health." Australian IOC board member Kevan Gosper told ABC radio the definition of doping was a concern. 'If you give an athlete a panadol to fix a headache, does that mean you've enhanced his potential performance? There is a grey area there.'

fact, at about the same time, the IOC Medical Commission added marijuana to the list of banned substances, thereby ensuring that there would be no repeat of the embarrassment caused by the positive test results of Ross Rebagliatti after winning a gold medal in snowboarding at Nagano. So, rather than seeing the list of banned substances reduced, it continues to grow, this time to add a substance with dubious performance enhancing qualities (and about which there are conflicting claims of its alleged detriment to human health).[5] For most athletic activities, marijuana is a performance inhibitor.

So far the "recreational drug" question has arisen in relation to marijuana and cocaine (see REBAGLIATI and LAMAZE). In 2000 two Rugby League players were suspended for testing positive to compounds popularly known as ecstasy. One of the players, Craig Field, is challenging the suspension he received on the basis that the rules permitting testing for non-performance-enhancing drugs are unreasonable.[6] This legal challenge is further discussed in Chapter 7 below.

Given this and other public debates surrounding doping policy, it was interesting to observe at the World Conference on Doping in Sport, that the IOC had established one of four pre-Conference working groups to report on "Prevention, Ethics, Education and Communication". It is useful to quote from this report at some length for, ultimately, the content of doping policy can only reflect the underlying characterisation of the ethical issue presented by doping:

> The Federal Sports Minister, Andrew Thomson, said he was 'gobsmacked' by the statements and was writing to the IOC seeking clarification...Former marathon champion and Australian Institute of Sport Director Robert de Castella said he would be 'alarmed and concerned' if Mr Samaranch's comments meant that he in any way condoned a relaxation of current anti-drugs regulations. 'I would shudder to think that we would go back to the dark ages of the '70s,' he said."

5 One of the more curious contributions to the debate on drug policy at the IOC organised World Conference on Doping in Sport was that of Dr Hap Davis, a sports psychologist from Canada, who submitted a paper entitled "Opinion: Cannabinoids are potential performance enhancing drugs and should be banned for use by Olympic athletes during and out of competition." A sample of his argument follows:

> "cannabinoids have been used medicinally for an estimated 4000 years to produce a state of calm and a relief from nausea. Likewise, psychological interventions are widely used to produce the same result. Thus, both pharmacology (cannabinoids) and psychology (relaxation techniques) can each enhance the mental status of the athlete both pre-competition and in competition."

This and other submissions to the Conference are available through the IOC's official website: <http://www.Olympic.org/doping>.

6 See *Craig Steven Field v National Rugby League Ltd*, filed in NSW Industrial Relations Court 27 June 2001.

The Ethical Basis of Sport

Competitive games are contests, which entail competition with a view to establishing a winner and loser, but this does not imply that winning is to be the only concern: rather, one can play to win, valuing the opportunity to exercise speed, strength and skill. For a good sports contest, though, there are certain prerequisites:

1. There is a presupposition of *equality of opportunity to compete* (equality under the rules), as clear outcomes of the form of competition created by the rules cannot be demonstrated unless all other variables are strictly controlled.
2. As no contest could exist without the opponent, a minimum of *respect for one's opponent* is essential, at least the respect which is due to a facilitator – i.e. to one whose co-operation and whose own level of performance are a major contributor to the very possibilities for excellence open to oneself in the endeavour chosen by both.
3. Although it is clearly possible to break the rules, to do so alters the conditions of the contest, so that a range of abilities not specified by the rules comes into play. A good contest will maintain the framework which ensures the integrity of the contest, and this requires *adherence to the rules and fair play.*
4. There is a *knowledge of relative abilities* which is a necessary outcome. This may be an occasion for conceit, but also for humility and generosity.
5. In games, there is a simple right and wrong, easily policeable by a clearly identified *legal authority.* At the same time, there is some possibility of differing interpretation and judgement. In playing games, students learn how to follow explicit rules, how to bend them and evade them, and how to operate within a system of penalties and consequences, both official and unofficial. Games are laboratories for value experiments.

In order to place emphasis on the primordial importance of ethics in sports competitions, various measures are proposed below. Although they are of a highly symbolic nature, they nonetheless stress, for all to see and hear, that ethics are essential and should be strictly adhered to:

1. An amendment to the Olympic Charter to include, in the text of the oath pronounced by the competitors' representative at the Opening Ceremony of the Olympic Games, the respect of ethical methods throughout the preparation for the Games. [the paper continued to suggest wording for the necessary amendment]

2. The oath should be taken not just by one competitor representing all the others; but it should be made a condition of participation that such an oath be taken by each athlete, possibly in the form of a written contract to compete fairly. Such a written document, in the form of an Athletes' Agreement, would contain direct statements such as "I am not in violation of the IOC Medical code and its anti-doping practices and procedures."[7]
3. In addition to the representatives of the competitors and judges, a representative of the coaches could also take a solemn oath.
4. Following the examples set by some national Olympic Committees, all competitors, coaches, medical staff and other persons involved in the training of the competitors participating in any sports event should be made to enter into an agreement with the organisers of said sports event that would specifically address the imperative need to strictly adhere to a defined code of ethics.
5. Sponsorship agreements between athletes and sponsors should include a clause prohibiting any form of doping and specifying the financial and other consequences for the athlete of being found positive for banned substances in a test by any legitimate testing authority.

---

[7] In this regard, note the following provisions of the *Membership Agreement - Athletes* used by the AOC in relation to participation in the Sydney Olympic Games:

"8. Doping Requirements and Use of Drugs

1 8.1 I Acknowledge that I have read the AOC's Anti-Doping Policy (see Schedule 4) and I agree:

(2) To observe and comply with the Anti-Doping Policy; and

(3) Not to use, attempt to use, have in my possession, attempt to have in my possession, traffic or attempt to traffic a "drug of addiction", "poison", and "restricted substance" (as each of these words and phrases is defined in the Poisons and Therapeutic Goods Act 1966 of the State of New South Wales) in contravention of the Poisons and Therapeutic Goods Act 1966.

4 8.2 I acknowledge that:

(1) the AOC has provided medical practitioners as part of the Team; and

(2) the Medical Code recommends that athletes should only use drugs and medications under the supervision of a physician.

I agree that I am not using and will not use any drugs and medications from the time of my selection until I am no longer a member of the Team without this use being under the supervision of a medical practitioner and all drugs and medications so prescribed being first approved by the Team Medical Director or his nominee."

For detailed comments on this and other aspects of the Australian Olympic Team membership agreement, see A Buti, "AOC Athletes' Agreement for Sydney 2000: The Implications for the Athletes" (1999) 23 University of New South Wales Law Journal 185.

The IOC document refers to "making the athletes" enter into certain types of agreements. However well-intentioned the IOC may be, there is no doubt that any individual capable of demonstrating that they became a party to an agreement by coercion or undue influence or illegitimate pressure (including commercial pressure) may well be able to escape being bound by the agreement on the basis of duress or unconscionable dealing.[8] Furthermore, proposed measure number 5 appears to contemplate the IOC dictating the contents of agreements between athletes and third party sponsors.[9]

We will further deliberate on the legal issues later.[10] Let us now consider each of the various policy justifications more closely.

Sports Ethics[11]

There is an historical belief that the essence of sport is competition between

---

8 See below, Chapter Seven, "Legal Challenges to Drug Testing".

9 According to Anglo-Australian legal principles, only the parties to a contract are bound by it, and none of the parties to an agreement is under any legal obligation to respond to suggestions from "third parties". It is thus hard to see on what basis the IOC can assert any legal foundation for mandating the terms of contracts between athletes and their sponsors. Nonetheless, where those same sponsors are members of the "Olympic Family" there are undoubtedly extralegal pressures that can be brought to bear. In such cases, the possibility of objection from the athlete on the grounds of duress or unconscionability may be difficult.

Note the provisions of the AOC Athlete Agreement dealing with the athlete's obligations to financial sponsors:

"8.3 In the event that I commit a doping offence (as defined in the AOC Anti-Doping Policy) by:
(1) returning a positive test result;
(2) providing a sample for testing (and which subsequently returns a positive test result); or
(3) committing any act or omission which otherwise constitutes a doping offence between the time I am accredited as a participant in the Games and midnight on 1 October 2000 (being the conclusion of the day of the Closing Ceremony of the Games) and in respect of which I am found to have breached the IOC Medical Code and also in respect of which a suspension of two years is imposed on me under the AOC's Anti-Doping Policy, I will repay to:
(a) the AOC all grants and other money paid to me by the AOC associated or in connection with my participation in the Games including, but not limited to the Medal Incentive Scheme Payments, the Olympic Dream Medal Reward Scheme and payments under this agreement; and
(b) Carlton and United Breweries all grants and other money paid to me by the "Foster's Sports Foundation".

10 See Chapter Seven, "Legal Challenges to Drug Testing".

11 There is an excellent, concise review of the usual ethical arguments in J Parry, "Ethics and

athletes based on their individually developed natural abilities, not on the most effective pharmacological agents.

What at first appears an attractive argument - that drug use destroys fair competition - deserves close scrutiny. First, it is not entirely clear that drug use does destroy fair competition. Secondly, banning the use of drugs will not guarantee the fair competition that we allegedly seek. Thirdly, there are other, far less intrusive, means by which we could ensure that our athletic contests are fairer.

The assumption underpinning the "fair competition" justification is that performance-enhancing drugs do in fact improve performance. This view has wide, but far from unanimous, support.[12] There is also no empirical evidence available to support the conclusion that those who use drugs actually improve their performance.[13] There may in fact be substances capable of improving the performance of athletes. But those who seek to ban a particular substance and support that ban with a program of mandatory testing must face a strong onus of proving the alleged effects of the drug.

Even were one to accept that performance-enhancing drugs at least have the potential to improve performance, or that athletes who take such drugs to improve performance should be penalised regardless of any actual results, other questions are raised. For instance, it has been argued that "since our genes decide our body chemistry, why shouldn't we if we choose, modify that chemistry in order to increase our athletic performance?"[14] The countervailing argument is that while our body chemistry is a natural synthesis of compounds, doping is not "natural" as it involves the consumption of synthetic substances. However, the practice of blood-doping, which is banned, does not fit this rationale, because it does not involve the introduction of "foreign" substances. Therefore, for this practice to fall

---

Doping", paper presented to IEC Scientific Conference on Doping in Sport (1999) <http://www.blues.uab.es/olympic.studies/doping/parry.htm>.
12 In relation to anabolic steroids, see E Zemper, "Drug Testing In Athletics" in R H Coombs and L J West (eds), *Drug Testing: Issues and Options* (New York, Oxford University Press 1991) at 124-125.
13 In fact in the American case of *Hill v National Collegiate Athletic Association and Stanford University* 7 Cal App 4th 1738, 273 Cal Rptr 402 (6th Dist 1990) at 413-419, the evidence presented suggested that performance-enhancing drugs actually were ineffective.
14 J Sumner, cited in K Donald, *The Doping Game* (Brisbane, Queensland University Press 1983) at 81.

within any definition of a prohibited practice, the legal definition of doping must be broadened to include any physiological substance taken in abnormal quantity or taken by an abnormal route of entry into the body".[15]

Were this definition to be adopted, one may then rightly ask why the consumption of amino acids, which purportedly increase the body's production of growth hormone, or the practice of carbohydrate loading, which purportedly improves endurance, are not similarly penalised? Thus, the simple proposition that drug bans, supported by mandatory testing, are an integral part of the effort to make sports more "natural" loses much of its force when any attempt is made to draw a line dividing fair and unfair practices.

Nonetheless, some argue that the aim of policy in this area ought to be to eradicate "unnatural" practices, or at least ensure that competition is between athletes, based on their "God-given" abilities. And, in any event, we don't want to see "drug users" become worshipped athletic heroes. But:

> there is already in existence a culture, professionally supported and promoted, that encourages the treatment of healthy athletes with drugs. Even if the "drugs" are simply those which are legally available (in terms defined by both the state and the IOC), such as vitamins and food supplements, the athlete is already developing the expectations and patterns of behaviour that might initially parellel illegal drug use, but which are to most athletes part of a common culture. Robert Voy, former chief medical officer for the US Olympic Committee, illustrates this point very clearly when he recorded the daily intake of legal drugs that a national track star was taking: vitamin E, 160mg, B-complex capsules, four times per day; vitamin C, 2000mg; vitamin B6,150mg; calcium tablets, four times per day; magnesium tablets, twice a day; zinc tablets, three times a day; royal jelly capsules; garlic tablets; cayenne tablets; eight aminos; Gamma-Oryzanol; Mega Vit Pack; supercharge herbs; Dibencozide; glandular tissue complex; natural steroid complex; linsine; Orchic testicle extract; Pyridium; Ampicillin; and hair rejuvenation formula with Biotin.[16]

Few readers would consider this to be a normal dietary intake.

---

15 E Zemper, "Drug Testing In Athletics" in R H Coombs and L J West (eds), *Drug Testing: Issues and Options* (New York, Oxford University Press, 1991) at 137.
16 B Houlihan, *Dying to Win: Doping in Sport and the Development of Anti-Doping Policy*, (Strasbourg, Council of Europe Publishing 1999) at 88.

If "sports ethics" refers to the creation of a "level playing field" that allows for fair competition, then why stop at regulating drug use? It is no doubt true that athletes from developed nations, with their Ministries of Sport and substantial public funding for sport, have a significant competitive edge. The medal tallies from any Olympic Games reveal the definite correlation between national wealth and Olympic success. Resources permit many nations to offer their athletes the finest facilities and coaches, and subsidies enable the athlete to dedicate himself or herself to the task of athletic success on a more or less full-time basis. What chance do athletes without these benefits have of competing on an equal basis? It is therefore ultimately self-deceiving to argue that banning drugs from sport will make competition fairer. Drugs, unlike the other acceptable means of enhancing performance, are at least equally fair.[17]

The main reason athletes use performance-enhancing drugs is to obtain or maintain a competitive edge. Many have argued that our society, by placing such a high premium on winning, is guilty of introducing the pressure which is persuasive. Certainly, the much publicised medal tallies at international competitions (particularly the Olympic Games) reflect the preoccupation of most of us with results. For many, to quote Vince Lombardi, the famous American football coach: "Winning isn't everything; it's the only thing". It is the winners in competition who attract the adulation of the media and through it the general public, which in turn leads to lucrative endorsements and government grants. In former times, some governments found the temptation to use performance at international sporting events as a measure of the superiority of a rival social system, not to mention a convenient means of

---

[17] Others have made this point: "Because only some athletes abide by the rules, the drug ban in effect creates monopoly benefits for drug users. The ban thus results in unfair contests between drug users and non-users....It is a perverse and ironic outcome that a drug ban instituted to create fair competition should promote unfair competition. Competition would be made fairer by removing the ban on drug usage, allowing all athletes to achieve their full potential. The ban deprives the majority of the benefits of drugs, leaving the minority who continue to use drugs with an unfair advantage". See "Unmask the Unfairness by Dropping Ban" *The Australian,* 17 August 1993 at 30.

A recent illustration of the problem of differential access to performance enhancing equipment was the controversy concerning the use of fitted bodysuits by swimmers. The controversy culminated in a reference to the Court of Arbitration for Sport in February 2000. The CAS ruled that the matter of deciding whether such suits constituted performance enhancing "equipment" within the meaning of the applicable competition rules was the sole responsibility of FINA, the relevant international federation. FINA ruled that the suits should be permitted. As part of the negotiations preceding the ruling, the manufacturers of the suits offered to provide suits, free of charge, for those athletes wishing to use them.

providing their own citizens with evidence to support their claims. It is not surprising that some athletes succumb to the pressure to succeed that leads them to take performance-enhancing drugs. If we are serious about our desire to eradicate drug-taking in sport, then we ought to reflect on our society's preoccupation with winning.[18]

Another aspect of sports ethics can be raised, if only for short shrift. That is the question of "cheating". Some argue that it is enough that the rules exist. If it is decided that athletes should not take steroids, then that, in itself, is sufficient reason for athletes not to do so. For the athlete to flout the rules is behaviour which is deserving of punishment. There is some force to this argument. Punishing an athlete who tests positive to steroids is only consistent with ensuring respect for the law. Yet, if, despite the law, we know that athletes continue to use steroids, are we not missing a vital point? Many have argued the same with respect to criminalisation of marijuana use. Yet annual surveys continue to reveal that substantial numbers of our citizens continue to engage in this illegal behaviour.[19] When we are aware of this level of disobedience, we must examine the law closely. Just as the United States government chose to repeal legislation banning the distribution and consumption of alcohol after the attempt to prohibit alcohol consumption failed, we might similarly opt to end the prohibition of substances if we can no longer justify it and the law is routinely ignored. If the law's underlying premises are flawed, putting more teeth into the law will not make it a better law.

A mandatory drug testing regime can undermine the civil liberties of the athletes affected. Any such intrusion can be balanced if there is a need for

---

18 In Canada, this was part of the agenda of the Commission of Inquiry into the Use of Drugs and Banned Practices Intended to Increase Athletic Performance. The Commissioner, Charles L Dubin, was appointed to examine the use of drugs in sport in Canada following the expulsion of Ben Johnson from the 1988 Olympic Games in Seoul. The Dubin Commission's recommendations have caused reflection, in Canada at least, into the preoccupation with winning that led to Johnson's disgrace. Refer to The Honourable Charles L Dubin, *Commission of Inquiry into the Use of Drugs and Banned Practices Intended to Increase Athletic Performance* (Ottawa, Minister of Supply and Services Canada 1990).
In Australia, the Senate Standing Committee on Environment, Recreation and the Arts, *Drugs in Sport: An Interim Report* (Canberra, Australian Government Publishing Service 1989) at 28-35, contains a summary of the reasons often advanced for taking performance-enhancing drugs. The same enquiry believed the argument based on fairness of competition to be unsound, because enormous disparities exist between competitors at all levels (at 48).
19 See R Fox and I Matthews, *Drugs Policy: Fact, Fiction and the Future* (Annandale, The Federation Press 1992) at 18-35.

such regulation. Of course that need must be appropriately demonstrated. That need is something that can be particular to the sport concerned, as well as commensurate with the values to which we in Australia subscribe.[20]

Health and Safety of the Athlete and the Public

Fairness in sport is not the only justification advanced. It may well be that the need to protect the health and safety of participating athletes justifies the present rules and the testing regime. By contrast to the alleged effects on performance of performance-enhancing drugs, there is sufficient empirical evidence to support the claim that such drugs may produce harmful physical and behavioural side effects, although the magnitude of harm varies among the different banned drugs. The potential side effects are numerous,[21] and in the worst cases can lead to death.[22] It has been argued by some that the belief that use of such drugs is widespread leads some athletes to use drugs they believe to be performance-enhancing in order to remain competitive, thereby putting their own health at risk.[23] However, many banned substances are medicinal. The athlete is penalised for improving his health.

In addition to the health risks posed to users of drugs, there are potential risks to others. It has been argued that anabolic steroid or stimulant use in competition (especially in team sports) produces unduly aggressive behavioural side-effects that may put competitors at risk.[24] However, aggressive play is often what the

---

20 Where athletes have been pressured to sign consents or where the terms of an agreement are unduly onerous, an athlete may be able to claim that the agreement ought not be binding. Where sanctions based on implementation of policy are excessive, the penalty may be held to be in unreasonable restraint of trade. These legal arguments are fully canvassed in Chapter Six: Legal Challenges to Drug Testing.
21 See K Donald, *The Doping Game* (Brisbane, Queensland University Press 1983) at 78-80 and H Opie, "Legal Regimes for the Control of Performance -Enhancing Drugs in Sport" (1990) 12 *Adelaide Law Review* 332.
22 For example, "Two Footballers Died After Horse Steroid Use" *Mercury*, 20 June 1991 at 32, cites the instance of steroid abuse leading to death of two young NSW country level rugby league players.
23 Here, the work of the Australian Sports Drug Agency may be important in two respects. Firstly, test results compiled by ASDA may provide more reliable information as to the extent of drug use. Secondly, research into the side effects of performance enhancing drugs may provide much needed information on the risks associated with their use.
24 The behavioural side-effects of anabolic steroid abuse have been the basis of some judicial support for drug testing in sport. *See R v Nathan Brendan Jones* (Unreported Decision, Supreme Court of Queensland, 21 April 1989).

coaches desire and demand. The psychological effects of performance-enhancing drug abuse may expose sporting organisations (who employ the athletes concerned) to vicarious liability for the wrongful acts of the athletes who injure other competitors or third parties.[25] Employer liability may also be argued, based on the employer's duty under statute and at common law to take reasonable precautions to provide a safe and healthy work environment,[26] which may justify penalising drug-taking.

This paternalistic concern for the health of our athletes seems curiously limited to health risks presented by ingestion of performance-enhancing drugs. It is acceptable common practice to inject painkillers to mask the pain of previous injuries, even though this may induce the athlete to continue to compete, at risk of causing irreparable damage to his or her body.[27] Further, the events themselves might be said to pose far greater risk to the athlete than the use of drugs to enhance performance. Every year in the United States competitors are killed or seriously injured in gridiron contests and in 1994 a world-wide audience was witness to the horrible death of an Austrian alpine skier. Anyone who has witnessed a luge race must have serious doubts about the insurability of a competitor!

It is unlikely that the safety of the public will be affected by athletes consuming performance-enhancing drugs. However, there may be some argument that "sporting stars" are role models for the public, especially the young, and thus there is a need to ensure that they "set the right example". This rationale has some merit, but is difficult to reconcile with the sponsorship of sport by companies responsible for the production of tobacco

---

[25] See *Bugge v Brown* (1919) 26 CLR 110; *Rodgers v Bugden and Canterbury Bankstown Rugby League Football Club Limited* (Unreported Decision, Supreme Court of NSW, 14 December 1990); and G M Kelly, "Negligence Actions Between Sports Participants: The Measure of Liability" (1992) 66 *Australian Law Journal* 329.

[26] See *Cotter v Huddart Parker Ltd* (1941) 41 SR (NSW) 33 at 37-38; and R Johnstone, "Pre-employment Health Screening: The Legal Framework" (1988) 1 *Australian Journal of Labour Law* 115.

[27] In 1976, the US football team, the Chicago Bears, settled a lawsuit brought by a player alleging that extensive injections of cortisone and other drugs caused irreparable damage to his knee. See "Bears Will Pay Butkus $600,000 in Damage Suit" *New York Times*, 14 September 1976 at 50. Also refer to J Barnes, *Sports and the Law in Canada* (3rd ed Toronto, Butterworths 1996) at 307-312 and the reported case: *Krueger v San Francisco Forty Niners* 234 Cal Rptr 579 (1987).

and alcoholic products.[28] We will deal with the matter of public image below.

The foregoing all relates to the testing for performance-enhancing drugs. What about testing for "recreational drugs" which have no proven performance-enhancing qualities? Presumably, the argument that use of such substances is to be discouraged on account of heath and safety concerns has more merit. However, at least in the case of marijuana, currently available evidence is inconclusive with regard to any harmful medical consequences.[29] There is a significant body of opinion that marijuana consumption is less harmful than either tobacco or alcohol usage.[30] Thus, even from the standpoint of health and safety, a policy of testing for use of all "recreational" drugs supported by sanctions for detected usage may not be supportable.[31]

As questionable as current anti-doping policy may be, there is a body of opinion which asserts that, from the perspective of health, it makes more sense to deregulate drug use in sport. Adherents of this view argue that, especially in the case of steroids, the problem is not use itself, but use in unsafe doses. This view is consistent with the published views of the IOC Medical Commission, who have said that "anabolic steroids can have long term effects by causing many health problems".[32] The reason for the IOC's uncertainty is lack of information concerning dosage quantities. The point is that the danger arises only when the quantity consumed exceeds a certain level. If this is true, then the proper course to take to reduce health risk is to develop knowledge of the safe level of usage and monitor the athletes to ensure that none ingests unsafe quantities of the drugs. Banning drugs is therefore not necessary in order to protect the health of competitors.

---

28 This may become a thing of the past if present Federal Government policy is implemented. It should also be noted that, if this justification is ultimately the most powerful, then there would be an equally strong argument for testing stars of the entertainment world generally for drug use, considering their influence on the young and vulnerable members of our society.
29 Australian Capital Territory Legislative Assembly, *Marijuana and Other Illegal Drugs, Third Interim Report of the Select Committee on HIV, Illegal Drugs and Prostitution* (Canberra, ACT Government 1991) at 20-28. A fairly typical conclusion is the following, taken from the *Report of the Expert Group on the Effects of Cannabis Use* (1981) UK, HMSO: "much of the research undertaken so far has failed to demonstrate positive and significant harmful effects in man attributable solely to the use of cannabis".
30 Ibid at 28.
31 Such as the policy of the New South Wales Rugby League, the NRL and the ARL.
32 *Drugs in Sport: An Interim Report of the Senate Standing Committee on Environment, Recreation and the Arts,* (Canberra, Australian Government Publishing Service 1989) Part 2 at 49.

Public Image and Confidence

Obviously the public and sponsors are interested in protecting the integrity of sport and the individuals who participate in it. The argument in support of drug-testing here is that the fans and sponsors who support sport would lose interest if either believed that the players were "cheating" or not performing at their best on account of substance abuse.[33] This concern has been most predominant in the United States, especially in sports which attract the interest of the gambling community. Here another concern is important, and that is the protection of confidence in any result.[34]

The importance of maintaining public confidence in sport and protecting the image of sport must be balanced against the right of athletes to individual autonomy and privacy. If this is to be advanced as a justification, just where do we draw the line? One might well argue that sporting organisations have an interest in ensuring that their competitors do not engage in what might generally be thought to be "immoral" behaviour. Does that justify, for example, maintaining surveillance over athletes to ensure that none is engaged in an extra-marital affair? This very issue has provoked great controversy in various democracies when it has involved elected public officials. Certainly if the American experience is instructive, then we can conclude that there is great diversity of opinion on the matter. If there is such a range of opinion on the question of the morality of public opinions, surely we might question this as a serious justification for the mandatory drug-testing of our athletes.

Thus, while sporting organisations might justifiably be concerned with maintaining the confidence of the public in the integrity of the sports they administer, such concern must be managed with care, lest it develop into sinister and intrusive regulation of those who participate in sport.

Discouraging Illegal Activity Generally

Pursuant to the Customs (Prohibited Imports) Regulations[35] and the various State and Territories Acts,[36] the importation, cultivation, sale and possession

---

[33] All drugs are relevant to this discussion, but probably this argument is mostly directed at the "recreational" drugs, which have the greatest potential to impair performance.
[34] See *Shoemaker v Handel* 795 F 2d 1136 (3d Cir 1986) at 1142.
[35] Promulgated under the Customs Act 1901 (Cth).
[36] For example, the Drug Misuse and Trafficking Act 1985 (NSW) and Drugs of Dependence Act 1989 (ACT).

of many of the drugs for which testing is conducted carry criminal penalties. Thus, sporting organisations have legitimate concerns aimed at preventing their most important assets, the athletes, from the prospect of criminal prosecution. Furthermore, the sporting organisations must be careful to protect their officials from being placed at risk of criminal liability for aiding, abetting, counselling or procuring the commission of an offence or acting with a common purpose in the commission of a crime.[37]

Generally, those who promulgate restrictive drug laws have not had to justify their existence. Many of us in Australia, as well as overseas, assume that the use of drugs is an evil that justifies a host of intrusive legislation and administrative practice. We seem to accept this as undeniable truth. We hope that, at least insofar as drugs in sport is concerned, we have provided a framework within which to assess the validity of the rules and practices which support them.

Only "genuine" legitimate interests of sporting bodies and the public interest can justify the banning of, and testing for, demonstrated performance enhancing drugs. In addition, given the dubious nature of the "fair competition" rationalisation, it may be necessary to require that such drugs also have demonstrated adverse health consequences before adding them to the banned list.

Conclusions

It is hard to draw any definite conclusions from this review. The continuing difficulties that consume sports administrators attempting to harmonise anti-doping strategies and policies illustrate the lack of consensus on questions of policy. Still, it is important that the debate continue, to ensure that the rules that are produced are ultimately justifiable. Notwithstanding all that has been said, it is still hard to look past the simple proposition that what produces the

---

[37] Although the potential scope of liability may seem wide, that scope has been somewhat limited by *Giorgianni v The Queen* (1985) 156 CLR 473 where the High Court (per Wilson, Deane and Dawson JJ) held that: "For the purpose of many offences it may be true to say that if an act is done with foresight of its probable consequences, there is sufficient intent in law, even if such intent may be more properly described as a form of recklessness. There are, however, offences in which it is not possible to speak of recklessness as constituting a sufficient intent. Attempt is one and conspiracy is another. And we think the offences of aiding and abetting and counseling and procuring are others. Those offences require intentional participation..."

widespread drug use that the sporting authorities fear is the tremendous rewards that success produces.

The most eloquent summary of this state of affairs is probably that of Justice Charles Dubin, who wrote the following in the conclusions of his report following the Ben Johnson scandal of the late 1980s:

> As a society we have created a climate in sport in which the only good is perceived to be winning and the manner of doing so of no consequence. Only the winner is accorded praise and financial reward without recognition of the outstanding achievements of those who also compete but do not come first. The role of the media in fostering and encouraging this narrow, superficial view of success cannot be ignored. I have detailed in this report the negative reaction by the media to outstanding performances by Canadian athletes that did not result in gold medals. This too has placed the wrong emphasis on what sport is all about.
>
> If winning a gold medal in Olympic competition is the only achievement worthy of recognition, then everything is permissible in order to win. Such a proposition is completely unacceptable. But I do not mean to say that we must now accept mediocrity. We must strive for a true excellence, not the hollow victory of the cheater.
>
> At its inception, participation in Olympic competition was available only to amateurs. That is no longer the case. Some participants are truly professionals; others are professionals in all but name. Indeed, in the high-profile Olympic sports, many participants devote virtually all of their time to sport to the exclusion of employment, study, or other vocations. In addition, significant financial rewards are available to them. The Olympic Games and other international athletic competitions have become substantial commercial enterprises, particularly with the advent of television. The financial rewards for those conducting competitions and potentially for the athletes who compete are now enormous.[38]

---

38 Even members of the Olympic Family are not immune. The standard Australian Olympic Committee agreement for team members provides for significant financial rewards based on performance.

"14.1 I acknowledge that the AOC has agreed to underwrite the funding of the rewards provided under the Olympic Dream Medal Reward Scheme so that Gold Medallists will receive $15,000, Silver Medallists $7,500 and Bronze Medallists $5,000. These amounts may be increased if the AOC secures a sponsor or other official supporter of the Olympic Dream Medal Reward Scheme."

The athlete who wins a gold medal in international competition or breaks a world record in a high-profile sport can become a millionaire overnight from commercial endorsements and appearance fees. Commercialization of amateur athletic competition need not be a corrupting influence, but it does increase the temptation for those who are inclined to cheat.[39]

And it is against this pressure that the IOC commits itself to lead in the fight against doping. In the following Chapters we will describe the key elements in this strategy, and how domestic Australian law interacts with these efforts.

---

39 The Honourable Charles L Dubin, *Commission of Inquiry into the Use of Drugs and Banned Practices Intended to Increase Athletic Performance* (Ottawa, Minister of Supply and Services Canada 1990) at 518-519.

CHAPTER 5

THE TESTING AUTHORITIES

Introduction

In chapter two we saw how the doping policies of the ASC, the AOC, the various International Federations and the National Federations employ the services of the ASDA to conduct testing. We also saw how ASDA emerged as a statutory authority in response to the need for a reliable and independent testing authority. In this chapter, we shall explore both the role and function of ASDA.

The ASDA Legislation

There is significant public disquiet about the concept of athletes who test positive "escaping punishment on the basis of a technicality".

This reaction is understandable, but it involves drawing a conclusion that is not necessarily correct. Public reaction to "drug cheats" is based on a perception of their guilt, having been convinced that a positive drug test means that there is no doubt that the athlete used a banned agent. However, the lawyer's typical reaction to the imposition of sanctions based on what is, in effect, a mandatory drug test is much different.

In the first place, being required to submit to a urine test, where the urine is collected under supervision, is a somewhat unusual and intrusive event. It is, however, a procedure which seems generally accepted as necessary and justifiable. But, to a lawyer and hopefully to most in our society, it is essential that such procedures be carried out properly, which means within the limits of the powers given to the various agencies and in accordance with their procedures. Therefore, the statute from which ASDA derives its power is extremely specific in terms of describing the protocol of drug testing. This is to ensure that test results are accurate beyond any reasonable doubt. As we shall see, even where a positive test result occurs, the subject is given the opportunity to challenge the accuracy of the result and the recording of any "offence".

As we shall see in later chapters, the athlete's rights do not end there. There are further questions to be asked about the appropriate sanction, if any, to be applied in the event of a positive drug test.

Whether a drug test is being conducted by ASDA or some other agency in another country, the legal concerns remain the same. Was the test conducted under appropriate conditions, in accordance with the required procedure and within the jurisdiction of the relevant testing authority?

It is not only the lawyers who express such concern. Professor Manfred Donike, formerly in charge of worldwide IOC accreditation of laboratories, states:

> There is a well known proverb in analytical chemistry that says errors made at the sample taking stage will determine the analytical result. In doping control, simple, reasonable measures have been laid down in the Procedural Guidelines to guarantee correct sample taking and to maintain the integrity of the sample.
> The "Chain of Custody" which begins with the urine voiding and ends with the analysis result report, must be impeccable before a positive finding can lead to sanctions.[1]

Athletes and "Technicalities"

There are numerous well-known examples of athletes avoiding suspension due to irregularities in procedure. These examples are drawn from Australia as well as overseas.

---

1 M Donike, "Laboratory Procedures", Doping is Cheating: Fight for a Clean Sport, IAAF 1st World Anti-Doping Seminar, 14-16 March 1991. The "Chain of Custody" argument was of great importance in the Modahl and Capobianco cases, discussed below.

KRABBE

In 1992, the German Athletics Association (DLV) requested its South African counterpart (the South African Athletics Association) to conduct drug tests on three German athletes who were training in South Africa. After collection, the samples were analysed at the IOC accredited laboratory in Cologne, Germany. The tests were conducted under the supervision of Professor Manfred Donike. Donike in fact was the man responsible for conducting further tests on samples conducted at previous Olympic Games. In fact, at the Seoul Olympics, Donike's further testing revealed that at least 50 male competitors had been taking steroids. Only 10 positive tests were announced.[2]

In the case of Katrin Krabbe, one of the German athletes, Donike's tests suggested that the urine samples had been tampered with. This conclusion was drawn on the basis that the three samples collected were identical and were the urine of the same female. On this basis it was not hard to conclude that there had been manipulation of the samples. Under the rules of the relevant international federation, the International Amateur Athletic Federation (IAAF), tampering with a sample is a doping offence.[3]

---

[2] A Jennings, *The New Lords of the Rings* (London, Simon & Schuster 1996) at 245.

[3] Interestingly enough, neither the ASC's Anti-Doping Policy nor the model Anti-Doping Policy recommended by the AOC to the various national federations in Australia deals directly with the problem of tampering with a sample or using masking agents to hamper efforts to detect prohibited substances. The IAAF Rules contain the following provision.
"Rule 55 – Doping
1. Doping is strictly forbidden and is an offence under IAAF Rules.
2. The offence of doping takes place when either:
(ii) an athlete uses or takes advantage of a prohibited technique...
7. The expression "prohibited technique" shall include:
(b) use of substances and methods which alter the integrity and validity of urine samples used in doping control."
The ASC Anti-Doping Policy does define "prohibited method" as being:
"a method prohibited under the anti-doping policy of:
(a) the relevant [international federation]..."
Assuming that one equates a "prohibited method" with a "prohibited technique", then it is fair to conclude that the ASC Anti-Doping Policy incorporates by reference provisions such as those of the IAAF Rules, Rule 55.
Likewise, the rules of the international federation governing swimming (FINA) contain a similar provision.
The issue of sample integrity is separately discussed below.
The Australian Sports Drug Agency Act 1996 provides in s 15C that tampering with a sample in any way constitutes a "notifiable event", which in practical terms, amounts to the same as having committed a doping offence. However, the anti-doping policy of the ASC, for example, does not make the occurrence of a "notifiable event" necessarily a doping offence (only refusal to provide a sample is considered a doping offence).

All three athletes tested were suspended by the DLV and the IAAF for four years. The athletes all appealed against their suspensions, contending that the test results were invalid and that the sanctions were inappropriate. The thrust of the argument regarding the test results was that the tests were not conducted in accordance with the applicable rules, being those of the DLV. As a result, if the test results were not valid, then no sanction could be imposed. Ultimately, the appeals were successful.

Aside from what were termed "minor irregularities in the sampling procedure", there was no provision in the DLV's rules for the conduct of drug testing out of competition.[4] These conclusions were reached by the DLV's own panel and confirmed by the IAAF Arbitration Panel, which concluded:

The DLV had acted contrary to its rules and procedures in the case of the request to test Krabbe [and the others] and had no basis for authorising the tests...

In some respects, the Krabbe case is similar to that of Australian cyclist Martin Vinnicombe, because the reasoning of the IAAF Arbitration Panel was based in part on the fact that the DLV rules made no provision for the collection of samples by anyone other than its own Doping Commission.[5]

SMITH-DE BRUIN

Another case involving tampering with a urine sample involved multiple gold medal winner, Michelle Smith-de Bruin, who was ultimately banned for four years for using a masking agent, in this case alcohol, in the urine sample. She was tested on 10 January, 1998 without prior notice at her home in Dublin, Republic of Ireland. Unlike Krabbe, Smith-de Bruin's tests were part of an established Out-of-Competition Doping Control Program authorised by FINA,

---

4 "Krabbe ban cut to only one year", *The West Australian,* 31 March 1993.

5 Vinnicombe successfully argued that tests carried out by the Canadian Anti-Doping Authority while he was in training in Pennsylvania could not result in sanctions, as the Canadian authority was not properly authorised in accordance with ASDA rules. As discussed in Chapter 2, Vinnicombe's sanctions were overturned on this basis. The ASDA legislation was subsequently amended to permit testing of Australian athletes overseas by agents acting on behalf of ASDA. As far as Krabbe is concerned, we must be careful not to confuse this legal challenge initiated by Krabbe with a subsequent challenge she made to sanctions imposed when she tested positive to Clenbuterol. The argument in this case centred on whether the DLV needed to prove an intentional commission of a doping offence. This issue is further explored in Chapter 8 below.

the international swimming federation. The sample was tested in the IOC Accredited Laboratory in Barcelona. On 30 January, 1998, the laboratory informed FINA that:

> Unequivocal signs of adulteration have been found in [Smith de-Bruin's] sample...The content of alcohol of the sample...is in no way compatible with human consumption and the sample shows a very strong whiskey odour. Its low specific gravity is also compatible with physical manipulation.[6]

A later analysis of the "B Sample" (see below) was performed on 21 May 1998 confirming the original test results. A hearing before the FINA Doping Panel was held on 24 July 1998 in Lausanne, at which Smith de-Bruin appeared, represented by counsel. Despite Smith de-Bruin's assertion that she had neither used a banned substance nor manipulated the sample she provided, the FINA Doping Panel concluded that a doping offence (within the meaning of that term in the FINA Rules) had been committed. The Panel found that there had been manipulation of the sample for which Smith de-Bruin was responsible. Accordingly, the swimmer was suspended for a period of four years.[7]

Crucial to FINA's determination in the Smith de-Bruin case is the fact that the testing out of competition was properly authorised and was carried out strictly in accordance with the required procedure.

Departure from sample collection protocol is not the only argument that has been used successfully to challenge the validity of a positive test result. As the ASDA rules for collection and analysis of samples clearly demonstrate, there is great concern over the integrity of the sample, particularly when it comes to ensuring that the sample has been dealt with in a manner consistent with accurate results. In particular, the rules attempt to ensure that the chain of custody of the sample remains unbroken. This was a significant issue in the attempted suspension of British athlete Dianne Modahl.

---

6 FINA Press Release, Lausanne, 6 August 1998.
7 The FINA Rules contain a provision essentially the same as IAAF Rule 55.7(b). The FINA Rules provide:
    "DC 1.2 The offence of doping occurs when:
      (b) a competitor uses or takes advantage of a banned procedure (see DC3)...
DC 3.1 Banned techniques include
      (b) use of substances and methods which alter the integrity and validity of urine or
          blood samples used in doping control."

MODAHL

Modahl was tested at an athletic event in Lisbon. Test results showed a high level of testosterone in her sample. Testosterone is a substance which is not banned absolutely, as it occurs naturally within the human body. However, the IOC Medical Code provides that the "administration" of testosterone is banned and that the presence of a testosterone to epitestosterone ratio of greater than six to one in the urine of a competitor constitutes an offence unless there is evidence that this ratio is due to a physiological or pathological condition. Test results showing a "T/E ratio" of greater than six to one must be followed by an investigation by the relevant international federation before the test result is declared positive. Modahl's sample revealed a T/E ratio of 42:1.

A hearing convened under the auspices of the IAAF, by the disciplinary committee of the British Athletics Federation (BAF), was held in December 1994. Despite representations by Modahl that the testing protocols were not adhered to and that there had been breaches in the chain of custody over the sample, she was found guilty of a doping offence and subjected to a four year worldwide ban.

Fortunately for Modahl, the rules of the BAF allowed for an appeal to an independent panel. The Independent Appeal Panel was satisfied that appropriate procedures had been carried out, but was concerned about possible degradation of the sample. In this case, the evidence was that the sample had been stored in unrefrigerated conditions for a period of two days. The pH level of the B sample (a portion of the original sample kept for later verification testing) was abnormally high and at levels consistent with bacterial degradation. The Panel accepted expert evidence which suggested that the increase in testosterone was due to the presence of bacteria.

The Appeal Panel's reasons included this passage:

> When we take all the factors put before us together we come to the conclusion we cannot be sure beyond a reasonable doubt of Mrs Modahl's guilt. On the evidence before us there is a possibility which cannot be ignored that the cause of the T/E ratio in the samples of her urine was not that testosterone had been administered but that the samples had become degraded owing to their being stored in unrefrigerated

conditions and that bacteriological action had resulted in an increase in the amount of testosterone in the samples. Mrs Modahl is therefore entitled to succeed in her appeal.[8]

CAPOBIANCO

A final example of the chain of custody problem is the case involving Australian sprinter, Dean Capobianco. In the first few months of 1996 Capobianco was tested several times, the last of which occurred on 27 May, just months before the 1996 Atlanta Summer Olympic Games. All but the 27 May test results were negative, including the results of a test conducted on 26 May. The 27 May test was carried out using high resolution mass spectrometry equipment at the IOC accredited laboratory in Cologne, Germany. The result of this test was reported as positive, revealing the presence of the banned anabolic steroid, stanozolol. After Capobianco attended at the testing of the B sample (also positive), Athletics Australia, Capobianco's national federation, was informed that Capobianco had tested positive. Capobianco maintained that it was impossible to explain how he could have tested negative on 26 May and positive the following day. The only explanation he provided is that there must have been some mistake made during the processing of the second sample.

In accordance with IAAF rules, he was granted a hearing before a tribunal of Athletics Australia. The Chairman of the Tribunal was Robert Ellicott QC, a member of the arbitral panels established by the IAAF and the Court of Arbitration for Sport (the workings of these tribunals is discussed in Chapter 5). Ellicott was also formerly Attorney-General of Australia.

---

[8] See D Modahl, *The Dianne Modahl Story: Going the Distance* (London, Hodder & Stoughton, 1995) at 241. The book gives a full account of Modahl's experience, including complete details of the various technical arguments relating to procedure and chain of custody. Modahl was reinstated by the IAAF Council in November 1996. She still contends that, despite her subsequent vindication, what she has lost can never be compensated. In her own words: "I have always protested my innocence, the British Athletic Federation (BAF) have accepted my innocence, but my story doesn't have the sort of happy ending you get in films with all the loose ends neatly tied. Time can never be reversed. People have asked whether Diane Modahl will ever run again but it isn't simply a matter of pulling on a pair of spikes once more. I was banned from 18 June 1994: the year that followed, in which I battled to clear my name, can never be added to the end of my career."
Subsequent to her exoneration by the BAF Appeal Panel, Modahl commenced legal action against the BAF seeking damages for wrongly banning her for alleged drug abuse. She was unsuccessful. Refer to *Modahl v BAF Ltd* (1999) 22 July (HL), available at <http://www.parliament.the-stationery-office.co.uk/pa/ld199899/ldjudgmt/jd990722/modahl>.

At the Athletics Australia hearing, Mr Ellicott determined that there was sufficient doubt as to the evidence against Capobianco to justify clearing him of the alleged doping offence. In particular, Ellicott was concerned about what had happened to the samples taken from Capobianco between the time of their collection in the Netherlands and their arrival at the laboratory in Cologne. Prior to the actual hearing, Athletics Australia requested documentation from the IAAF regarding the processing of samples taken from Capobianco. They were most concerned to establish that proper procedures relating to "chain of custody" had been followed.

At the hearing, the evidence was presented. It consisted of signed "Doping Control Form" with signatures of Capobianco and the IAAF Doping Control Officer; a statutory declaration from the Officer; a document identifying the sample tested as bearing the same control number as that on the signed Doping Control Form; the report of the analysis of the A sample (test date 19 June 1996); and further documentation relating to the testing of the B sample.

Mr Ellicott found that the evidence did not establish that the sample had remained in the custody of the anti-doping officials to an extent to rule out the possibility of error. Specifically, he found that there was no evidence that applicable doping control rules relating to the storage and transportation of the sample had been followed. These rules relate to placing the samples in an appropriate container, delivery of the samples to a courier, ensuring the samples remain in custody of the courier at all relevant times and arrival of the samples at the testing laboratory with the seals on the container intact.

Furthermore, there was no evidence about what had happened to the samples between the date of their arrival at the laboratory on 28 May 1996 and the date of the testing, 19 June 1996. Perhaps in deference to the Modahl case, Ellicott also indicated that there was no evidence that the samples had been stored in a safe area and under refrigeration (to avoid degradation of the sample).

Perhaps in anticipation of a technical challenge, the IAAF Rules included a provision which was intended to operate to "cure" technical but insubstantial departures from procedures established in the Rules. This technique of legal drafting is fairly common in regulatory statutes.

However, in his reasons Ellicott expressed a somewhat adverse opinion as the the effect of this "curative" rule. He wrote:

this rule does not, in my view, allow a Tribunal to ignore gaps in evidence which should be provided in order to enable the Tribunal to form a view...that the sampling and testing procedure was carried out properly and that there was no reasonable possibility of tampering.[9]

The purpose of the rules relating to custody of the sample and detailing procedures for transportation and dealings with it are there, according to Mr Ellicott, to eliminate any risk of tampering with the evidence. This risk might well be exacerbated in a case such as Capobianco's, where the samples were transported over distance and national frontiers and were stored for lengthy periods.

Ellicott expressed concern for the position of athletes who faced substantial penalties for drug use, where the evidence establishing the doping offence consisted of test results from such samples. In language often associated with criminal law determinations, he wrote:

> [an athlete is entitled] to expect that if a charge is laid against [him or her], he or she will be provided with the documents that evidence the custody of the samples and that the IAAF or National Federation will place evidence before the Tribunal that the chain of custody had not been broken.[10]

Under the IAAF Rules, the International Federation can refer the determination of the National Federation to arbitration by the IAAF Council. The IAAF is the only international federation whose rules provide for this form of appeal to an internal body (see Chapter 6). The hearing was ultimately held in March 1997 and the reasons of the IAAF arbitrators were delivered and published on 17 March 1997. In their decision, the IAAF panel held that the IAAF had fulfilled its burden of proof to show that a doping offence had been committed. The panel was satisfied that the evidence as to how the sample was dealt with was sufficient to demonstrate compliance with the applicable Rules. Accordingly, as there was insufficient doubt as to the accuracy of the test or the identity of the sample, the evidence establishing that Capobianco had tested positive to stanozolol was accepted. Consequently, Capobianco was suspended and was therefore ineligible to compete in national or international competition for a period of four years from the date of provision of the sample (27 May 1996).

---

9 Athletics Australia Doping Control Tribunal, Reasons of R. Ellicott, QC (17 July 1996) ("Ellicott reasons") at 10.
10 Ibid.

> Interestingly enough, the IAAF panel did state in their reasons that evidence regarding the chain of custody should have been made available to Capobianco prior to the first hearing, held by Athletics Australia. However, the panel did conclude that, despite the deficiencies and errors in the documentation, these deficiencies did not amount to a breach of the IAAF Rules or "Procedural Guidelines for Doping Control".
>
> Since the IAAF determination, the IAAF Council determined that the sanction for such offences should be reduced from four to two years.[11] Subsequently, Capobianco's sanction was reduced in accordance with the rule change.

Other Rules and Regulations

These cases all demonstrate the degree of concern about ensuring compliance with appropriate protocol, although absolute compliance is not required. The concern here is with the reliability of the evidence on which a positive finding is based. It is for this reason that the IOC Medical Code contains detailed provisions dealing with accreditation of laboratories, testing procedures and sampling procedures in doping controls.[12] The various international federations, such as the IAAF,[13] also prescribe detailed procedures for testing and dealing with samples. Finally, the ASDA, in its legislation and regulations, prescribes similarly detailed procedures.

This plethora of rules presents several problems. First of all, where the rules are inconsistent, there may be uncertainty as to which rules should be followed. At present, the anti-doping policies of both the Australian Sports Commission and the Australian Olympic Committee oblige member federations to support drug testing by the Australian Sports Drug Agency. ASDA's procedures are presently governed by Commonwealth legislation, which was last amended in 1996. However, it is possible that international federations may prescribe procedures which are slightly different from those applied by ASDA. ASDA is presently attempting to solve this problem by moving many of the procedural

---

11 IAAF Press Release, 31 July 1997. The sanction for a first doping offence for various substances (including anabolic agents) was reduced from four years to two years.

12 IOC, *Medical Code,* at Chapter VI "Testing Procedures", Appendix B "Procedure for Accreditation of Laboratories", Appendix C "Sampling Procedures in Doping Controls".

13 "Procedural Guidelines for Doping Control", IAAF, April 1992.

requirements from the legislation, amendment of which requires Parliament to act, to the Regulations, which can be amended without Parliamentary action. This move in itself required statutory amendment, which is presently in process. Nonetheless, the problem of potentially inconsistent, or at least different, procedural requirements remains and no amount of flexible drafting by ASDA and/or the drafters of Commonwealth legislation can totally accommodate this.

Inconsistent Policies

As we saw in Chapter Two, there are numerous national and international bodies regulating sport and doping activity in particular. Each has its own interest. Bodies forming part of the Olympic Movement can probably be counted on to adopt consistent uniform doping policies and procedures, which are ultimately derived from the IOC *Medical Code*. Bodies dependent on Commonwealth agencies, particularly the Australian Sports Commission, will probably adhere to the model ASC anti-doping policy and be content to rely on ASDA-specified procedures for the conduct of drug tests. Indeed, the model doping policy for national sporting organisations produced by the ASC does this.

However, even the general anti-doping policies adopted by the ASC and the AOC have some inconsistencies,[14] although efforts are being made to make the policies essentially identical. The problem, however, is the desire for bodies to preserve their autonomy.

There are several issues that arise as a result of inconsistent policies. It is hard to imagine, for example, the IAAF deciding not to publish its own guidelines for doping control. Ultimately, therefore, despite efforts being made to assist ASDA by amending its legislation to make procedural rules more flexible, the problem of too many sets of potentially different rules is likely to remain.

The International Position

As a general rule, the regulation of doping on an international level is governed by the Olympic Charter and the IOC. The *Medical Code* sets out the IOC's position on the regulation of doping:

---

14 These policies are discussed in detail in Chapter 7. These policies differ on questions of legitimate therapeutic use of banned substances as well as policies which apply to inadvertent use.

the IOC shall establish an IOC Medical Code which shall provide for prohibition of doping, determine the prohibited classes of substances and prohibited methods, provide for the obligation of competitors to submit themselves to medical controls and examinations and make provision for sanctions to be applied in the event of a violation of such Medical Code...[15]

Chapter II of the Code defines and prohibits doping:

Doping contravenes the ethics of both sport and medical science. Doping consists of:

1. the administration of substances belonging to prohibited classes of pharmacological agents, and/or
2. the use of various prohibited methods.[16]

In February of 1999 the IOC convened a conference on doping in sport. The conference led to the formation of the World Anti-Doping Agency (WADA). The proposed Mission Statement of the WADA stated:

The mission of the Agency shall be to promote and coordinate at international level the fight against doping in sport in all its forms; to this end, the Agency will cooperate with intergovernmental organisations, governments, public authorities and other public and private bodies fighting against doping in sport, inter alia, the International Olympic Committee (IOC), International Sports Federations (IF), National Olympic Committees (NOC) and the athletes...[17]

WADA is still in the process of establishing its position within the international frameworks of doping control. Athletes should remain aware of developments in relation to doping control practices and procedures that arise as a result of WADA's activities.

At the first meeting of the board of directors of WADA in January 2000, the following priorities were set as agenda items:

- Develop protocols with the international sports federations (IFs) for conducting out-of-competition testing before the 2000 Olympic Games in Sydney;

---

15 IOC, *Medical Code* at 2.
16 IOC, *Medical Code* at Chapter II.
17 WADA Mission Statement.

- Design a process for the accreditation of testing laboratories that may include the designation of a reference lab. The labs' compliance with ISO standards is also contemplated;
- Enhance the results management system for doping controls in major sporting events, including the Olympic Games; Encourage and monitor peer-reviewed research, especially regarding the detection of EPO, HGH, and other substances; Determine methods for extending sanctions to all individuals involved in doping, not only athletes;
- Explore the concept of athletes holding "passports" that record health and or testing information;
- Establish contact with appropriate agencies with expertise in areas relevant to the fight against doping, including existing independent anti-doping agencies, and to use the existing resources of other agencies;
- Educate athletes, coaches, and administrators on the risks involved with taking prohibited substances;
- Begin work on drafting a WADA Anti-Doping Code;
- Initiate the process of harmonizing anti-doping rules in sport and national legislation;
- Work with governments to stem the trafficking of prohibited substances and their movement across borders; and
- Achieve a wider diversity among Board members, especially to include more women.

Clearly, standardising drug testing protocols and working toward uniformity of sanctions and national approaches is a task to which WADA is well-suited. However, this work is at an early stage. Athletes must be aware of the various doping control practices and procedures of the relevant national or international sporting association or federation which concerns itself with the athlete's sport.

The future clearly lies in the direction of greater international co-operation. Substantial progress was made when Government ministers and other authorised government officials responsible for anti-doping within their national jurisdictions came together at an international drugs in sport summit organised by the Government of Australia in late 1999.

The summit was hosted by Jackie Kelly MP, Minister for Sport and Tourism and Minister Assisting the Prime Minister for the Sydney 2000 Games, and chaired by the then Australian Minister for Justice and Customs, Senator Amanda Vanstone. In the communique released following the close of the conference, participants affirmed their commitment to both drug-free sport and international co-operation. It is worth quoting at length from the communique issued following the conclusion of the conference:

"Participants at the summit:

1. Affirmed their belief that ethical sport plays a vital role in the well-being of their societies and, consequently, their conviction of the need for strong government leadership and action in the fight against doping in sport.

2. Confirmed that the role of governments in the fight against doping at the national level is to work with relevant sporting organisations to establish comprehensive national anti-doping programs based on the principles of independence, transparency, integrity, accountability and sound science, derived from an anti-doping policy that promotes public health among young sportsmen and sportswomen and the value of, and ethical basis for, doping free sport and respect for athletes' rights.

3. Confirmed governments' individual and collective commitment to take action within all relevant areas of governmental responsibility to eradicate doping in sport through the development of effective national anti-doping laws and policies, the establishment and conduct of national drug testing programs, support for research on prevention and detection methods, provision of anti-doping education and information services, and reducing the flow of prohibited substances.

4. Acknowledged governments also have a responsibility to contribute to the effectiveness of the international fight against doping in sport by working cooperatively with other governments, international sports organisations and the International Olympic Committee (IOC) to develop effective approaches for combating doping in sport.

5. Affirmed their commitment to the World Anti-Doping Agency (WADA) and its development towards an independent, transparent and accountable agency that has broad support and respect among governments, inter-governmental organisations, as well as international and national sporting organisations, in particular athletes, and acknowledged the significant work of the IOC and several inter-governmental bodies in its establishment."

The communique also contained the following policy commitment:

"Recognising the need to adopt a strong and definitive position on anti-doping, and in cooperation with relevant national sporting organisations, participants agreed:

1. To develop national anti-doping policy frameworks that promote the ethics of doping free sport and respect for athletes' rights and education of athletes and young people;

2. Governments, the Olympic movement and sporting organisations must be involved and work together to develop and implement anti-doping policies;

3. The principles of fairness, ethics and equity should underpin anti-doping policies (eg, the protection of athletes' rights);

4. Policies should comprehensively address all elements of anti-doping programs, including drug testing, education, national and international consistency, collaboration, research, sanctions and appeals;

5. To increase deterrence, there should be a system of internationally applicable and equivalent sanctions across all sports, such as a two-year minimum ban for first-time offenders;

6. Policies should include an independent system for prior approval to use substances from a predetermined list when there are genuine therapeutic reasons, no therapeutic alternatives, subject to appropriate competency based approval, accountability and verification procedures, to protect the system from abuse;

7. When hosting major sporting events, governments should adopt criteria that require promoters and organisers to ensure effective anti-doping programs are in place for those events;

8. Where appropriate, governments should provide legislative backing for anti-doping policies and programs.

On the matter of drug testing itself, the communique stated the following:

Recognising that high quality drug testing programs are an essential feature of a comprehensive national approach to anti-doping, participants agreed that:

2.1 Governments should work with their national sporting organisations to establish high-quality drug testing programs.

2.2 Governments should fund or otherwise enable high quality national drug testing programs in whole or in conjunction with national sporting organisations.

2.3 The elements of a high quality drug testing program include:

    2.3.1 Year round, no notice, out-of-competition testing.

    2.3.2 The strategic application of drug testing resources so as to most efficiently and effectively maximise the deterrent effect.

    2.3.3 Protection of athletes' rights throughout the sample collection, analysis and result management, and appeals and arbitration. Recognising the importance of establishing high quality drug testing programs that are based on the principles of world's best practice, participants agreed that:

1. Drug testing should be conducted in accordance with internationally accepted procedural standards, specifically the International Standard for Doping Control.

2. Sports drug testing laboratories should be accredited by an independent agency.

3. Accreditation standards should assess laboratories on the basis of their scientific capability, quality management and ethical standards.

3. International Collaboration

Participants recognised that international collaboration between government, the Olympic movement and sport is an essential component of progressing the fight against doping in sport. Participants agreed that:

3.1 International collaboration can be built by the use of existing or the establishment of bilateral and multilateral anti-doping agreements between and among countries through which they can harmonise anti-doping policies and promote cooperation on research, drug testing, education, sanctions and adjudication. To this end, they would encourage states from all regions to accede

THE TESTING AUTHORITIES

to the Anti-Doping Convention (ETS No. 135, Strasbourg, 16 November 1989) and use the Convention as a tool for coordinating their national anti-doping policies.

3.2 Participants expressed their support for the World Anti-Doping Agency (WADA). The WADA can provide international leadership and coordination for a range of anti-doping activities. For the WADA to operate effectively it needs to involve athletes, all sports and governments from all regions.

3.3 It is essential that the WADA undertake its functions always having regard to the principles of independence, accountability, transparency and expertise in its actions.

3.4 The functions of the WADA should be to:

- 3.4.1 promote and coordinate the fight against doping;

- 3.4.2 reinforce the ethical basis for anti-doping and protect the health of athletes;

- 3.4.3 establish and maintain a list of prohibited substances;

- 3.4.4 coordinate no notice, out of competition testing;

- 3.4.5 develop analytical standards;

- 3.4.6 promote harmonised sanctions;

- 3.4.7 develop education programs;

- 3.4.8 promote and coordinate peer reviewed research.

3.5 Particular attention should be paid to address concerns regarding the WADA's regional, gender and athlete representation, and governance.

3.6 Pursuant to the Canadian Proposal to the summit, it was agreed to establish an interim International Inter-governmental Consultative Group on Anti-Doping as described in Appendix 1.

3.7 It was further agreed that the Consultative Group would undertake its function taking into account the issues raised in the Summit Declaration on the World Anti-Doping Agency in Appendix 2.[18]

As an interim measure, the participants at the summit agreed to establish an international intergovernmental consultative group on anti-doping, comprised of nations representing all continental regions. The consultative group will work to promote the work of WADA by coordinating worldwide governmental participation in WADA as well as harmonisation of the policies of the various governments in this area.

Prior to the Sydney Olympic Games, WADA conducted 2043 out-of-competition urine tests involving 27 summer sports in 82 nations.[19] WADA's role has been enhanced by agreements with various international federations for it to be the appropriate testing authority.

In Australia, the IOC position is applied through ASDA, discussed below.

The Australian Position

The efforts of the Australian Government to discourage the use of drugs in sport throughout the 1980s saw the establishment of ASDA as a statutory authority within the Department of the Environment, Sport, Territories and Local Government portfolio. The Agency was established in 1991, following passage of the Australian Sports Drug Agency Act 1990 (Cth) ("the Act"). The Act has been amended five times since then.[20] ASDA's policies and procedures are at the forefront of world practice in this area and ASDA has been used as a model by other countries seeking to establish their own drug testing authorities in sport.[21]

The Agency's mission is to provide leadership in the development of a national strategy concerning drugs in sport. The objects of the Agency are:

---

18 The communique can be found at <http://www.drugsinsport.isr.gov.au>.
19 See <http://www.wada-ama.org>.
20 These amending Acts were passed in 1991-2, 1992-93, 1993-94, 1994-95, 1995-96 and 1999.
21 This is evidenced by the various agreements between ASDA and overseas bodies whereby ASDA is used by them for the conduct of drug tests: a number of these are described in Chapter 2. Further detail on this can be found through ASDA's website
http://www.ausport.gov.au/asda.html.

(a) to deter the use of scheduled drugs or doping methods in sport; and
(b) to encourage the development of programs to educate the sporting community about matters relating to drugs in sport; and
(c) to advocate the international adoption of consistent and effective anti-doping programs; and
(d) to co-ordinate the development of a consistent and effective national response to matters relating to drugs in sport.[22]

The Agency's educational goals impose on the Agency a requirement to formulate an education policy that is accessible by all Australian sporting organisations through the provision of information to raise the awareness and knowledge of the sporting community. Their services for the community include the distribution of a range of resources on drugs in sport for all groups, including the popular *Drugs in Sport Handbook,* a free-call 1800 telephone hotline service and seminars and workshops.[23]

To achieve its primary objective of providing a drug free sporting environment, the Agency conducts more than 3,000 tests per year on competitors in over 50 Olympic and non-Olympic sports. Furthermore, the Agency is sub-contracted by many Australian professional sporting associations to conduct both competition and out-of-competition testing.[24] The Agency also provides technical support on drugs in sport issues and policy development to Australian sporting organisations. This includes:

(i) implementation of the National Drugs in Sport Frame work;
(ii) assisting National Sporting Organisations to develop a drug testing and education policy; and
(iii) working with state governments to establish complementary drug testing legislation.[25]

The Athletes' Legal Position in Australia

ASDA has set out certain testing procedures, which are designed to protect the athletes' rights. What follows is a general description of the athletes' legal position under the ASDA regulations. It is, however, recommended

---

22 Australian Sports Drug Agency Act 1990 (Cth) at s 8.
23 <http://www.ausport.gov.au/asdamain.html>.
24 Ibid.
25 Ibid.

that an athlete seek legal advice should any enforcement of these rights become necessary.

- ASDA is under an obligation to provide certain information to athletes. This includes information regarding testing procedures and sample collection. Furthermore, athletes are entitled to receive a copy of an information sheet. This sheet describes the competitor's legal position and the consequences of failure to provide a sample or returning a positive test result.[26]

- Test results may be invalidated where the procedural requirements for sealing the sample have not been met, the laboratory used for testing the sample is not accredited, or the sample has been tampered with.[27]

- Should the athlete return a positive result (or fail to provide a sample) then the athlete is entitled to present his or her case to the Administrative Appeals Tribunal (AAT).[28]

- The ASDA will enter the athletes on the Register of Notifiable Events and notify both the competitor and other relevant bodies (subject to the decision of the Administrative Appeals Tribunal).[29] The relevant National Sporting Organisation will then decide whether to prosecute the athlete or not. The ASDA cannot prosecute athletes nor impose any punishment on them.

---

26 Australian Sports Drug Agency Act 1990 Regulations 11(1)(f) and (3).
27 Australian Sports Drug Agency Act 1990, s 17M(4).
28 Ibid at ss 17N(2)(b) and 17V.
29 Ibid at ss 17R and 17S.

CHAPTER 6

DISPUTE RESOLUTION IN SPORTS: APPEALS AND ARBITRATION

In any system where rules and penalties are prescribed, disputes are inevitable. Where organisations and individuals have much at stake, it is particularly important to ensure that disputes are capable of being resolved impartially and speedily by respected institutions applying recognised principles.

As the professional lifetime of the athlete tends to be substantially shorter than that enjoyed by other professionals a relatively short suspension may cause irreparable damage to the athlete's career. Furthermore, should it eventually be determined that the athlete was innocent of a doping infraction, the athlete's value to sponsors may be much reduced because of the taint of suspicion of drug use.

It is not only on the athlete's side that the stakes are high. Federations in sports with successful professional leagues are concerned that, in the event a suspension proves to have been wrongly imposed, the federation may face crippling liability.

REYNOLDS

Harry "Butch" Reynolds, an Olympic gold and silver medal winner and world record holder in the 400 metres, competed in a track meet in Monte Carlo, Monaco on 12 August 1990. Immediately after the competition, Reynolds was tested for performance enhancing drugs as part of a program of random testing. Each of the two samples of Reynolds' urine taken tested positive to the banned steroid Nandrolone. The tests were conducted by an IOC approved laboratory in Paris.

In November 1990 the International Amateur Athletic Federation issued a press release stating that Reynolds had been suspended as a result of the test results and offered a hearing by The Athletics Congress of the United States (now known as USA Track and Field), the relevant United States' national federation. The suspension was for a period of two years, thereby eliminating Reynolds from competition in the 1992 Barcelona Summer Olympic Games.

Reynolds immediately brought suit in the Federal Court for the Southern District of Ohio, arguing that the drug test had been given negligently, and the results were in error (see *Reynolds v TAC* 935 F 2d 270 (1991). The Court determined that Reynolds needed to exhaust his administrative remedies before he could present his case in the civil courts. This determination was as a result of the provisions of the US Amateur Sports Act (36 USC. §§ 371-396 1988).

To exhaust his administrative remedies, Reynolds participated in an independent arbitration before a panel of the American Association of Arbitrators in June of 1991. The jurisdiction of the AAA panel was established under the constitution of the United States Olympic Committee and the Amateur Sports Act. At this arbitration, Reynolds was exonerated on the basis that there was strong evidence that the urine samples provided to the Paris laboratory were not Reynolds'. The IAAF refused to lift Reynolds' two year suspension, as the arbitration was not conducted under the IAAF rules.

Reynolds then appealed his suspension to the relevant national federation, The Athletics Congress (TAC), as required by IAAF rules. After two weeks of deliberations, the TAC Doping Control Review Board completely exonerated Reynolds. The IAAF reopened Reynolds' case pursuant to IAAF Rules, which allowed the IAAF to conduct an independent arbitration where it appears that one of its member foundations such as TAC has "misdirected itself". This arbitration was held on 10 and 11 May 1992 in London, England. At the conclusion of the hearing, at which the IAAF and TAC were parties and Reynolds attended and gave evidence, the panel concluded that the drug tests were valid and Reynolds' two year suspension was upheld.

Soon after this, Reynolds commenced legal action in the US Federal District Court alleging breach of contract, breach of contractual due process, defamation and tortious interference with business relations (see *Reynolds v IAAF* 1125.ct 2512 (1992). He sought damages as well as a temporary restraining order that would allow him to compete in races leading up to the US Olympic trials in June 1992. Although he prevailed in his action for the restraining order and qualifying to compete in the Olympic trials, the IAAF announced that every athlete who competed with Reynolds at the US Olympic trials would be ineligible to compete in the Olympic Games at Barcelona. Despite a last minute attempt (before a judge of the Supreme Court of the United States) by the TAC to overturn the orders entitling Reynolds to participate in the trials, Reynolds eventually qualified for the Olympic team as an alternate for the 400 metre relay. The IAAF still refused to permit Reynolds to compete at the 1992 Olympics and TAC removed his name from the US Olympic team roster. The IAAF then increased Reynolds' two year suspension by four months, as punishment for participating in the US Olympic trials.

In September 1992, Reynolds resumed his court action in Ohio. The IAAF did not respond to Reynolds' complaint, despite having been given appropriate notice. A default judgment was entered in Reynolds' favour and ultimately Reynolds was awarded some US$27 million in damages, including treble punitive damages. The District Court found that the IAAF "acted with ill will and a spirit of revenge towards Mr Reynolds." In particular, the Court referred to "the suppression of evidence, threats levied against Reynolds and his fellow athletes, and the extension of Reynolds' suspension for an additional four months". More than $20 million of the award was in the form of punitive damages for these acts. The balance of the award represented estimates of the loss of potential earnings Reynolds suffered as a result of his wrongful exclusion from competition. The IAAF refused to submit to the jurisdiction of the US courts and announced that it would simply ignore the decision.

When Reynolds commenced proceedings against four of the IAAF's corporate sponsors (to intercept sponsorship payments), the IAAF eventually intervened and ultimately succeeded in persuading the US Circuit Court of Appeals that the US Federal Courts lacked jurisdiction over the dispute. The money judgment and the injunctions were reversed (see *Reynolds v IAAF* 23F 3d 1110 (1994)).

The sheer size of the damages award in Reynolds' case shows just how high the financial stakes can be for organisations in this area. That may well explain the nervousness of FIFA (the governing international federation for soccer, or association football as it is known) about obliging itself to impose standard two year suspensions for doping infractions.

Reynolds' experiences also illustrate the importance of establishing an agreed procedure for challenging test results and/or penalties imposed. The IAAF remains the only international federation with its own internal appellate process. Others now submit disputes to the jurisdiction of the Court of Arbitration for Sport (CAS).

Litigation and Alternative Dispute Resolution

Given the delay and expense involved in traditional litigation of disputes, in commercial contracts parties often agree to an alternative form of dispute resolution. With sporting activity, there may be additional reasons for settling complaints outside the civil courts.

The Reynolds' experience shows the obvious fear by the IAAF of the financial consequences of an adverse judgment. On the athlete's side, there are also many reasons why litigation is best avoided. One advantage of litigation is that a binding legal ruling can emerge. Persistent problems may need the finality of binding legal rulings. The Olympic Movement is making every effort to direct disputes to CAS, the operations of which are discussed below.

The CAS offers arbitration services in disputes relating to sporting activity. Before describing how the CAS works, it is worth briefly contrasting traditional and non-traditional dispute resolution processes.

Litigation: the Traditional Way of Resolving Disputes

We use Australian civil procedure to describe the process of litigation. Similar processes are in use throughout the common law world. Litigation in jurisdictions based on continental or "civil law" is conducted differently. The main points of distinction involve the use of the inquisitorial process, rather than the common law's adversarial process, and the fact that judges in civil jurisdictions are trained from early in their career to operate as judges, rather than selected from amongst the community of lawyers.

The litigation system of dispute resolution is an adversarial system. During litigation both sides present their case and are then given an opportunity to scrutinise and test the case put forward by the other side. The role of the judge is limited to deciding issues of fact and applying the law (as well as ensuring that the trial is run fairly and efficiently). The judge will not, however, engage in testing of the evidence or cross-examination of witnesses. A judge will then examine the cases put forward by both parties and make a ruling in favour of one party or the other.

The options open to a judge in most disputes are very limited and it is difficult, if not impossible, for a judge to impose a form of compromise on the parties. The judge must find that either one party or the other is right and make an order accordingly. The outcomes that are possible through a negotiated settlement or mediation are more varied. In such a case the parties may come to any compromise which they can both live with. Unless agreed to by the parties, the mediator cannot "impose' a settlement on the parties.

Alternatives to Litigation: Alternative Dispute Resolution (ADR)

There are plenty of obvious drawbacks to the traditional litigation process. Some of those problems can be addressed within the context of the traditional model, while some cannot. As a result, there has been increasing interest in alternatives to litigation. Collectively, these alternatives are referred to as "alternative dispute resolution" (ADR).

ADR is a process which encourages the disputants to reach their own solution and where the primary role of the neutral third party is to help the disputants to solve their problems.

Successful forms of ADR address the disadvantages of the traditional form of dispute resolution. Some of those disadvantages are:

- cost of proceedings;
- delay in reaching a solution;
- the judge is often not conversant with the technical details of the dispute;
- the adversarial nature of the process is seen by many as not being conducive to reaching sensible compromises; and,
- litigation is often viewed as inflexible and impractical.

There are various alternatives, which are used to achieve a more effective resolution of disputes. One response to the shortcomings of litigation has been the growth in both number and importance of specialised tribunals. This does not so much represent a change in process as a change in adjudicator. The panel in such a tribunal is more likely to have the detailed knowledge required to resolve complex technical, economic, environmental, medical or scientific problems, which can arise. If well chosen, the Panel is likely to be "business friendly".

Another response has been a growth in alternative forms of dispute resolution, particularly arbitration and mediation.

Arbitration

Arbitration involves an adjudicative process with a decision arrived at, not by the parties themselves, but by an adjudicator. The parties lose control of the process. The law permits certain matters in dispute between parties to be submitted to a third, independent person for decision. That person is selected by the parties or their nominee and is referred to as an arbitrator or umpire. Even though this process is generally outside the court system, the parties cannot totally exclude the courts. About the only thing that cannot be settled by arbitration is a criminal case (for obvious reasons). Otherwise, the scope for the use of arbitration in civil matters is virtually unlimited.

Purpose of arbitration

The main objective of arbitration is to obtain finality and an enforceable result (called an "award"), at the same time as avoiding the costs, delays and formalities of the court system. In addition, arbitration offers the possibility of selecting an arbitrator. In Australia there is uniform Commercial Arbitration legislation.[1]

Advantages of Arbitration:

- Dispute settled more expeditiously than litigation;

- Proceedings are private, therefore adverse publicity is avoided;

- Parties can arrange the hearing at mutually convenient times;

---

1 For example, Commercial Arbitration Act 1984 (NSW).

- Proceedings are normally less formal and complex than litigation;

- For technical disputes, the parties can normally select arbitrators with the necessary expertise;

- Arbitration can sometimes make it easier to resolve international disputes. Often parties are reluctant to submit their dispute to the courts of another jurisdiction, and arbitration supported by international recognition of foreign arbitral awards legislation may be more acceptable;

- Arbitration can be more flexible. For example, an award can have an element of periodic review built into it; and

- For the IFs and IOC, there is a reduction of exposure to massive litigation damages and restraint of trade arguments.

Both grievance and salary arbitration have been used with great success in sporting disputes. North Americans are well familiar with the annual resolution of salary disputes in baseball and ice hockey by binding arbitration. It is now the practice of the IOC to empower, using members of CAS (see below), an ad hoc panel of arbitrators to resolve disputes arising during the Olympic Games. At the recent Sydney Olympic Games, the ad hoc panel was able to convene hearings and provide reasoned decisions within 24 hours of a dispute arising.

There are some **Disadvantages of Arbitration:**

- Selecting a mutually acceptable arbitrator can sometimes be difficult.

- Some arbitrators lack the necessary technical expertise and also are insufficiently experienced in handling disputes. Errors in handling the evidence and the procedure may result in court applications making the process more time consuming and expensive.

- Sometimes arbitration can be more expensive than litigation. Parties must themselves pay the costs of the arbitrator and the facilities.

- Parties often lack the advantage that proper discovery offers, that is, parties can lack a full understanding of the case of their opponent, thereby resulting in failure to define the issues for hearing fully.

- Appeal rights can be uncertain, as the uniform legislation provides that an appeal lies to the Supreme Court on any question of law arising out of an award, but only with the consent of the other parties or with the leave of the court.

- Lack of precedent may make the arbitration process too uncertain for some parties.

- For the athlete there is usually a restriction in damages or remedies available.

The Court of Arbitration for Sport has addressed some of these disadvantages. Importantly, especially in doping matters, the CAS is building up a body of decisions on doping disputes that will increasingly define the legal norms in this area. This development has been much strengthened in Australia by a recent decision of the New South Wales Court of Appeal, confirming the ability of parties to agree to exclude appeals from decisions of the Court of Arbitration for Sport (see *Angela Raguz v Rebecca Sullivan* below).

How does an arbitration arise?

Parties may agree to arbitrate, either by agreeing to arbitrate an existing dispute or by having provided in their contract that any future dispute will be referred to arbitration. For example, the contract used by the Australian Olympic Committee for athletes on the Australian team competing at the Sydney Olympics provides:

> Subject to the provisions of the Olympic Charter, any dispute relating to:
>
> (1) my selection or non-selection as a member of the Team by the AOC; or
> (2) this agreement or any matter arising in relation to it,
>
> and whether arising during the term of this agreement or after its termination, will be solely and exclusively resolved by the Court of Arbitration for Sport according to the Code of Sports-Related Arbitration.
>
> The Court of Arbitration for Sport will rule on its jurisdiction and has exclusive power to order provisional and conservatory measures. The decisions of the Court of Arbitration for Sport will be final.

> In the interests of speedy and expert resolution of any such disputes, I hereby surrender any right I may have to commence proceedings in a court in relation to any such dispute or to file any appeal, review or recourse to any state court or other judicial authority from any arbitral award, decision or ruling issued by the Court of Arbitration for Sport. In particular, and without restricting the generality of the foregoing and for further and better assurance notwithstanding that such provisions have no applicability, I agree that neither party will have the right of appeal under section 38 of the Commercial Arbitration Act of any of the Australian states or to apply for the determination of a question of law under section 39(1)(a) of such Act.

This contract attempts to exclude the courts altogether. Indeed, the AOC Membership Agreement for Athletes contains an extensive provision dealing specifically with the athlete's agreement not to commence legal proceedings. While it is not possible to exclude the Courts absolutely, it is possible to provide that parties are obliged to go to arbitration before they go to the Courts. Indeed, Butch Reynolds was required to exhaust his internal remedies with the IAAF before the US Federal District Court would hear the merits of his claim.

The use of these clauses (sometimes called *Scott v Avery* clauses after a 19th century English case of the same name) has been affected by the provisions of the uniform arbitration legislation, which (effectively) allows courts to hear disputes despite the presence of a *Scott v Avery* clause: Uniform Commercial Arbitration legislation s 55. A court may, if it chooses, stay legal proceedings brought where there is an agreement to refer the dispute to arbitration: s 53. This the court will do, if it is satisfied that there is no reason not to refer the matter to arbitration and that the applicant is ready and willing to co-operate in the process of conducting the arbitration. Likewise, a Court, under s 38 of the legislation, may decide to hear an appeal of an arbitration award.

Nonetheless, s 40 of the legislation provides that the Court should not grant leave to appeal an arbitration award where the parties have agreed to binding arbitration and do not consent to the appeal going ahead.

RAGUZ v SULLIVAN

> This dispute concerned which of two judokas should be nominated as the Australian representative for the Sydney Olympic Games in the women's under-52kg category. The CAS decided in Ms Sullivan's favour. Ms Raguz sought leave to appeal the decision in the NSW Supreme Court. The case was considered by the NSW Court of Appeal.

As part of the selection process both Ms Raguz, Ms Sullivan and the Judo Federation of Australia signed various documents over a period of time, which created an arbitration agreement to submit disputes to the CAS for appeal. These documents expressly excluded the option to appeal the decision of the CAS to any domestic court.

The question for the Court of Appeal was whether the Supreme Court had jurisdiction to hear Ms Raguz's application in the light of the arbitration agreement. Ms Raguz relied on s38 of the Commercial Arbitration Act 1984 (the Act), which gives the Supreme Court jurisdiction to entertain an appeal from an award in two cases:
i) if the parties to the arbitration agreement give their consent; or,
ii) if the Supreme Court grants leave.

There was no consent in this case. The Court's power to grant leave is subject to s 40 of the Act which prevents the Court from granting leave if there is an exclusion agreement, in writing, between the parties to the arbitration agreement which excludes the right of appeal.

The Court of Appeal found that several interlocking documents signed by Ms Raguz, Ms Sullivan and the Judo Federation of Australia constituted a multipartite contract which contained both an arbitration agreement and an exclusion agreement.

The Court held that these agreements excluded it from interfering with the decision of the CAS and Ms Raguz's application for leave to appeal was dismissed (see *Angela Raguz v Rebecca Sullivan*, New South Wales Court of Appeal 240 (1 September 2000)).

Uniform legislation

Commercial arbitration is governed by statutes in each of the States and Territories. These Acts dated back to the nineteenth century and were recently reformed. Australia now has essentially uniform arbitration legislation. The legislation does leave the conduct of the arbitration to the parties in most cases and applies generally by default (that is, if the parties haven't so provided). Many of the legislative provisions expressly preserve the right of the parties to exclude them and come to their own agreement.

Apart from the matter of *Scott v Avery* clauses, the legislation also deals with:

- powers of the arbitrator (ss 14, 24);
- attendance of witnesses;

- awarding of costs (s 31); and,
- excluding the right to appeal (ss 38, 39).

The conduct of arbitration proceedings

In general, the arbitrator has a wide discretion as to the manner in which proceedings are conducted. The uniform legislation provides that the arbitrator is not bound by the rules of evidence and may proceed as he or she thinks fit.

Decisions by the arbitrator will be made according to law. However, the parties may agree to relieve the arbitrator of this obligation and accept the "wisdom of Solomon". Of course, in such a case, parties would have to ensure that they did not rely on any previously obtained legal advice.

Arbitrators are bound by the rules of "natural justice". Broadly speaking, this means that the parties must be given the opportunity to hear and respond to the case against them and the arbitrator cannot be biased.

The manner of proceedings is otherwise very similar in most cases to a trial, and parties are normally represented by counsel. The result of the arbitration will be that the arbitrator will make an "award", which is the same as a judgment. Normally, this award will be final and binding on the parties. However, the parties are free to agree on an appeal process.

The role of the courts after an arbitration

The courts will retain the right of judicial review. That is to say that courts will retain the power to set aside an arbitrator's award for abuse of process (ie, misconduct by the arbitrator), remove arbitrators for misconduct or exercising undue influence, incompetence or unsuitability, terminate proceedings in the event of undue delay, extend time and impose terms and conditions on orders. The uniform legislation attempts to reinforce the finality of arbitrations by prohibiting appeals to courts where the parties have signed a written "exclusion agreement" excluding such an appeal except in limited cases.

Also, the grounds for judicial review were narrowed in the uniform legislation. Now parties can only apply to have the award set aside if there is an "error of fact or law on the face of the award".

Enforcement of an arbitration award

Arbitration awards based on a written submission are enforceable by leave of the court like a judgment or other court order. Even foreign arbitral awards can be enforced in State and Territorial courts pursuant to the Arbitration (Foreign Awards and Agreements) Act 1974 (Cth).

Mediation

This is a process designed to allow the parties to solve their own dispute by agreement. Unlike traditional forms of dispute resolution such as arbitration and litigation, it does not work by referring the dispute to an impartial third party for judgment. Its essential features are:

- There is no decision. Parties are encouraged to reach their own, mutually satisfactory solution, which may not involve the application of rules.

- Parties do not agree in advance to accept the decision of the mediator (unlike arbitration). Furthermore, in some jurisdictions, judges have the power, at any stage of court proceedings, to order the parties to enter either arbitration or mediation to try to reach a settlement.

- Procedures are generally informal, although there is a basic requirement that conciliators or mediators should act fairly and be neutral.

- Mediation is often used as a first resort, failure of which leads to either arbitration or litigation.

As a form of dispute resolution, mediation is only available when there is some good faith between the parties, as will hopefully be the case where the parties are bound to each other in a long term agreement. Where the parties do not have this good faith, mediation is most likely to fail.

One potential pitfall of mediation is that parties may be reluctant to "give the game away", by engaging in a good faith process. This will especially be the case where they are deliberately preserving their ability to sue later on (ie, keeping their powder dry). The legal system has attempted to deal with this problem by rules designed to afford the protection of "legal privilege" to any admissions made in the course of a genuine attempt to settle a dispute.

The Court of Arbitration for Sport (CAS)[2]

Parties involved in sport related disputes, including allegations of drug taking, be they clubs, sporting federations or associations or sponsors, generally have three possible options available for a successful resolution of a dispute:

a) resort to the body that has been established by the relevant national or international federation to deal with the dispute;

b) commence litigation in the civil courts, provided the courts have jurisdiction to hear the matter; or,

c) submit the dispute for arbitration.

Arbitration is a private, independent and impartial legal institution authorised by the state legal system, which enables disputes under private law to be settled. It allows for the resolution of sport related disputes in a cost efficient and time effective manner. Furthermore, when endorsed, possibilities of appealing the decision of the arbitration panel or board are extremely limited.

In 1983, the IOC session in New Delhi officially ratified the statute of the Court of Arbitration for Sport (CAS). Its mission was to secure settlement of sports related disputes. To achieve this, it entrusted panels of arbitrators with the task of pronouncing an award. When the CAS was conceived, it was under the umbrella of the IOC. However, on 22 June 1994 in Paris, an agreement between the IOC, Summer Olympic International Federations (SOIF) and Winter Federations (AWIF) and the Association of National Olympic Committees (ANOC) and 31 international sports federations constituted the International Council of Arbitration for Sport (ICAS). While the Paris Agreement started the harmonisation of procedural rules between national and international federations, it also affirmed the essential conditions of independence and objectivity which allowed the pronouncement and enforcement of awards equivalent to judgements from state courts. To help this process of harmonisation, in 1996, the ICAS established two decentralised courts in Sydney, Australia and Denver, USA.

---

2 For a more complete discussion of the CAS, see T Kavanagh, "Doping Cases and the Need for the International Court of Arbitration for Sport" (1999) *University of New South Wales Law Journal* 721; M Reeb (ed), *Digest of CAS Awards 1986-1998* (Stoempfli Editions, Berne 1998); and MJ Beloff, T Kerr and M Demetriou, *Sports Law* (Oxford, Hart Publishing1999).

This development has increased the effectiveness of this arbitral institution by bringing it closer to those who seek to make use of it. Consequently, since its inception, the CAS has dealt with over 140 cases.

Furthermore, the CAS at the request of the IOC, International Federations, National Olympic Committees or associations recognised by the IOC, may prepare advisory opinions about legal issues with respect to the practice or development of any activity related to sport. With the consent of the party instituting the advisory mechanism, the opinions can be made available to the general public.

Arbitration before the CAS allows for the following advantages:

- a single jurisdiction is provided for;
- as a general rule, the parties themselves choose the applicable law. Where no agreement/ compromise is reached, Swiss law applies;
- the arbitrators are specialists in sports law;
- the procedure is flexible enough to incorporate the unique circumstances of any given case;
- it is a confidential process, as hearings are not open to the public;
- initiating the process is relatively inexpensive; and
- in principle, the working languages of the CAS are French and English.[3]

The users of the CAS include any individual or legal entity with the capacity and power to agree to arbitration, for example an athlete, a sports club, association or federation. These parties may be represented or assisted during hearings by counsel of their choice, who may or may not be a lawyer.[4]

The task of the ICAS is to facilitate the settlement of sport related disputes through arbitration and to safeguard the independence of the CAS and the rights of the parties. To this end, it looks after the administration and financing of the CAS.[5] The ICAS comprises 20 top level jurists who are appointed for a renewable period of four years.[6] These members cannot appear on the list of CAS arbitrators nor act as counsel to any of the parties to proceedings before the CAS. Their tasks include:

---

3 Court of Arbitration for Sport, *Guide to Arbitration* at 11 – 13.
4 CAS, Code of Sports-Related Arbitration, R30.
5 Ibid at s 2.
6 Ibid at s 4.

- adopting and modifying the "Code of sports-related arbitration";
- elect the CAS president and two vice presidents;
- elect the presidents of the two CAS divisions;
- designate the personalities who constitute the list of CAS arbitrators;
- look after financing of the CAS;
- appoint the CAS secretary general; and
- set up regional or local, permanent or ad hoc arbitration structures.[7]

The CAS, which is overseen by the ICAS, is split into two divisions:

- The Ordinary Arbitration Division: concentrates on disputes arising from all legal relations between parties and for which it has been decided to submit the matter to the CAS. For example; sponsorship contracts, television contracts, contracts regarding the rights of the athlete, etc.
- The Appeals Arbitration Division: is responsible for resolving disputes concerning the decisions of disciplinary tribunals or similar bodies or federations, associations or other sports bodies.[8]

In the ordinary arbitration division, there are two stages to the process. First, a written phase and then a hearing phase. These may sometimes be preceded by an attempt at conciliation, which may be renewed at any time in the process.[9]

Before recourse to the arbitration proceedings, the parties must either have an arbitration clause in their contract consenting to the jurisdiction of the CAS, or they have subsequently reached agreement allowing the CAS to hear the case. Once this is satisfied, a party may make an application outlining a brief statement of the facts and legal arguments, including a statement of the issue to be submitted to the CAS for determination. The parties may then freely choose one or three arbitrators from a list published by the ICAS. The opposing party then explains their position in a written answer. Finally, they will be summoned to a hearing to put their case, for the taking of evidence and for the oral pleadings. It is then the task of these arbitrators (the Panel) to resolve the dispute that has been referred to them. Once the panel has reached a determination, which has been communicated to the CAS, the determination becomes a binding award. The award is made

---

7 Ibid at s 6.
8 Ibid at s 20.
9 Ibid at R 47.

by a majority decision, or, in the absence of a majority decision, by the president of the panel.[10] If one of the parties refuses to execute the award, the opposing party has recourse to the state courts to obtain its execution.

In the Appeal Division, the arbitrators determine on the basis of the rules and regulations of the federation or association concerned by the appeal and, subsidiary, the rules of law chosen by the parties or the law of the country in which the sports body is domiciled.

During the proceedings of an Olympic Games, the ICAS establishes an ad hoc Division of the CAS. This ad hoc Division is charged with the responsibility to provide for the resolution by arbitration of any dispute which may arise during the Olympic Games and which results from or affects the holding of the Olympic Games. In such a case, the Rules of Arbitration have been modified to provide a speedy resolution and are contained in the "Rules for the Resolution of Disputes Arising During the Olympic Games".

The National Sports Dispute Centre

As stated earlier, in 1996 the Australian Olympic Committee (AOC) established a registry of the CAS in Sydney. This Oceania Registry, as it is known, provides arbitration for disputes relating to the Olympics. When the AOC announced the establishment of the Oceania Registry they also, along with the Australia and New Zealand Sports Law Association (ANZSLA), announced the establishment of an arbitration body which represented all sports within Australia.[11] This body, the National Sports Dispute Centre (NSDC), is equally controlled by the AOC, ANZSLA, the Australian Sports Commission (ASC) and the Confederation of Australian Sport.[12]

The aim of the NSDC is to reduce the expense and time consumed in sporting disputes. To this end, it provides services in arbitration and mediation and a tribunal service. The NSDC may arbitrate in any dispute, if requested to by all parties to that dispute or if there exists an arbitration

---

10 Ibid at R46.
11 B Doyle, "National Sports Dispute Centre Pty Limited" in "200 Towards 2000" ANZLA 7th Annual Conference, 23-25 October 1997, Newcastle.
12 Ibid.

clause in a contract or constitution.[13] Similar principles apply with regard to the NSDC's mediation services.[14]

The NSDC provides two forms of tribunal assistance. Firstly, if a sporting body already has in place its own tribunal, then the NSDC can supply the names of suitably accredited tribunal members from its panel of accredited tribunal members. Secondly, the NSDC has its own tribunal service which acts in accordance with NSDC rules. This tribunal may hear a matter in the first instance, but may also act as an appellate tribunal from other domestic sporting tribunals.[15]

In addition, the NSDC also operates as a referral service for lawyers who possess suitable backgrounds in legal issues pertaining to sport.[16] The NSDC is a relatively recent development. Its effectiveness will depend on whether Australian sports bodies are willing to refer their disputes to the NSDC.[17]

---

13 Ibid.
14 Ibid.
15 Ibid.
16 Ibid.
17 Ibid.

CHAPTER 7

LEGAL CHALLENGES TO DRUG TESTING

Introduction

Given the substantial rewards that accompany successful competitive performance, it's not surprising that athletes challenge attempts to impose penalties. In this chapter, we will look at the most frequently-raised legal challenges:

- Failure to follow appropriate testing protocol
- Lack of procedural fairness
- Defects in the evidence
- Absence of intent to engage in doping activity
- Penalty is excessive and in restraint of trade.

Failure to Follow Appropriate Testing Protocol

Most of the recent challenges to drug-testing fall here. The athlete's argument is likely to be that a test is invalid where the procedures for the collection, security and scientific testing of samples do not conform to those established by law or practice. Problems have also arisen where the tests are conducted overseas and do not conform to Australian standards. The legal challenges that ensue are likely to be protracted and expensive[1] and harmful to the reputation and legitimacy of the Agency and its objectives. Hence, the Agency is concerned with ensuring that its procedures are consistent with international practice and are followed throughout Australia.[2]

It is essential that administrators carefully observe the details of their sport's'doping policies. Furthermore, establishing uniform procedures is important.

> **VINNICOMBE**
>
> Vinnicombe was tested by the Canadian Anti-Doping Authority while competing overseas. He returned a positive result to Stanozolol. As a result, ASDA entered Vinnicombe's name on the Register of Defaulting Competitors and the relevant sporting organisations imposed a penalty of two years' suspension. Vinnicombe subsequently instituted proceedings against ASDA, the ASC, the Australian Professional Cycling Council Inc (APCC) and the Australian Cycling Federation Inc (ACF) challenging the validity of the test results and the penalty that followed. The parties, with the exception of ASDA, eventually agreed to submit certain questions to a referee. The referee's conclusions on the questions enabled the parties (with the exception of ASDA) to settle the dispute.

---

1 For example, see *Brew, Krabbe* and *Moller v Deutscher Leichtathletik Verbund (DLV)*, IAAF Panel, London, 24 June 1992, where the identification of the competitor giving the sample was challenged. Also, in a case involving American sprinter Butch Reynolds a dispute over the labeling of the urine samples to be tested led to a US District Court awarding damages in the amount of $AUS 39 million to Reynolds: see "Record $39 Million Damages to Reynolds, But Who Pays?" *The Australian,* 5-6 December 1992 at 30. The International Amateur Athletic Federation, which was ordered to pay the damages to Reynolds, was ultimately successful in obtaining a reversal of the default judgment entered against it on grounds of lack of jurisdiction: see *Reynolds v International Amateur Athletic Federation,* 23 F 3d 1110, Fed App 158 (6th Cir, 1994).

2 Section 8 of the Australian Sports Drug Agency Act 1990 (Cth), provides:
"The objects of the establishment of the Agency are:
(a) ...
(b) to encourage State and Territory governments and National, Sate and Territory sporting organisations, to adopt uniform drug sampling and testing procedures; and
(f) to encourage the development and maintenance of drug testing laboratories accredited by the International Olympic Committee; and
(g) to promote and encourage the adoption, at an international level, of uniform sampling and drug testing procedures, and of educational programs relating to the use of drugs in sport".

Although, subsequent to the testing, Vinnicombe admitted to having taken Stanozolol, the referee, Mr R Ellicott QC determined that this admission could not be the basis for entering his name on the Register of Defaulting Competitors and the subsequent imposition of the suspension by the sporting organisations. Mr Ellicott then, having accepted Vinnicombe's evidence as to the manner in which the testing was conducted as the only available evidence, concluded that the procedures used by the Canadian Anti-Doping Authority (CADO), despite conforming with Canadian Doping Control Standard Operating Procedures and international protocol, did not conform to the requirements of the ASDA Act and the ASDA Regulations.

The referee concluded that the failure to comply with the statutory requirements was material. He listed nine material breaches of the *ASDA Act* and the *ASDA Regulations,* including such matters as failure to inform Vinnicombe of his entitlement to have a representative present, failure to ask Vinnicombe to accompany the CADO officers to a drug control facility, and failure to obtain the signature of a chaperone on the Drug Testing Form. In fact, no Drug Testing Form was even provided. These failings relate to critical matters, such as the chain of custody of the sample and the provision of proper information to Vinnicombe. As a consequence, Vinnicombe could not be taken to have returned a positive test result within the meaning of the *ASDA Act*. This finding led to a settlement of the dispute between Vinnicombe, APCC, ACF and ASC, with Vinnicombe being allowed to compete without suspension as a professional cyclist. See *Vinnicombe v Australian Sports Drug Agency* (Unreported Decision, Federal Court of Australia, NSW District Registry, No G0065 of 1992).

The implications of this finding are substantial for drug-testing in sport. As noted in Chapter 6, the result of the determination in the case of Butch Reynolds was the award of substantial damages against the IAAF, the authority under whose aegis the testing was conducted. We would be remiss if we did not also mention the possibility of actions in defamation being commenced in similar situations. While it seems generally acceptable to promote the goal of a drug-free environment in sports, care must be taken to ensure that the means of eliminating drugs in sport are consistent with the norms of a free and democratic society. The following extract from the referee's decision in the Vinnicombe case makes the point quite eloquently:

> the fact that Vinnicombe took the drug Stanozolol must not be allowed to cloud the issue so far as the role of ASDA is concerned. The ASDA Act, itself, prevents the finding of a positive test result, even if a

competitor has taken drugs, if the appropriate procedures are not followed. The strict procedures are there to protect the competitor, the organisations, the government and sport generally. They have been worked out no doubt after considerable consultation to protect competitors and to prevent fraudulent practices. The procedures are strict but not difficult to follow for those involved in sport. If they are not followed the competitor who has, in fact, taken drugs may go free.[3]

The foregoing comment is of course premised on the view that public policy justifies testing athletes for drug use. The importance of the procedural safeguards is magnified, once one accepts that there may be less than unanimous acceptance of underlying policy (see Chapter 4 above).

MODAHL

British runner Diane Modahl tested positive to testosterone after an athletic event in Lisbon in June 1994. Despite test results revealing a testosterone: epitestosterone ratio of 42:1 (substantially in excess of the assumed normal ratio of 6:1), Modahl maintained that she had not committed a doping offence and that the test results were erroneous. In support of her argument she questioned the testing process. In particular, she demonstrated that her sample had been stored unrefrigerated in the office of the Sports Medicine Centre for three days and then transferred to refrigerated premises where the urinalysis was completed. Further evidence revealed that the B sample recorded an unusually high pH, which was consistent with bacterial degradation of the sample. This was submitted as a possible explanation for the high testosterone level. When Modahl appealed the imposition of sanctions, the Appeal Panel of the IAAF concluded:

> On the evidence before us, there is a possibility, which cannot be ignored, that the cause of the T/E ratio in the samples of her urine was not that testosterone had been administered but that the samples had become degraded owing to their being stored in unrefrigerated conditions, and that bacteriological action had resulted in an increase in the amount of testosterone in the samples.

Modahl's four year suspension was lifted.

---

3 *Vinnicombe v ASDA,* unreported Federal Court of Australia, NSW District Registry (No G0065 of 1992) Referee's Decision at 13.

Lack of Procedural Fairness

Recent challenges have shown that a failure to adhere to the "rules of natural justice" will undermine any anti-doping policy. Natural justice consists of two components:

Hear the other side (audi alteram partem): a person is entitled to know the nature of any accusation made against them and to be given a fair opportunity to state his or her case; and,

Free from bias (nemo judex in causae sua): no one should judge his own cause. Any tribunal exercising authority to which the rules of natural justice apply must be free from any bias.[4]

For our purposes, "hear the other side rule" *(audi alteram partem)* is the more important, for it has been the more significant focus of procedural challenge.[5]

A preliminary question concerns the application of the rules of natural justice to the actions of a sporting organisation or ASDA. The rules of natural justice clearly apply to government agencies like ASDA. The High Court of Australia proposes:

> The law has now developed to a point where it may be accepted that there is a common law duty to act fairly in the sense of according procedural fairness in the making of administrative decisions which affect rights, interests and legitimate expectations, subject only to the clear manifestation of a contrary statutory intention.[6]

There is some doubt about the applicability of natural justice to private bodies.[7] However, there is sufficient judicial and extra-judicial support for

---

4 For more detailed discussion see J R S Forbes, *The Law of Domestic or Private Tribunals* (Sydney, Law Book Company 1982) at 56-61. See also *Ridge v Baldwin* [1964] AC 40.
5 In any event it is not clear whether officials of the relevant sporting organisation can sit on a tribunal dealing with the rights of an affected athlete. It would obviously be more in accord with the rules of natural justice for this situation to be avoided. However, in *Krakouer v Croxford* (Unreported Decision, Supreme Court of Victoria, 9 April 1985), the presence of two executive officers of the Victoria Football League (now the Australian Football League) on a disciplinary tribunal did not invalidate the decision: see also *Stollery v The Greyhound Racing Control Board* (1972) 128 CLR 507.
6 *Kioa v West* (1985) 159 CLR 550 at 569 per Mason J.
7 See *McInnes v Onslow - Fane* [1978] 1 WLR 1520 at 1535.

the idea that sporting tribunal disciplinary decisions that affect the liberty and financial interests of athletes attract the application of the rules of natural justice.[8]

From a practical perspective, there are particular procedural pitfalls that can lead to successful legal challenge of a decision rendered by either ASDA or a sporting organisation. The most critical issue is the matter of providing the athlete with the opportunity to make a case. The "hear the other side rule" means generally that the affected person has the right to be heard.

SAXTON AND DAVIES

An example of legal challenge based on denial of this right is the much publicised case of Andrew Saxton and Andrew Davies. Both were members of the British Olympic Team who were sent home from the Barcelona Olympics following the return of positive tests to Clenbuterol. This decision appeared to have been made on an ad hoc basis and certainly without any hearing at which the athletes were represented. Although the responsible British sporting organisation subsequently decided that no further penalty would be imposed, an issue remains as to whether they were denied natural justice.

Specifically, did the failure to notify the athletes of the commission of any known offence or the failure to provide them with an opportunity to explain the test result amount to a denial of natural justice?[9] It is clear that, at the very

---

8 See *Gray v Canadian Track and Field Association,* Supreme Court of Ontario, Toronto Weekly Court, Montgomery J, unreported, 18 July 1986; *Quirke v Bord Lutchleas Naheireann,* High Court of Ireland, Burr J, unreported, 25 March 1988; *Xuereb v Viola* (1989) 18 NSWLR 453 at 496; GM Kelly, *Sports Law: An Australian Perspective* (Sydney, Law Book Company 1981) at 73-83; M J Beloff, "Pitch, Pool, Risk...Court? Judicial Review in the Sporting World" (1989) Spring, *Public Law* 95 at 101-103; and JRS Forbes, *The Law of Domestic or Private Tribunals* (Sydney, Law Book Company 1982) at 97-212.

9 See S Rofe, "Recent Developments in Drugs in Sport: Overview of Legal Cases and the Implications to Sport" conference paper, *Drugs in Sport Legal Challenges Briefing,* Australian Institute of Sport, 26 November 1992 and see also E Grayson, "Drugs, Sport and the Olympics", (1992) 142 *New Law Journal* 1171. Martin Vinnicombe, in his challenge of a positive test result to Stanozolol, also argued that failure to provide him with an opportunity to be heard before the imposition of a penalty amounted to a breach of the rules of natural justice by ASDA, the ASC and the relevant sporting organisations.

least, prior notice that a decision adversely affecting interests is to be made is the minimum content of procedural fairness.[10]

A more spectacular example is that of Harry "Butch" Reynolds, the American sprinter, who was subjected to suspension by the International Amateur Athletic Federation for testing positive for steroid use. Reynolds successfully argued in the United States District Court that the suspension was wrongfully imposed and was awarded substantial damages. A full discussion of Reynolds' legal action is contained in chapter five. The US District Court stated that:

> It is this court's conclusion that the IAAF hearing was not conducted in good faith, was not conducted by an unbiased decision-maker, was not in accordance with the IAAF's own rules and regulations, did not accord Reynolds a full and fair opportunity to participate and resulted in a decision that was not fair and impartial but rather was arbitrary and capricious.[11]

There are other more technical but difficult issues. Firstly, any decision rendered must be:

> based upon some material that tends logically to show the existence of facts consistent with the finding and...the reasoning supportive of the finding, if it be disclosed, [must not be] logically self-contradictory.[12]

In other words, the finding and any resulting decision must follow the evidence.

As far as the evidence itself is concerned, disciplinary tribunals are not generally required to apply the rules of evidence as strictly as trial courts.[13] However, in light of the legal challenges that have already been made or threatened, it may be advisable for sporting organisations to comply as closely as possible to the strict rules of evidence developed for court proceedings.[14]

---

10 See M Allars, *Introduction to Australian Administrative Law* (Sydney, Law Book Company, 1990) and also *Lloyd v Marine Council* (1987) 14 ALD 521.

11 *Reynolds v IAAF* (Unreported Decision, United States District Court, Southern District Ohio, Eastern Division, c-2-92-452, 1992).

12 *Mahon v Air New Zealand* [1984] AC 803 at 821.

13 *Briginshaw v Briginshaw* (1933) 60 CLR 336 at 361-362 per Dixon J; *Rejfek v McElroy* (1965) 122 CLR 517; *Hardcastle v Commissioner of Police* (1986) 53 ALR 593.

14 These rules would include the exclusion of hearsay, opinion evidence, evidence as to the character of witness and similar fact evidence. For a general text which explores these and other rules with greater detail, see D. Byrne and J D Heydon, *Cross on Evidence* (Sydney, Law Book Company 1991).

Another concern is whether the athlete involved has the right to counsel at any stage of the proceedings. Denying an athlete legal representation at the proceedings of a sporting organisation may not amount to a denial of natural justice.[15] In one interesting development, Lord Denning held there was a right to legal representation where a sporting tribunal was deciding a matter of serious importance to the participant in terms of his reputation and livelihood.[16] However, the relevant sporting organisation in that case had no provision at all in its rules respecting the right to counsel. In a later case, the same judge upheld a Football Association rule prohibiting legal representation before its tribunal.[17] Administrators must therefore be wary of failing to make provision for the right to counsel.

The 1992 amendments to the ASDA Act[18] were to some extent informed by the need to pay heed to the rules of natural justice. Notably, s 16(1) of the amended Act provides that, following the return of a positive test result, ASDA must essentially provide the competitor with an opportunity to present any information or evidence to invalidate the result. Section 16(2) lists the bases on which ASDA may invalidate the test result. Section 16(4) obliges ASDA to provide the athlete with written reasons for deciding that a test result is valid. As if to underline the importance of adherence to the rules of natural justice, s 16(4)(b) provides that ASDA must inform the athlete that application may be made to the Administrative Appeals Tribunal for review of the decision. The ASDA procedures provide an adequate model for sporting organisations who wish to develop their own procedures in accordance with the requirements of natural justice.

Defects with the Evidence

The proof of security of chain of custody of the urine samples from the athlete providing the sample to testing laboratory, has led to legal challenges as to the validity of the drug testing. Athletes have argued that the security of the urine samples has not been maintained.

---

15 See M J Beloff, "Pitch, Pool, Risk...Court? Judicial Review in the Sporting World" (1989) Spring, *Public Law* 95 at 102-103.
16 See *Pett v Greyhound Racing Association Ltd* [1969] 1 QB 125.
17 See *Enderby Town Football Club v Football Association Ltd* [1971] 1 Ch 591.
18 Australian Sports Drug Agency Amendment Act 1992 (Cth).

CAPOBIANCO

Australian athlete, Olympic Sprinter Dean Capobianco, challenged the chain of custody procedure. He was suspended for four years after the IAAF found him guilty of a doping offence. The IAAF's arbitration panel overturned a decision by Athletics Australia (AA) to allow Capobianco to compete because of flaws in the chain of custody of a urine sample taken from the sprinter. The IAAF was appealing a finding by the AA arbiter, that the IAAF could not prove the positive sample (for the steroid Stanozolol) was Capobianco's. Capobianco disputed that the samples which tested positive were his, alleging fault in the chain of custody between when they were taken and when they were tested. The AA Arbiter was not satisfied by the chain of custody of Capobianco's urine sample between the race venue in Holland and the testing laboratory in Cologne, Germany. The procedures adopted by AA's Anti Doping Control Tribunal and the conduct of its Chairperson, Mr Ellicott QC, were carried out within the spirit of natural justice.

Mr Ellicott rightfully held that due to the fact that not all information with regard to the chain of custody was available, AA were unable to substantiate the charge against the client. While AA had no control over the documentation or over the officials who were involved in the drug testing, it was their duty to produce relevant information, to prove beyond reasonable doubt that the offence was committed. This is in accordance with Rule 4.4 of the Australian Olympic Committee Anti Doping Policy. However, the IAAF panel, without providing reasons, rejected the AA arbiter's decision.[19]

On 27 September 1996, the IAAF Council referred the matter to the Arbitration Panel. The Arbitration Panel handed down its decision on 17 March 1997. The Arbitration Panel expressed concerns about the availability of all relevant material concerning the client's samples. This evidence should have been available to the client and Athletics Australia prior to the hearing before Mr Ellicott QC. Furthermore, it was shown that there were some deficiencies and errors in the documentation of the chain of custody, for example the log book. However, the Arbitration Panel claimed that there was no clear demand of special written documentation of chain of custody in the IAAF Rules or "Procedural Guidelines for Doping Control".

---

19 Refer to T*he Sydney Morning Herald,* 17 March 1997; *The Canberra Times*, 18 March 1997; *The Australian,* 18 March 1997; and *The Age,* 18 March 1997.

DRUGS, SPORT AND THE LAW

> The Arbitration Panel claimed that under Rule 55.9 of the IAAF, a departure or departures from the procedures set out in the "Procedural Guidelines for Doping Control" shall not invalidate the finding that a prohibited substance was present in a sample, unless this departure was such as to cast real doubt on the reliability of such a finding.
>
> However, this would seem to contradict the IOC Medical Code, Article 5, which restates Rule 4.4 of the Australian Olympic Committee Anti Doping Policy [20]. Furthermore, clause 1.2 of Appendix D of the "Laboratory Analysis Procedures" states:
>
>> Proper chain of custody controls shall always be enforced during all testing and specimen handling. Only authorised personnel may handle specimens to be tested and they shall sign chain of custody forms to document when specimens are in their possession.
>
> Furthermore, under the IOC, "Medical Commission: Requirements for accreditation and good laboratory practice", clause 5 states:
>
>> Documentation of all aspects of the testing process must be available. This documentation will be maintained for at least two years, and will include: chain of custody documents... The laboratory should be prepared to maintain documents for any specimen under legal challenge for at least five years.
>
> The above indicates that there could be a case where the IAAF Rules are in conflict with the Rules of the IOC. While the lawyer for the IAAF, Herbert Smith, claimed in a correspondence to Mishcon de Reya[21] (dated 14 November 1996) that all IOC registered laboratories were independent laboratories and that IAAF had no contractual entitlements to the laboratories' original documents, without these documents being available to the IAAF, there is no guarantee that the chain of custody was maintained.

The Vinnicombe and Capobianco cases illustrate that, not only is it important that testing procedures be followed, it is essential that agreement be reached on standardized procedures at the national and international level.

---

20 Rule 4.4 of the Australian Olympic Committee Anti Doping Policy states:
"Minor irregularities, which cannot reasonably be considered to have affected the results of the otherwise valid tests, will have no effect on such results. Minor irregularities do not include the chain of custody of the sample."

21 Lawyers for Capobianco.

Amendments to the ASDA Act were made after the Vinnicombe incident by providing for overseas testing of Australian athletes by "approved" foreign anti-doping agencies.[22] It remains to be seen whether this provision will eliminate the problem evidenced in the Vinnicombe case.

Absence of Intent: The "Inadvertency" Defence

Given that doping offences do not appear to require any related mental element, there is further concern about mandatory testing. Generally, a doping offence occurs where a urinalysis records a positive test result for a banned substance. Doping policies are all drafted to operate this way. It is not relevant how or why the substance was ingested.[23] It is therefore possible that if a banned substance enters an athlete's body without his or her knowledge, for example by means of ingesting a beverage "spiked" by

---

22 Australian Sports Drug Agency Amendment Act 1992, s 66B.
23 For example, under the IAAF Drug Testing Programme, rule 55 (2) states:
   "The offence of doping takes place when either
   (i) a prohibited substance is found to be present within an athlete's body tissue or fluids..."
Similar definitions can be found in the doping policies of other organisations and Ifs. For example, the Australian Sports Commission's Anti-Doping Policy provides in s. 3.1:
   "A person commits a doping offence if:
   (a) a prohibited substance is present within the person's body tissue or fluids unless:
   (i) the person uses the prohibited substance for a therapeutic purpose, or
   (ii) there are exceptional circumstances
   (b) the person uses or takes advantage of a prohibited method
   (c) the person refuses to provide a sample for testing when requested by a drug testing authority
   (d) the person is involved in trafficking, or
   (e) the person knowingly assists, or is knowingly involved in the commission of a doping offence by an other person."
"Exceptional circumstances" are further defined in the Policy as follows:
Exceptional circumstances exist if the presence of the prohibited substance is beyond the person's control. For example:
   (a) the person has a natural Testosterone:Epitestosterone ratio above 6:1, or
   (b) the person is administered the prohibited substance in hospital without their knowledge.
Exceptional circumstances do not exist merely because the person:
   (a) took the prohibited substance inadvertently, or
   (b) they did not know the substance was prohibited.
The onus of proof is on the person who claims that:
   (a) they used a prohibited substance for a therapeutic purpose, or
   (b) there are exceptional circumstances.

another or, in the case of marijuana, by means of passive inhaling of the drug,[24] then that athlete may be subjected to the same sanctions as one who voluntarily or deliberately ingests a banned substance with the specific intention of improving performance.

Of course, some rules provide for consideration of the athlete's intent when it comes to determination of sanctions. In one recent case, the sanction to be applied was reduced on account of the athlete's claim that he had inadvertently ingested prohibited substances.

> ## RICHARDSON
>
> British 400 metre runner Mark Richardson tested positive for nandrolone in October 1999 and was subjected to a two year ban. Richardson claimed that he had inadvertently ingested nandrolone through contaminated food supplements he was using.
>
> Despite initially engaging the IAAF in an arbitration, Richardson subsequently withdrew from the arbitration process and agreed to submit to a determination by IAAF Council. Richardson never challenged the "legality" of rules based on strict liability, as he agreed to be bound by the IAAF Rules. In March 2001 a request for early reinstatement of Richardson was refused. However IAAF Council decided to reinstate Richardson on 14 June 2001. This was justified by the IAAF's "exceptional circumstances" rule.[25] Council were strongly persuaded by two factors:
>
> 1. The fact that Richardson chose not to challenge its "strict liability" rule; and

---

24 The chromatography testing done by all IOC approved laboratories, including the Australian Government Analytical Laboratories (who perform such analysis for ASDA) can trace elements of marijuana metabolites passively inhaled. See L Uzych, "Drug Testing of Athletes" (1991) 86 *British Journal of Addiction* 25 at 29.

25 Rule 60 – Sanctions
   "...8. In exceptional circumstances, an athlete may apply to the Council for reinstatement before the IAAF's period of ineligibility has expired.
Where an athlete has provided substantial assistance to a Member in the course of an enquiry into doping carried out by that Member, this will normally be regarded by the Council as constituting exceptional circumstances.
However, it is emphasised that only truly exceptional circumstances will justify any reduction. Details of the procedure and the criteria for application are to be found in the 'Procedural Guidelines for Doping'."

2. Substantial voluntary efforts by Richardson to educate fellow athletes of the dangers of food supplements.

Note however that Richardson was still recorded as having committed a doping infraction. Aside from the moral stain associated with this record, there may be other more material consequences. The athlete may be obliged to return funding or lose eligibility and his or her corporate sponsorship may be affected.

WATSON

Alex Watson, a modern pentathlete, was disqualified from the Seoul Olympics on the grounds that test results showed a level of caffeine in his urine in excess of the allowable level. Though Watson admitted to having ingested a number of cups of coffee, the level of caffeine detected was not simply explainable this way. Watson argued that his drinks had been tampered with. See "Watson: a Victim", *The Age,* 26 September 1988.

LAYCOCK

Ron Laycock, an elite level Australian weightlifter, tested positive to Stanozolol after the Australian Weightlifting Championships in September 1993. Despite the positive test and the notification of the Australian Weightlifting Federation, Laycock was not withdrawn from the Australian team competing at the World championships in November of that year. The AWF maintained that its doping policy required a full hearing to be convened prior to imposing any sanction and that it was not possible to do so in sufficient time before the World Championships. The AWF had been notified of the positive test result only eight days prior to the event. There was some evidence that the AWF tried to persuade Laycock to withdraw voluntarily. Eventually, the AWF convened an independent committee to conduct a hearing, at which Laycock argued that his food had been spiked. The tribunal did not accept the argument and Laycock was given a two year suspension in accordance with the standard doping policy of the ASC.

Clearly, there are moral concerns inherent in creating an offence of absolute or strict liability. Yet the doping infraction itself is not a criminal offence, nor is it enforced by the State. Organisations secure the consent of participants to the rules they apply. Yet the practical effects, to the athlete, of a sanction may well exceed any realistically possible criminal penalty. Thus, while we concede that the legal argument against absolute liability in doping cases may be a weak one, there is still much value in understanding the approach taken to strict liability in our courts.

The practice of imposing sanctions on the basis of strict or absolute liability for doping offences is wrong in policy and possibly also in law. According to Australian criminal law, in cases where the law requires proof of criminal intent, there will be a common law defence of honest and reasonable mistake. However, as a doping infraction is not a criminal offence, this defence will not apply.[26] In *He Kaw Teh v the Queen*,[27] Gibbs CJ remarked:

> if it is held that guilty knowledge is not an ingredient of an offence, it does not follow that the offence is an absolute one. A middle course, between imposing liability and requiring proof of guilty knowledge or intention, is to hold that an accused will not be guilty if he acted under an honest and reasonable mistake as to the existence of facts, which if true, would have made his act innocent.

While a doping offence is not strictly speaking a statutory offence, the general principles laid down by the High Court in *He Kaw Teh* would apply, as the rules that prescribe the elements of a doping offence affect an athlete's right to work. The actions of sporting organisations, in promulgating rules prescribing doping offences, would be subject to the a general principle elucidated by Denning LJ in *Abbott v Sullivan*[28] :

> [bodies] which exercise a monopoly in an important sphere of human activity, with the power of depriving a man of his livelihood, must act in accordance with the elementary rules of justice.

The Supreme Court of Western Australia, in *Maynard v Racing Penalties Appeal Tribunal of Western Australia*,[29] held that these "elementary rules of justice" implicitly make available a defence of honest and reasonable

---

26 See *Maynard v Racing Penalties Appeal Tribunal of Western Australia* (1994) 11 WAR 1. See comment by T Buti and H Opie, "Drug Testing in Horse Racing: Honest and Reasonable Mistake as a Defence" (1994) 4 ANZSLA *Newsletter* 6.
27 (1985) 157 CLR 523 at 533.
28 [1952] 1 KB 189 at 198.
29 (1994) 11 WAR 1.

mistake. The Court also applied principles set out in *He Kaw Teh* [30] so as to read into the rules of the sporting organisation concerned a "defence" of honest and reasonable mistake.

In the *Maynard* case, the Court was concerned with a doping offence described in Rule 175 of the Rules of Racing (the Rules), which provided that racing stewards were authorised to punish:

> (h) Any person who at any time administers, or causes to be administered, any prohibited substance as defined...
> (ii) which is detected in any pre- or post-race sample on the day of any race.

Maynard was convicted of causing a prohibited substance to be administered to a horse contrary to Rule 175(h)(ii) of the Rules and was disqualified from training for three years by the stewards of the Western Australian Turf Club. Maynard contended that the prohibited substance had been administered for a legitimate medical purpose three weeks prior to the race day on which the horse's urine sample was extracted. He gave evidence that he had obtained the opinion of the veterinary surgeon who administered the drug that the horse would be ready to race in 14 days. Further evidence was adduced that the Australian Equine Veterinary Association recommended that this particular substance, depro-medol (a cortico-steroid used to treat inflammation), would pass through the horse's system by excretion within 21 days. Maynard accordingly argued that he had not intentionally committed a breach of the Rules and was acting under an honest and reasonable mistake. Following an unsuccessful appeal against his exclusion, Maynard applied to the Supreme Court of Western Australia seeking the Court's declaration as to the proper construction of Rule 175(h)(ii). The Full Court held by a majority that the proper interpretation of Rule 175(h)(ii) included an implied "defence" of honest and reasonable mistake that a horse is drug free in race day. Ipp J, speaking for the Court, said:

> In my opinion, a presumption applies to the Rules of Racing that honest and reasonable mistake will be a defence to offences created thereby, unless an intention to exclude that defence plainly appears

---

30 The High Court judgments can be read as requiring that for statutory offences the "defence" of honest and reasonable mistake will apply, unless "excluded by the words of the statute creating the offence or by the subject matter with which it deals". (per Gibbs CJ 528 and Brennan J at 565).

from the rule in question. In my view there is nothing in the words of Rule 175(h)(ii) that can be said plainly to lead to the exclusion of that defence. It would have been possible for the Rules of Racing to provide for such an exclusion, but they do not do so. The declaration sought by the applicant is that Rule 175(h)(ii) requires the negation of an honest and reasonable but mistaken belief that any prohibited substance administered or caused to be administered had been excreted by the race day and therefore would not be present in the blood or urine. I consider that the implication of such a provision (subject to the qualification that the person charged must first properly raise the issue) is in accordance with the elementary rules of justice. In the same way as the rules of natural justice have been held to be a necessary implication, by operation of law, to the Rules of Racing, so do I consider that the elementary rules of justice are so necessary. It could hardly be unnecessary for the Rules of Racing not to conform with elementary rules of justice. I would therefore grant a declaration that it is implicit under Rule 175(h)(ii) that, provided there is evidence which raises the question (cf *He Kaw Teh v The Queen* at 535), there can be no finding that an infringement has been committed unless there has been a negation of an honest and reasonable but mistaken belief that any prohibited substance administered or caused to be administered to a horse had been excreted by the race day and therefore would not be present in the blood or urine".[31]

The Full Court of Western Australia[32] subsequently overruled *Maynard*. Harper was a licensed trainer under the Rules of Trotting, which are similar to the Rules considered by the Court in *Maynard*. Harper was convicted by the stewards of the Western Australia Trotting Association. Two concurrent eight month disqualifications were imposed, pursuant to Rule 346 of the Rules of Trotting:

> Where a ... sample taken from a horse is shown to contain a drug ... and the stewards have not given permission for the administration of a drug...
>
> (a) the trainer or other person in whose custody or under whose control the horse was at the time shall be deemed guilty of an offence...[33]

---

31 *Maynard v Racing Penalties Appeal Tribunal of Western Australia* (1994) 11 WAR 1 at 23-24.
32 *Harper v Racing Penalties Appeal Tribunal of Western Australia* (1995) 12 WAR 337.
33 Rule 365B contains a deeming provision: "For the purposes of these Rules, where a sample from a horse is found to have contained a substance described in this Rule in excess of the maximum quantity appearing opposite the substance then the horse shall be deemed to have had administered to it a drug or a drug capable of reducing that substance."

However the Rules provide a defence. Under Rule 346A, a trainer or other person,

> shall not be guilty of an offence if he shall satisfy the Stewards that he took all reasonable and proper precautions to prevent the administration of a drug to the horse herein referred to.[34]

Harper was found guilty by the Stewards because two of his horses returned blood samples on race day which recorded total carbon dioxide levels in excess of the permitted 35 millimoles per litre. Harper argued that the level of carbon dioxide was caused by a feed supplement which had been administered to the horses and that he had acted in good faith and did not believe he was infringing any rule.

Harper's appeal to the Racing Penalties Appeal Tribunal was dismissed. Harper appealed to the Supreme Court of Western Australia.

As in *Maynard*, the Court in *Harper* concluded that the Rules of Trotting were not part of the "statute law" of Western Australia and section 24 of the *Criminal Code* (WA) did not apply to the Rules of Trotting. However, the Court went on to hold that there was no need for the Stewards to negate a claim of honest and reasonable mistake on the part of the person charged with the offence. Anderson and Owen JJ:

> With all respect to the majority in *Maynard's* case, we do not subscribe to the view that policy requires the implication of a term that would require the stewards positively to negate honest and reasonable mistake on the part of a licensed person before proceedings to disqualify that person for non-compliance with the Rules. There are a number of reasons for this ... the very survival of the industry as well as substantial government revenue would seem to depend on encouraging the public to bet on horse racing, that is, to bet on the outcome of each race... It may well be anticipated that unless racing is perceived to be fair and honest, people may be discouraged from betting. This might be thought to justify stringent controls in respect to the administration of drugs to horses and the enforcement of those controls by preparatory means.

---

34 Rule 128 states: "when any horse which has been brought to a race-course for the purpose of engaging in a race is found by the Committee of the Club or the Stewards to have had administered to it any prohibited substance ... the trainer and any other person who was in charge of such horse at any relevant time, may be punished, unless he is satisfied that he had taken all proper precautions to prevent the administration of the prohibited substance."

> That an application of the Rules may seriously affect the rights and privileges of the licensed person is every reason to ensure that the licensed person should be accorded natural justice within the framework of the rules. But it does not follow that the content of the obligation to accord natural justice includes an obligation not to impose a penalty for breach of the Rules of Trotting unless honest and reasonable mistake is first negatived. Nor does it follow that, in the circumstances of this industry, a rule of the type under consideration is necessarily repugnant to the rules of natural justice. It may well be the case that those familiar with every aspect of the industry and with long experience in it have come to the conclusion that to ensure the integrity of racing and to maintain public confidence in its integrity, there is need to impose very stringent controls and that those who wish to participate in racing for rich rewards will have to accept that the privilege of doing so may well be taken from them if for any reason, even without actual fault on their part, they present a doped horse for racing.[35]

However, the result of *Harper* is not that a defence of honest and reasonable mistake is inapplicable. The case does not maintain that the offence in question is one of strict liability. Rather, the licensed person will still have the opportunity to satisfy the Stewards that he or she "took all reasonable and proper precautions to prevent the administration of the drug".[36] *Harper's* case places the onus of proving the presence of an honest and reasonable mistake on the alleged offender. In *Maynard* the Court had placed the onus of disproving such a mistake on the Stewards. *Harper* is therefore still consistent with the idea that such offences are not to be construed as offences of strict liability.

Further, even if *Harper's* case is followed, it remains to be seen whether the reasoning in the case will be applied in the context of other sports.

On any reasonable interpretation of *Harper*, it would be inappropriate to apply any sanction where an athlete tests positive to a banned substance on the basis of an honest and reasonable mistake.[37] As a practical matter, it may

---

[35] *Harper v Racing Penalties Appeal Tribunal of Western Australia and Another* (1995) 12 WAR 337 at 349.
[36] Ibid at 350.
[37] This may, implicitly, have been the basis on which Australian swimmer Samantha Riley was permitted to continue to compete, notwithstanding that she tested positive to a banned substance in competition. Of course, in such cases, the norm is to consider the intention of the athlete (if at all) at the stage of determining the appropriated sanction. Guilt effectively needs to be conceded. Only were sporting organisations to incorporate the equivalent of Rule 346A of the Rules of Trotting in their doping policies would lack of intent establish a defence.

be that making available a defence of honest and reasonable mistake will make proof of the commission of a doping offence difficult. However, such difficulty is not sufficient to exclude the defence, as Brennan J remarked in *He Kaw Teh*:

> A pragmatic concern about unmeritous acquittals does not warrant the imposition of strict liability.[38]

If doping offences are interpreted as either requiring a certain mental element or attracting the defence of honest and reasonable mistake, there may be a significant problem in cases of inadvertent consumption of certain banned substances, particularly those used in medication for coughs, hay fever and in the treatment of asthma.

LAUMANN

Silken Laumann, a world-class Canadian rower, was tested during the 1995 Pan-American Games in Argentina. Test results revealed the presence of the banned stimulant, pseudoephedrine, in Laumann's urine. Laumann argued the test result was as a result of her use of the over-the-counter decongestant medication, Benadryl. She maintained that she had no intention of enhancing her performance. Furthermore, Laumann established that she had consulted a doctor about the medicine, seeking advice on whether she could take it without risk of ingesting a banned substance. Complicating matters was the fact that Benadryl was produced in different versions, the Benadryl D taken by Laumann containing the banned pseudoephedrine. Laumann and her team-mates were stripped of the gold medals they had won in the quadruple-sculls event at the Pan-American Games.

Laumann was subsequently reinstated by FISA, the international federation for rowing. No sanction was imposed. According to FISA's executive committee, there was "no intentional or negligent use of a banned substance." And, in any event, despite being free to compete, Laumann was still recorded as having committed a doping infraction and was therefore ineligible for a medal. However, FISA lacked the jurisdiction to restore the medals which had been stripped by the Pan-

---

38 *He Kaw The v the Queen* (1985) 157 CLR 523 at 580. Note, however, that if an athlete has not taken effective precautions "to avoid the possibility of the occurrence of the external elements of the offence" the defence of honest and reasonable mistake may not be successful: ibid at 567 per Brennan J.

American Sport Organisation. See "Laumann cleared in 'fairy-tale ending'", *Toronto Star,* 8 April 1995, at pE1.

RILEY

In 1995 world record holding swimmer Samantha Riley was subjected to a routine random drug test while at the World Swimming Championships in Rio de Janeiro. Testing revealed the presence of a propoxephrine metabolite known as dextro proproxephrine, a substance commonly found in digesics. Following notification of the positive result in the A sample, Riley accepted the result and waived her right to require the testing authority to test the B sample. On 3 January 1996 Riley made written submissions to FINA, the relevant international federation. A hearing was convened before a single member of the FINA executive, some six days later, for the purpose of determining what sanction, if any, should be applied. At the hearing Riley argued that she had been given an unlabelled headache tablet by her coach when she complained of a headache. She also admitted that she had undergone a number of prior drug tests and she and her coach had attended an ASDA athlete and coach education programme on the dangers of inadvertent doping. The FINA hearing resulted in no sanction, but a simple warning being administered. Riley's coach was subsequently barred from participating in "all swimming activities" for a period of seven months. At the hearing Riley's representatives relied on the decision of the Supreme Court of Western Australia in *Maynard v Racing Penalties Appeal Tribunal of Western Australia and Others* (1993-94) 11 WALR 1, discussed above.

ANDREA RADUCAN

The case of Romanian gymnast, Andrea Raducan, clearly demonstrates the importance of strict liability in doping offences. At the Sydney 2000 Olympic Games the 16 year old gymnast was stripped of her gold medal in the women's individual artistic gymnastics event on the grounds that she had tested positive to the banned stimulant pseudo-ephedrine. The IOC acknowledged that Raducan innocently took over-the-counter medicine prescribed by her team doctor to treat a cold and that she gained no competitive advantage from the substance. However, the IOC pointed out that her offence carried a penalty of strict liability.

With much public sympathy, Raducan appealed to the Court of Arbitration for Sport. A three member panel dismissed her appeal and held that the IOC had made the right decision "as a matter of law and in fairness to other athletes". The CAS noted that Raducan's age, weight, need for medication and reliance on her doctor were "irrelevant". The panel noted that the crux of its decision was the positive test:

> "It is the presence of a prohibited substance in a competitor's bodily fluid which constitutes the offence irrespective of whether or not the competitor intended to ingest the prohibited substance." The Court added that it was "aware of the impact of its decision on a fine, young elite athlete. It finds in balancing the interests of Miss Raducan with the commitment of the Olympic Movement to drug-free sport, the Anti-Doping Code must be enforced without compromise."

While it may be argued that it is the athlete's responsibility to ensure that any medication ingested does not contain a banned substance, this is made difficult, as the broad categories of banned substance list a number of drugs and "related compounds". Furthermore, athletes with a genuine desire to comply with doping rules must depend on the availability of up-to-date information on what substances and compounds are on the banned list. Without this, it may be practically impossible for the athlete to be aware of the potential breach. The experience of the British weightlifters, Andrew Saxton and Andrew Davies, illustrates this problem. Both were banned from the 1992 Barcelona Olympics after having tested positive for the steroid Clenbuterol, which was treated by the IOC Medical Commission as a banned substance in the "related compound" category. Both athletes appeared to be completely unaware of the listing of their medication by the IOC Medical Commission and had not, prior to the Olympics, been informed of that fact by their athletic and medical advisers.[39] Following their exclusion from the Barcelona Olympics, further proceedings against both athletes were discontinued.

Despite the fact that these rules are always strictly interpreted, there has been a case where an exception to the rules was allowed. Eric Lamaze admitted ingesting a banned substance, but defended himself by arguing that he was so distraught at the time that he could not be said to have been acting voluntarily; he was in fact the victim of "automatism". The court accepted that Lamaze was the victim of an extraordinary set of circumstances and as a result his life-ban was overturned.[40]

---

39 E Grayson, "Drugs, Sport and the Olympics" (1992) 142 New Law Journal 1171.
40 The Lamaze case is discussed below.

The cases of Riley, Raducan and Laumann have similar facts and yet three different results emerge. The cases were decided by three different organisations with different interests. The fact that vastly different results can emerge from very similar situations demonstrates the extraordinary power of the various adjudicative bodies. The full impact of this power can be felt when National Federations are tempted to allow the interests of the sport they administer impact on their decisions. For example, in Riley's case it could be argued that FINA was influenced by the qualities of the athlete involved and its desire to protect the image of the sport. This demonstrates an advantage of the CAS, which is a truly independent adjudicative body.[41]

Therapeutic use

Most doping codes exclude genuine therapeutic use from the definition of a doping offence. However, to use this defence, you must normally notify the appropriate authorities.

> **LYNCH**
>
> Andrew Lynch, an AFL player with the Brisbane Lions, was subjected to a disciplinary hearing by the Australian Football League following detection of DHEA, a banned anabolic steroid. Lynch claimed that his use of the substance was therapeutic, as he suffered from chronic fatigue syndrome, for which DHEA was an effective medication. No sanctions were imposed, as Lynch had relied on advice from ASDA that he would not be in breach of policy if his use were therapeutic. The AFL Anti-Doping Code contains the following provisions regarding therapeutic use:
>
> 7.1 Where a Player through his Club has received authorisation from the AFL Medical Commissioner to use a substance otherwise prohibited under this Code then, solely for the Player concerned and subject to the conditions attaching to the authorisation, the substance concerned will be deemed not to be prohibited under this Code. The authorisation must be in force before the Player concerned provides a sample for testing.
>
> 7.2 All applications for therapeutic use of an otherwise prohibited substance must be made on behalf of a player solely by his Club Medical Officer to the AFL Medical Commissioner. The application must include a description of the Player's medical condition, length

---

41 For a discussion of the CAS see Chapter Five.

of treatment and verification there is no alternative medication that does not contain prohibited substances. The AFL Medical Commissioner may require the provision of additional information and may also require the Player to undergo a medical examination by the AFL Medical Commissioner or his nominee.

7.3 The AFL Medical Commissioner will determine the application according to the following criteria:

(1) the Player would experience significant impairment of his health if the prohibited substance were withheld;

(2) no enhancement of the Player's normal level of performance would result from the administration of the prohibited substance as medically prescribed;

(3) the Player would not be denied the prohibited substance if he were not competing in an AFL Competition; and

(4) no permitted alternative medication can be substituted for the prohibited substance.

(5) no authorisation may be given in respect of anabolic steroids.

The process of gaining approval for therapeutic use of a prohibited substance was streamlined in 1999 when the Australian Sports Drug Agency Amendment Act 1999 (Cth) was passed. The amendments created the Australian Sports Drug Medical Advisory Committee (ASDMAC). The ASDMAC replaces former Medical Advisory Committees which were part of the ASC.[42]

Restraint of trade

To date, the most effective sanction applied against defaulting athletes has been the suspension. The imposition of a suspension against an athlete invokes the response that it constitutes a restraint of trade. As Scott J stated in *Gasser v Stinson:*

> in a sport which allows competitors to exploit their ability in the sport for financial gain and which allows that gain to be a direct consequence of participation in competition, a ban on competition is, in my judgement, a restraint of trade.[43]

British shot putter, Paul Edwards, went to the High Court in London, arguing that his four year suspension was an unreasonable restraint of trade.[44] In the

---

[42] For a discussion see H Opie, "Medico-Legal Issues in Sport" (2001) 23 *Sydney Law Review* 375 at 392-395.

[43] Scott J (Unreported Decision, High Court of Justice, Chancery Division, 15 June 1988, No CH-88-G-2191 of 1988) at 37.

[44] "The Drug", *The Weekend Australian,* 21-22 June 1997.

1988 *Gasser v Stinson and Holt* case,[45] the same court judged that a two year suspension from competition for testing positive to drug use was reasonable in the circumstances. The basis of the decision was that the penalty was held to be reasonable in view of the interest of the IAAF in deterring athletes from taking performance-enhancing drugs and ensuring a drug-free sport.

The unreasonable restraint of trade argument emerged in two Australian cases.[46] Both concerned athletes tested positive for banned drugs.

PATE AND HALL

Cyclists Stephen Pate and Carey Hall, both athletes tested positive to an anabolic steroid following success in the 1991 World Championships. They were stripped of their medals and penalised with a fine and deferred suspension by the international cycling body, the Union Cyclists Internationale (UCI). In addition, the Australian Professional Cycling Council Inc (APCC) imposed a two year ban on the athletes, which prevented them from competing in any professional cycling event in Australia. In effect, this precluded the cyclists from competing in World Championships for the duration of the ban, as in order to qualify, they would need to have competed at the Australian Championships at which the national team was to be chosen. Pate and Hall challenged the ban imposed by the APCC on the basis that it constituted an unreasonable restraint of trade. They explained that, if they lost the opportunity to win medals at the World Championships, they would miss out on opportunities to compete in Europe and Japan and also miss substantial sponsorship opportunities. They estimated that the ban could cost them as much as $AU 200,000 per year.[47] Even this substantial amount pales when compared to the $US 6.8 million awarded to Butch Reynolds on account of lost earnings during the period he was banned from competing by the IAAF. The stakes here are enormous, commensurate with the growth of the magnitude of the sports industry.

Pate and Hall's argument centred on the fact that the international body had imposed a penalty less severe than that imposed by the

---

45 *Gasser v Stinson and Holt,* Scott J (Unreported Decision, High Court of Justice, Chancery Division, 15 June 1988, No CH-88-G-2191 of 1988).
46 Vinnicombe considered bringing civil action on the basis of restraint of trade, but did not proceed.
47 See T Gaspar, "Pate and Hall Set the Pace" (1992) 2 *ANZLA Newsletter* at 9-10.

APCC. Their general proposition was that it would be unreasonable for a national sporting organisation to impose a greater penalty than its international counterpart. The challenge instituted by Pate and Hall was eventually resolved by an out of court settlement.

ROBERTSON

Unfortunately for the limited legal budget of the APCC, yet another cyclist who tested positive for steroid use launched a legal challenge to his penalty. Bill Robertson tested positive for Nandolone on 26 December 1991 and was disqualified from holding an APCC license for two years. After exhausting his rights of appeal within the sporting organisation, Robertson commenced proceedings claiming his disqualification was void as it constituted an unreasonable restraint of trade.[48] Robertson's challenge was successful. There could be no doubt that a two year suspension constituted a restraint of trade, as it prevented Robertson from earning income as a professional cyclist. The APCC was thus bound to show that the restraint was reasonable in that it afforded "no more than adequate protection to the interests of the [APCC] and of the professional cycling industries in Australia". As the APCC did not defend the case (having already presumably exhausted its budget for legal advice and assistance), it was not surprising that the Court found that the penalty was unreasonable in that it was in excess of that provided for in the rules of the relevant international organisation.

It is interesting to speculate what the outcome of this case might have been had the APCC chosen to defend it. One argument that might have been made is that the APCC had an interest in continuing to receive assistance from the ASC. Any sporting organisation which is

---

48 Robertson also argued that the APCC had imposed a penalty that was too severe as it was in excess of the penalty which would have applied under the rules of the Federation Internationale du Cyclisme Professionel (FICP) and the Union Cyclists Internationale (UCI). The basis for this argument was that the APCC was a member of FICP, which in turn is a member of the UCI. The UCI rules would have provided for a sanction in the form of a fine and a deferred three month suspension for a first offence. Waddell CJ held that these rules only applied to international events or to foreign riders competing in domestic events. As Robertson was a domestic rider competing in a domestic event, the UCI rules were held not to apply and therefore the APCC was free to impose its own sanction, which, in turn, was based on the ASC's Doping Policy, which it had adopted. See *Roberston v Australian Professional Cycling Council Inc* (Unreported Decision, Supreme Court of New South Wales per Waddell CJ, 10 September 1992).

> in breach of the ASC's Doping Policy will be denied financial or other assistance by the ASC.[49]

Restraint of trade: the legal principles

Let us examine the restraint of trade doctrine in more detail. Firstly, we explore the relevant legal principles concerning the restraint of trade doctrine. Secondly, the issues that are likely to be raised in any restraint of trade challenge to a suspension for a doping offence.

The general approach since *Nordenfelt v Maxim Nordenfelt Guns and Ammunition Co Ltd*[50] has been that contracts to restrain a person's liberty of action in carrying on his or her trade, business, occupation or profession and all restraints of trade of themselves are contrary to public policy and therefore void, unless the restraint is (i) reasonably necessary to protect the interests of the person in whose favour it is imposed; (ii) not unreasonable as regards the person restrained; and (iii) not unreasonably injurious to the public.

The essence of the restraint of trade doctrine is that it considered undesirable for persons to be deprived of their means of livelihood without reasonable cause. It follows that the actions of a sporting organisation in refusing to allow an athlete to compete, whether by means of refusing to issue a licence or otherwise, constitute, on the face of it *(prima facie)* at least, a restraint of trade. This is so because the doctrine applies once the athlete's means of obtaining his or her livelihood is affected. Once it has been established that the penalty constitutes a restraint of trade, it then remains to be considered whether the restraint is reasonable or not. Two considerations guide the courts:

- It is a matter of striking a fair balance between relevant and legitimate interests of the parties, with a passing glance at the interests of the public.[51]
- The reasonableness of the restraint will turn on the particular circumstances of each case.

The courts may overturn excessive penalties. The imposition of sanctions that will effectively end an athlete's career will receive close scrutiny by the courts.

---

49 ASC,*Revised Doping Policy*, September 1992, s 6.3.
50 [1894] AC 535 at 565.
51 JRS Forbes, *Disciplinary Tribunals* (Sydney, Law Book Co 1990)

One might assert that it seems to be consistent with the purpose of imposing discipline to ensure that the penalty fits the crime. Presumably, if it is open to an athlete to argue that the sanction imposed for drug taking constitutes as unreasonable restraint of trade, then it is equally open to an apprehended felon to make the same argument. The difference between the two cases is that we accept (as an a priori assumption) that incarceration of felons, with the effect of removing their means of livelihood, is a reasonable way to protect the public interest in securing a society free from crime. In the case of the athlete's use of banned substances, are we equally prepared to make the same assumption?

The courts determines, as a matter of law, whether in the circumstances a restraint of trade is reasonable.[52] The court will be guided by a determination as to whether the penalties imposed for drug taking are, in its view, more than reasonably necessary to protect the legitimate interests of the sporting organisation concerned. Included in this determination will be the effect of the restraint on the athlete concerned and the impact on the public of the imposition of the penalty.

In cases involving the application of a penalty for breach of an ethical rule of a profession or association, courts will not invalidate the penalty unless "it goes beyond what can reasonably be related to the maintenance of [the group's] honour and standards".[53] Thus, any penalties imposed for breach of doping policy cannot go beyond what is reasonably necessary to protect the interest of promoting drug-free sport.

Where possible, sporting organisations should attempt to document their decision regarding the appropriate penalty, so as to be able to present credible evidence at any later judicial proceeding. In addition to the substance of the penalty, courts will review the manner in which it is imposed. Therefore, a rule may be reasonable in the view of the court, but may be applied unreasonably. Examples of this might be the imposition of the penalty retrospectively.[54]

In deciding on the length of the period of restraint is an important consideration.[55] When the restraint stems from disciplinary measures, the

---

52 *Lindner v Murdoch's Garage* [1950] 83 CLR 628 at 645.
53 *Pharmaceutical Society of Great Britain v Dickson* [1968] 2 All ER 686 at 689-690.
54 *Hughes v Western Australian Cricket Association Inc* [1986] 69 ALR 660.
55 *Halsbury's Laws of England,* at para 35 and cases cited therein.

courts appear concerned to deny excessive or draconian penalties as valid restraints of trade.[56] The courts frown on any penalty which would effectively end an athlete's career, or rules which are imposed retrospectively.[57] Concern has also been directed at rules which are rigid and provide for arbitrary exercise of control over players.[58] Furthermore, rules, which allow a player a right to be heard or a right of appeal may not satisfy the courts. The relevant appeals committees may not necessarily make decisions which a Court would find acceptable in determining whether the restraint was reasonable.[59] In any case, the Court cannot review the merits of the case, except in an extreme situation of unreasonableness.[60]

In deciding whether a restraint is unreasonable, the enquiry into the effects on the covenantor or even third parties is not restricted to economic effects. Non-economic effects, such as effects on personal lives, should be discussed.[61] In *Adamson v New South Wales Rugby League Pty Ltd* (the "League's Draft Appeal case"), Wilcox J considered the effect of the restrictive covenant on personal autonomy:

> the internal draft is contrary to the common law principle that people are entitled to practise their trade as and where they wish, exercising and developing their skills as they see best and making their own decisions as to their employment and lifestyle. Instead, the draft imposes upon a player a requirement which limits his freedom to select his employer, his coach and his team mates... The more fundamental question is, however, in a free society, can anyone justify a regime which requires a player to submit such intensely personal decisions to the determination of others?[62]

Thus we consider the effect of a drug testing program on the civil liberties of an athlete.

---

56 *Greig v Insole* [1978] 3 All ER 449 at 502-503; and *Hughes v Western Australian Cricket Association Incorporation* (1986) 69 ALR 660 at 703.

57 *Greig v Insole*, ibid at 504; and *Hughes v Western Australia Cricket Association Incorporation* ibid, at 703. Also see S and L Owen-Conway, "Sports and Restraint of Trade" (1989) 5 *Australian Bar Review* 208 at 223.

58 *Hall v VFL and Clark* [1982] VR 64 and *Foschini v VFL and South Melbourne Club Ltd* Supreme Court of Victoria (Unreported Decision, 15 March, 1983 No 968 of 1982).

59 *Buckley v Tutty* (1971) 125 CLR 353 at 379, and *Foschini v VFL and South Melbourne Club Ltd*, ibid at 21.

60 *League Draft Appeal* case (1991) 103 ALR 319 at 353-354 per Wilcox J.

61 Ibid at 341 per Wilcox J, cf at 323 per Shepperd J.

62 Ibid at 355.

The court must consider whether the restraint acts against the public interest.[63] The factor of public interest, and thus notions of public policy, have received less attention by the courts, as they are intimately connected with the determination of what is reasonable between the parties. However, the courts in the sport cases have emphasised various considerations of public interest or policy in assessing player restraints. In *Buckley v Tutty,* the High Court explained that the law treats unreasonable restraints as unenforceable,

> because it is contrary to the public welfare that a man should unreasonably be prevented from earning his living in whatever lawful way he chooses and that the public should unreasonably be deprived of the services of a man prepared to engage in employment.[64]

In *Greig v Insole,*[65] public interest factors weighed most strongly with Slade J in his consideration of the Test and County Cricket Board's proposed competition ban on players who had signed to play in cricket competitions organised by a private promoter. These factors included the likelihood that the bans would effectively end the careers of two of the cricketers concerned and that, if talented players were driven out of first class cricket, temporarily or permanently, the cricket going public would be deprived of a great deal of pleasure. These cases support the Owen-Conways'[66] conclusion that, "the public interest in being able to observe talented players is of major importance".

Civil liberties concerns

A program of mandatory drug testing (refusal to submit to testing is deemed to be an infraction of all doping policies) necessarily raises the question of interference with liberty. Determining whether the program constitutes an unlawful or unreasonable interference with the athlete's civil liberties may affect the outcome of a challenge based on principles of restraint of trade.

Although citizens of Australia are not currently afforded protection of their civil liberties by means of a constitutionally entrenched Bill of Rights, the common

---

63 *Beetson v Humphries*, Supreme Court of NSW (Unreported Decision, 30 May 1980, No 10950 of 1980).
64 *Buckley v Tutty,* above n 56 at 380.
65 *Greig v Insole*, ibid at 503.
66 See S and L Owen-Conway, "Sports and Restraint of Trade" (1989) 5 *Australian Bar Review* 208 at 223.

law has a long tradition of concern for the protection of civil liberties, rooted in the philosophies of liberalism and individualism which underpin our political system. Included in the notions of individualism and liberalism is the principle of individual autonomy, that individuals should be allowed to determine their own course of action in accordance with their own morality and preference. This underlying respect for individual autonomy is closely linked to the right of privacy: the right to be free from, amongst other things, bodily intrusion or unwanted access by others to personal information and attention.[67]

Even though the law does not recognise any general right of privacy in Australia,[68] Kirby P in *Carrol v Mijovich* [69] stated that our common law has "vigilantly defended the privacy of the individual". Furthermore, privacy protection is recognised under Article 17 of the International Covenant of Civil and Political Rights (the Covenant), to which Australia is a party, but has given only limited effect in the form of the Privacy Act, 1988 (Cth). The Covenant was ratified by Australia on 12 August 1980. On Article 17, the Commonwealth declared that it reserved the right to compromise the privacy rights of individuals "in the interests of national security, public safety, the economic well-being of the country, the protection of public health or morals, or the protection of the rights and freedoms of others".[70] The Information Privacy Principles contained in the Privacy Act 1988 (Cth) reflect the recommendations of the Australian Law Reform Commission's report on Privacy, published in 1983, which in turn were drawn primarily from guidelines emanating from the OECD. The Information Privacy Principles of the *Privacy Act* will apply to the ASC and ASDA (as they are both agencies created by the Commonwealth government), and similar principles will apply to other sporting organisations administering sport in Australia by virtue of the Privacy Act Amendment (Private Sector) Act 2000 (Cth).

The various drug testing programmes in Australia, and for that matter overseas, can be regarded as an infringement of individual autonomy

---

67 This much was recognized by the High Court in *Coco v R* (1994) 120 ALR 415 in the context of a challenge to the admissibility of wiretap evidence. The High Court judgments all contain language expressing the view that there needs to be clear and unambiguous statutory language to justify the interference with a fundamental right or freedom. Although the High Court did not need to articulate a general right of privacy it is clear that the various judgments contain both explicitly and implicitly a recognition of the fundamental importance of individual privacy. In this case, the individual's common law right to be free from trespass was secured by judicial insistence on clear statutory expression.
68 See *Victoria Park Racing Co v Taylor* (1937) 58 CLR 479.
69 (1991) 25 NSWLR 441 at 446.
70 Aust TS (1980) No 23, annex.

because they violate the privacy of the athlete being subjected to testing. Such persons are required to urinate in the presence of the designated drug officer. As, in our society, the act of urination has traditionally been regarded as private, its observation by another, especially under the dictate of law or policy, must be regarded, prima facie, as an invasion of privacy.[71]

There is also the question of the potential use of any information collected during the testing process. It is possible that an athlete's urine sample may reveal personal medical information that normally would be protected by the confidentiality of the doctor-patient relationship.[72] Ordinarily, it is for the patient to decide to whom access to such information is to be given. Thus, the intrusion of an agency empowered to collect such information must be viewed as a potential threat to confidentiality.

In addition, the potential for abuse of the individual's right to control access to personal medical information is threatened by a potentially excessive collection of data. Principle 1 of the Information Privacy Principles contained in the Privacy Act 1988 (Cth) states that:

> Personal information shall not be collected by a collector for inclusion in a record or on a generally available publication unless:
>
> (a) the information is collected for a purpose that is a lawful purpose directly related to a function or activity of the collector; and
> (b) the collection of the information is necessary for or directly related to that purpose.[73]

The only information that ASDA can justifiably collect is that related to the objects of ASDA. Those objectives are outlined above and generally relate to the goal of a drug-free sporting community. Testing for performance-enhancing drugs is a primary means of achieving that objective. However, given that ASDA's strategy includes "out of competition testing" it is conceivable that some of the information collected will relate to behaviour of

---

[71] E Kaplan and L C Williams, "Will Employees' Rights be the First Casualty of the War on Drugs" (1983) 31 *Kansas Law Review* 755 at 761.

[72] It is generally accepted that the doctor-patient relationship is one that the law treats as a relationship of confidence. Thus the law protects the patient from the unauthorized disclosure of confidential medical information. See, generally, D J Laster, "Breaches of Confidence and of Privacy by Misuse of Personal Information" (1989) 7 *Otago Law Review* 31 at 38.

[73] Privacy Act 1988 (Cth), s 14.

the athlete that is not related to his or her performance in sport. There are privacy concerns about such information being collected by ASDA, even though the process by which the information is collected is an integral part of ASDA's strategy.[74] A good example of the potential difficulty inherent in this justification is testing for marijuana use.[75] A positive test result for marijuana may be recorded weeks or even months after consumption, but any intoxication resulting from marijuana use typically lasts only a few hours following ingestion.[76] Even assuming that marijuana consumption posed a threat to the stated goals of ASDA (which as we indicated above is doubtful), we cannot be sure that a positive test result to marijuana is related to athletic performance. The possibility of involuntary ingestion and the very doubtful enhancing benefits of marijuana only reinforces the privacy concerns in mandatory drug-testing of athletes.

Where the substance is clearly not related to performance enhancement, the public policy justification for imposing a sanction on the basis of a mandatory test is weak.

LAMAZE

Eric Lamaze, a Canadian equestrian rider, tested positive to a banned stimulant in July 2000. The stimulant was contained in a diet supplement he used. Lamaze was suspended as a result of this positive test. Subsequently, the Canadian Equestrian Federation "reconsidered" and elected to overturn the ban, on the basis that the contents of his diet supplement had been changed, adding the banned stimulant, without any change to the product labelling or other notification to users. Unfortunately for Lamaze, while under suspension, he was subjected to another test, this time testing positive

---

74 It is frequently argued that if testing were limited to competitions athletes could beat the drug bans by timing their ingestion of performance-enhancing drugs appropriately.

75 The Australian Rugby League drug testing program includes standard testing for marijuana use.

76 E Lock and M Jennings, "The Constitutionality of Mandatory Student-Athlete Drug Testing Programs: The Bounds of Privacy", 38 *University of Florida Law Review* 596 at 601-602. Urinalysis can detect only past consumption of drugs, not levels of intoxication and it does not measure past or present impairments or improvements. See F A Hanson, "Some Social Implications of Drug Testing" (1988) 36 *Kansas Law Review* 899 at 904; J Morgan, "the Scientific Justification for Urine Drug Testing" (1988) 36 *Kansas Law Review* 683 at 692-694; and D J Greenblatt, "Urine Drug Testing: What Does it Test?" (1988-89) 23 *New England Law Review* 651 at 660, 664.

to cocaine, a substance with which he had had repeated past difficulties. He was subjected to a life ban, this being his second positive test result. Given the proximity of the ban to the Sydney Olympic Games, Lamaze invoked his right to arbitration on the question of the life ban. At the arbitration, Lamaze's counsel persuaded the arbitrator, Professor Ed Ratushny, that when his client accepted a cigarette containing cocaine, he was so distraught at the ban for use of the diet supplement that he could not be said to have acted voluntarily. Lawyers sometimes refer to the state that Lamaze was argued to have as "automatism". As a result, the life ban was overturned. Referring to Lamaze's history of drug abuse and his "Cinderella story", Professor Ratushny described the sequence of events leading to the ban:

> "An erroneous determination of a drug infraction, resulting in a lifetime ban, following a 'storybook comeback', leading to a chance encounter, combined with an extraordinary mental condition" established the "extraordinary circumstances" necessary under Canadian anti-doping rules to warrant overturning the ban.

Lamaze immediately sought reinstatement on the Canadian Olympic Team. This effort was unsuccessful, as the agreement signed by all Canadian athletes (as with the Australian Athletes' Participation Agreement) contained a clause entitling the athlete to be excluded from the team for unlawful drug use. See *In the Matter of an Application by Eric Lamaze for a Category II Reinstatement Pursuant to the Canadian Policy on Doping in Sport and the Doping Control Regulations,* Canadian Centre for Ethics in Sport, Ed Rathushny, QC, Adjudicator, Ottawa (19 September 2000). Also refer to R MacLeod, "Equestrian Rider's Ban Overturned" *The Globe and Mail,* 19 September 2000, at S1.

Possible criminal penalties

Testing for some banned substances, such as cocaine and heroin (and, in the case of the Australian Rugby League, marijuana), exposes athletes not only to economic penalties (including loss of funding, forfeiture of prize money and potential loss of endorsement opportunities) but also to criminal sanction. Thus, for athletes, provision of a urine sample may lead to a criminal conviction. Any such risk is exacerbated by the fact that urine samples do not fall within the scope of the rule, which provides for a privilege against self-incrimination. This privilege essentially provides a person with the option of not providing information where to provide it would tend to expose the person to the imposition of a civil penalty or conviction of an offence. In Australia, the rule extends only to oral and documentary disclosure.[77] As Gibbs CJ stated in *Sorby* v *Commonwealth*:[78]

> The privilege [against self-incrimination] prohibits the compulsion of the witness to give testimony but it does not prohibit the giving of evidence, against the will of a witness, as to the condition of his body. For example, the witness may be required to provide a fingerprint, or to show his face or some other part of his body so that he may be identified...

Thus, presumably, the privilege against self-incrimination will not apply to the collection of a urine sample for the purpose of analysing the level of prohibited substances in an athlete's body.

Given the potential application of the criminal law to some of the activities which may be revealed by drug testing, there are further concerns relating to the civil liberties of athletes. To some extent, mandatory drug testing erodes the presumption of innocence, as no reasonable basis is required before the athlete is required to submit to testing.[79] Randomly selected athletes are forced to undergo testing in a manner normally reserved for those reasonably suspected of having committed an offence. Failure to submit to the test will result in a determination that the athlete has committed a doping offence and the athlete will be subject to sanctions.[80] The absence of any prerequisite for testing that there be a reasonable suspicion that an athlete has engaged in prohibited drug-taking conduct is disturbing considering the privacy concerns with urinalysis testing. [81]

---

77 *King v McLellan* [1974] VR 773, *Sorby v Commonwealth* (1983) 152 CLR 281 at 292-293; see generally, D Byrne and JD Heydon, *Cross on Evidence,* (4th ed, Sydney, Law Book Company 1991) at 677-687.
78 (1983) 152 CLR 281 at 292.
79 Recall that this is what led the Quebec Superior Court to declare the mandatory testing of prison inmates to be in violation of the provisions of the Canadian Charter in *Re Dion and the Queen* (1986) 30 CCC (3d) 108 (Que Sup Ct). Also refer to J Barnes, *Sports and the Law in Canada* (3rd ed Toronto, Butterworths 1996).
80 Note that this will be the case even where the substance detected is not one for which use or possession carries criminal penalties.
81 It is difficult to predict what probative value would be assigned to evidence of a drug test in the context of a criminal trial for possession or use of a controlled substance. Also, it should be noted that despite frequent, highly publicized incidents in the United States involving star athletes and the use of controlled substances, criminal prosecution ordinarily does not follow. This fact might lead some to observe that there is one law for the famous and another for those unfortunate enough not to belong to that category.

Given that doping offences do not appear to require any related mental element, there is further concern about mandatory testing. Generally, a doping offence occurs where a urinalysis records a positive test result for a banned substance. It is not relevant how or why the substance was ingested.[82] It is, therefore, possible that if a banned substance enters an athlete's body without his or her knowledge, for example by means of ingesting a beverage "spiked" by another[83] or, in the case of marijuana, by means of passive inhaling of the drug,[84] then that athlete may be subjected to the same sanctions as one who voluntarily or deliberately ingests a banned substance with the specific intention of improving performance.

Given that doping offences do not require proof of any intent (and we have already expressed concern about the practice of imposing sanctions on the basis of strict or absolute liability for doping offences), it would seem even more inappropriate to impose criminal sanctions as a result of a positive test result.

Regulators should be aware that a mandatory drug testing regime poses a number of problems from the standpoint of the civil liberties of the athletes affected. While noting the potentially deleterious effects of such a regime on those civil liberties, any such intrusion can be balanced by the need for such regulation. That need is something that can be particular to the sport concerned as well as commensurate with the values to which we in Australia subscribe.

Consent to drug testing

Where an individual has expressly or implicitly consented to the imposition of the drug test, no longer is a justifiable privacy expectation

---

[82] For example, under the IAAF Drug Testing Programme, rule 55 (2) states:
   "The offence of doping takes place when ...
   (i) a prohibited substance is found to be present within an athlete's body tissue or fluids."

[83] Alex Watson, a modern pentathlete, was disqualified from the Seoul Olympics because test results showed a level of caffeine in his urine in excess of the allowable level. He argued that his drinks had been tampered with. See "Watson: a Victim", *The Age*, 26 September 1988. In 1994, weightlifter Ron Lacycock, at a hearing convened to determine what penalty should attach to his alleged steroid use, argued that his drink had been tampered with.

[84] The chromatography testing done by all IOC approved laboratories, including the Australian Government Analytical Laboratories (who perform such analysis for ASDA), can trace elements of marijuana metabolites passively inhaled. See L Uzych, "Drug Testing of Athletes" (1991) 86 *British Journal of Addiction* 25 at 29.

violated.[85] Likewise, one who has consented to a procedure may not complain later that the procedure involved a violation of his or her civil liberties. The intrusive nature of the drug test and the range of sanctions that apply to offenders are such that the prospect of being subjected to urinalysis is one which creates fear in the athlete. The athlete should be informed in advance of the nature of drug testing procedures in order to obtain his or her consent. This is necessary to allay any fears the athlete may have about the drug testing procedure and thus to protect the tester from allegations of committing the crime of assault. (Assault is any act which intentionally or recklessly causes another person to fear immediate and unlawful personal violence.[86] At common law, assault is seen as the threat or attempt to apply force, with actual force to the person of another being referred to as battery.[87])

If the tester actually engages in physical contact with the athlete without consent, there is additionally the possibility of commission of the tort of trespass to the person. This may lead to a claim for damages against the drug tester, the authority responsible for the conduct of the test and/or any relevant sporting organisation. It follows that an athlete's consent cannot be procured by a promise and that any consent given is subject to the possibility that it may later be withdrawn.

In order for consent to be valid it must be genuine. That is to say, it must be given voluntarily and on an informed basis.[88] It therefore is the responsibility of sporting organisations to inform the athletes within their jurisdiction of the existence and the nature of their drug testing programme. The most convenient and obvious manner of disseminating such information is to append it to the rules and regulations of the sporting organisations or include it in any written contract entered into between that organisation and an athlete. In the typical situation confronting athletes (where adherence to a drug testing programme is a prerequisite to sanctioned competition) the genuineness of any consent procured will be an issue. In addition, any athlete

---

85 *Chabot v Manitoba Horse Racing Commission* [1987] 1 WWR 149, 33 DLR (4th) 714 (Man CA). Also refer to J Barnes, *Sports and the Law in Canada*, (3rd ed, Toronto, Butterworths, 1996) at 45, 103.

86 *Fagan v Metropolitan Police Commissioner* [1968] 3 All ER 422 and *Vallance v The Queen* (1961) 108 CLR 56.

87 In Criminal Code jurisdictions such as Queensland, Tasmania and Western Australia, no distinction is made between assault and battery. Assault includes both actual force and the threat or attempt to use it.

88 *Chatterton v Geson* [1981] 1 QB 432 at 443 and *F v R* (1983) SASR 189.

receiving financial assistance from the ASC will, as a matter of course, be required to submit to that organisation's rules and regulations. These include the agreement of the athlete to submit to testing by ASDA on demand.

Insofar as an athlete may claim, after being asked to submit to a drug test, that any consent procured was invalid, there are some legal limitations. In the first place, the criminal law will only vitiate consent that is extracted by force or threat of force.[89] This is hardly likely in the context of sports drug testing.

Outside the context of the criminal law however, the choice offered to the athlete bears all the hallmarks of duress.[90] The athlete is effectively provided with two alternatives: submit to testing and compete, or fail to submit and be excluded. From a legal perspective, the submission by the athlete to the testing will not be considered to have been procured by duress, so long as the condition imposed on the athlete is reasonable and justifiable on grounds of public policy.[91]

Notwithstanding the fact that, from a technical perspective, the testing of an athlete is permitted only where the athlete consents, we refer to the current regime in Australia as one involving mandatory drug tests, for, in reality, submission to drug-testing is the only practical alternative open to the athlete. This "practical compulsion" may vitiate consent and render any contractual arrangement between the athlete and the sporting organisation voidable. However, it is arguable whether the athlete has been induced to

---

89 This often arises in sexual assault cases: see *R v Clarence* (1888) 22 QBD 23.
90 We are aware that the meaning of duress in the criminal law context is much more restrictive than in the commercial law context. For purposes of the criminal law, duress is essentially limited to situations where the accused is acting "under a threat that death or grievous bodily harm will be inflicted unlawfully upon a human being if the accused fails to do the act...": *R v Hurley* [1967] VR 526 at 529. The threat does not need to be made to the accused, it must relate to "a human being": *R v Brown* (1986) 43 SASR 33 and *R v Palazoff* (1986) 43 SASR 99. Given that the means by which consent is procured is often contractual, we think it appropriate to apply commercial law norms in this context. We are however mindful of the fact that this application would be inappropriate in the context of a prosecution of a drug testing authority for criminal assault.
91 A commonly encountered legal analogue is that of the settlement of an outstanding legal claim. Thus, where a party claims money damages for the commission of a tort and the potential defendant offers a lesser sum than the amount claimed, which is accepted in exchange for the promise not to pursue the claim, the compromise will be indefeasible. This notwithstanding that the compromise was secured in the shadow of considerable pressure introduced by the claimant. Courts are loathe to upset such compromises, notwithstanding the existence of a threat of litigation, for the simple reason of promoting the settlement of disputes, the benefits of which to society at large are obvious.

enter the contract which includes an obligation to submit to drug-testing by "illegitimate" pressure from the sporting organisation.[92] While athletes might prefer not to be subject to any obligation to submit to drug-testing, it is more the desire to compete than any other "pressure" which has induced the athlete to agree to the rules of the sporting organisation.

Where the athlete's consent is procured by means of a contract with the sporting organisation, there is additionally the possibility that any consent given may be vitiated by the claim, on the part of the athlete, that the contract was tainted by unconscionabilty. The essence of this claim lies in the superior bargaining position enjoyed by the sporting organisation and the athlete's reliance on the organisation for his or her livelihood. Where the actions of the sporting organisation can be characterised as taking advantage of its superior bargaining position relative to the weakness of the athlete's position, the risk of consent being considered by the law to be invalid is increased.[93] In New South Wales, the Industrial Relations Commission has the power, by virtue of sections 105 and 106 of the Industrial Relations Act 1996 (NSW), to alter the terms of contracts of employment where those terms are unfair, harsh, unconscionable or against the public interest.

FIELD

Craig Field is a rugby league player employed by the Wests Tigers Rugby League Football Club Limited ("Wests"). On 12 February 2001, Field was tested by ASDA officials while he attended a weight training session organised by his club. The tests were conducted

---

92 See *Universe Tankships of Monrovia v International Transport Workers Federation* [1983] 1 AC 366 and *Crescendo Management Pty Ltd v Westpac Banking Corp* (1988) 19 NSWLR 40 at 46 where McHugh JA said (speaking of the elements of duress): "The proper approach in my opinion is to ask whether any applied pressure induced the victim to enter into the contract and then asked whether that pressure went beyond what the law is prepared to countenance as legitimate? Pressure will be illegitimate if it consists of unlawful threats or amounts to unconscionable conduct. But the categories are not closed".

93 For a thorough discussion of the nature of unconscionability in Australia see *Commercial Bank of Australia Limited v Amadio* (1983) 151 CLR 447. See also s 275(1) of the Industrial Relations Act 1991 (NSW). The Fair Trading Act 1957 (NSW), Contracts Relief Act 1980 (NSW) and Trade Practices Act 1974 (Cth) will also apply if any contract challenged is one for service not of service. A complete discussion of the Australian doctrine of unconscionability is contained in D W Greig and J L R Davis, *The Law of Contract,* (3rd ed, Sydney, Law Book Co 1985) at 1099-1114. See also BD Ward, "The Player Contract - A Comparative Analysis: In Search of Equity and Fairness" in *The Law of Professional Team Sports*, (University of Melbourne 1991).

under a contractual arrangement between the New South Wales Rugby League and ASDA. Field's A and B sample tested positive to benzoylecgonine, a metabolite of cocaine. Field was subsequently charged with having committed a Doping Offence and eventually suspended for a period of 6 months. Field had pleaded guilty to the commission of the offence and restricted his submissions to those in mitigation of sentence. Given Field's substantial salary, the effect of his suspension is considerable in financial terms. Field has just commenced proceedings in Industrial Court for an order declaring the relevant clauses of the NSWRL's Anti-Doping Rules to be unfair, insofar as they provide for urine testing for non-performance enhancing drugs. Field's statement of claim was filed on June 27, 2001.

It may well be the case therefore, that the consent of the athlete provides little justification for the imposition of drug testing, given the manner by which that consent is procured. Certainly, from the perspective of the athlete's civil liberties, we doubt the validity of any consent based on the athlete's need to submit to organisational rules in order to compete.

What is the legitimate interest of the sporting federation?

Protection from arguments of unreasonable restraint of trade and the legitimisation of drug testing is dependent on an understanding and acceptance of the underlying goal of eradicating use of banned substances. The testing itself must be fair, impartial and subject to proper scrutiny. Furthermore, it is necessary to consider the form of sanction used to support any ban. The sanction must also be fair, uniformly applied, justifiable and effective. All of these criteria must be satisfied before any regime of drug regulation can be justified.

It is worth quoting the objects originally listed in the Australian Sports Drug Agency Act 1990 (Cth). Section 8 provided:

> The objects of the establishment of the Agency are:
>
> (a) to encourage the practice of sport free from the use of drugs, in a manner consistent with the objectives of protecting :
>
> (i) the health of competitors; and
> (ii) the values of fair play and competition; and
> (iii) the rights of those who take part in sport; and

(b) to encourage the development of programs to educate the sporting community at large about the dangers of using drugs in sport; and

(c) to provide leadership in the development of a national strategy concerning drugs in sport; and

(d)...

Objects (a) to (c) deal with substantive concerns, while the remaining four ((d) - (g)) are more focused on establishing a measure of procedural uniformity, reflective of a concern for procedural justice.

Interestingly, subsequent amendment to the legislation has eliminated any reference to the objectives of an anti-doping program itself. The amended ASDA Act, s 8(a), simply refers to the object of: "deter[ing] the use of scheduled drugs or doping methods in sport...". There is no coherent objective.

However, deletion of express reference to the substantive justification for a drug testing policy does not eliminate it from judicial consideration in a challenge based on the application of principles of restraint of trade.

Various justifications have been advanced for the drug testing of athletes. With Olympic athletes, the emphasis has been on the need to curtail "cheating" and the need to protect the health of competitors. With the possible exception of drugs such as cocaine, heroin and amphetamines, which are psychomotor stimulants and thus may be performance-enhancing, the IOC has not historically been interested in so-called "recreational drugs". Therefore, drugs such as LSD and marijuana were not originally prohibited by the IOC Medical Commission and those international federations and national bodies incorporating its list of prohibited substances.[94] Following the controversy over Ross Rebagliati's positive test to marijuana at the Nagano Winter Olympic Games, the IOC Medical Commission added marijuana to its list of banned substances. By contrast, professional and collegiate sporting organisations in the United States are concerned primarily with abuse of "recreational drugs". This may be a reflection of the preoccupation of those bodies with the public image of and public confidence in the sport they

---

94 The IOC Medical Commission does list marijuana as a restricted drug but does not mandate its inclusion in testing. The authors are informed that some international organisations wish to commence testing for marijuana.

regulate.[95] This may be either a reflection of, or caused by, the intense media coverage often given to drug problems in American sports, particularly those at the professional level.[96] The extent of the problem in the United States was dramatically illustrated by the cocaine-related deaths of college basketball star Len Bias and professional football player Don Rogers within the same week in 1986.[97] In Australia, the only sporting organisations to demonstrate concern for "recreational drugs" as well as those with proven performance-enhancing qualities is the Australian Rugby League and the Australian Jockey Club, which conduct tests and impose sanctions for marijuana use. Positive test results lead to the imposition of penalties.[98]

Ultimately, whether any suspension or ban on an athlete for testing positive to a banned substance will run foul of a unreasonable restraint of trade action will depend on the specific facts of the case. Serious attention must be given to the questions of the appropriate penalty and the manner in which it is imposed, plus the justification or legitimate interests of the sporting body sought to be protected by the drug testing programme.

For a discussion of the various justifications advanced to support drug testing in sports, refer to the discussion of the development of doping policy in Chapter Three.

---

95 This concern is mirrored by such organisations' approach to the question of gambling. The following is extracted from R C Berry and G M Wong, *Law and Business of the Professional Sports Industries, Volume II: Common Issues in Amateur and Professional Sports* (Boston, Little Brown 1986) at 477: "The problems associated with illegal gambling and the influence it may exert on professional and intercollegiate sports are of special concern to athletic administrators and others since gambling affects the integrity of the games, the games themselves, and public confidence in athletes and sports".

96 E Lock, "The Legality Under the National Labor Relations Act of Attempts by the National Football League Owners to Unilaterally Implement Drug Testing Programs" (1987) 39 *University of Florida Law Review* 1 at 3, and E Zemper, "Drug Testing in Athletes" in R H Coombs and L J West (eds), *Drug Testing: Issues and Options* (New York, Oxford University Press, 1991) at 117-118.

97 "Drug Use Tied to Rogers' Death" New York Times 29 June 1986 and J Trossman, "Mandatory Drug Testing in Sports: The Law in Canada" (1988) 47 *University of Toronto Faculty of Law Review* 191 at 193.

98 Although, the AFL did at one stage propose bans for marijuana. *The West Australian*, 7 December 1995. The AFL does test for marijuana, but for statistical purposes only.

CHAPTER 8

THE FUTURE

Although there is no consensus on the policy objectives of the doping rules, the efforts to eradicate doping in sport will continue. The work of the CAS is likely to increase, particularly in Australia, where there is now judicial precedent supporting the role of the CAS.[1]

In this book we have highlighted a number of issues in the application of the doping rules. They will continue to generate debate;

- The content of the list of banned substances
- The role of the CAS and the IF's
- Whether inadvertent breaches of the doping rules ought be excused or dealt with more leniently
- The role of the IOC and sponsors in the work of WADA
- The appropriate level of sanction and restraint of trade
- The need to secure the consent of the athlete to agreements.

The banned substances

Ought we to continue to test for substances that have no real performance enhancing effects? Likewise, should we be testing for substances that,

---

1 *Raguz v Sullivan*, NSWCA 240 (1 September 2000) where the New South Wales Court of Appeal ruled that an exclusion agreement (agreement to use the CAS and not to appeal any ruling to the domestic courts) effectively prevented the athlete from appealing a decision of the CAS.

though possibly performance enhancing, are not a threat to the health or safety of the athlete? Obviously, the answers to these questions depend on the underlying policy of the relevant anti-doping code. There is no consensus on this policy. As noted in Chapter Seven, there is pending, in NSW, a challenge to the fairness of a contract incorporating rules which authorise testing for non performance-enhancing substances (see Field: Chapter Seven).

Also, given the number of cases that have involved athletes use of cold and flu remedies or pain relief (for legitimate reasons and generally with no performance enhancing effect), we might reconsider banning some substances outright, possibly in favour of a more sophisticated approach to regulating their use. It may be a question of whether the absolute ban is sufficiently important to justify weathering the inevitable questioning that occurs whenever athletes like Andrea Raducan or Samantha Riley are sanctioned or stripped of their medals.

The question of banning recreational drugs is also a vexed one, particularly as there is clearly little or no question of any performance enhancement. However, as the recent case of Eric Lamaze illustrates, a National Olympic Committee (and possibly the IOC as well) may wish to continue such testing, in order to distract attention from the tarnished public image of the IOC.

The CAS and the IFs

The Court of Arbitration for Sport is an integral part of the strategy for ensuring consistency in the application of doping policies. In addition, the CAS is quickly developing a body of principles capable of consistent application. However, we submit that we will continue to see some International Federations expressing concern about the degree to which their own disciplinary decisions may be questioned by the CAS.

Interestingly enough, at the World Conference on Doping in Sport, the most politically sensitive issue was the question of standardising minimum sanctions for doping offences. Two of the International Federations were unwilling to agree to a minimum two year ban for the first doping offence. These were the UCI (cycling) and FIFA (association football). These Federations expressed great concern (particularly FIFA) about potential civil liability in the event such a ban were to be overturned. Both Federations expressed a preference for a flexible approach, with the CAS capable of reviewing the penalty on application by the athlete or Federation concerned.

The view was expressed that the CAS was capable of developing principles for the consistent determination of appropriate penalties.

This is just one of the areas where the CAS is likely to have increased activity. Virtually all important International Federations provide in their doping policies for appeals to the CAS.

Problems of inconsistency are likely to continue. So long as the relevant National or International Federation remains the first body to determine the applicable sanction, the CAS is only likely to become involved where the athlete seeks to appeal. If therefore, the athlete succeeds in persuading the NF or IF either not to apply a sanction or to apply a minimum sanction, then the CAS will not become involved. By contrast, where the athlete is subjected to a lengthy ban, then the CAS will in all likelihood have the opportunity to review the matter. The only exception to this will be cases arising during the Olympic Games, when the ad hoc panel of the CAS is immediately involved.

One issue that appears to have been overlooked is the question of conflict of interest. Where the athlete in question is popular and a benefit to the sport's public appeal, the relevant sporting federation will undoubtedly have an interest in either avoiding the imposition of a penalty or minimising the penalty it applies. If one doubts this, try to imagine the difficulty the Professional Golfers' Association would have were Tiger Woods to test positive to a banned substance.[2] As the major draw at any tournament in which he competes, were he to be excluded from competition, there would be a marked decline in attendance and television ratings.

A further issue may be dissatisfaction on the part of some sports federations with decisions rendered by the CAS. A case in point (though not involving a doping infraction) is a decision made by CAS to allow the result of a Paralympic wheelchair race to stand. The race was marred by a collision between several competitors. A referee at the event had ruled in favour of an appeal by a Japanese competitor and ordered that the race be rerun. The CAS, following an appeal of the referee's decision by the Canadian team, ordered the result to stand. The CAS decision drew condemnation from the chairman of the athletes committee of the International Paralympic

---

2 There have in the past been suggestions of professional golfers using beta blockers to enhance their performance.

Committee, who argued that the CAS lacked the necessary technical knowledge to rule on the matter.

The Inadvertent Breach

All relevant anti-doping policies penalise doping, regardless of whether the athlete intended to ingest the prohibited substance. Yet there is sympathy for those who clearly did not intend to gain any competitive advantage. Balanced against this is the concern that allowing exceptions for inadvertent use will effectively gut anti-doping policies.

Similar concerns exist with respect to therapeutic use, though allowing the athlete to register and seek approval for such use should limit the number of cases of this nature.

WADA, the IOC and Sponsors

In Chapter Five, we noted the continuing efforts to harmonise international approaches to doping. WADA will be at the forefront of these efforts, assisted by the consultative group formed following the Sydney Drugs in Sport Summit in 1999. We need further consideration of co-ordinating the efforts of the various national doping authorities with those of WADA.

Given the concerns expressed at the World Conference on Doping in Sport regarding the independence, accountability and transparency of WADA, the continuing involvement of the IOC and sponsors in the work of WADA is bound to come into question in the future.

The IOC has been accused of turning a blind eye to drug use in the past. Even the supposedly squeaky clean United States Olympic Committee (USOC) has been accused of covering up positive drug tests. As a result of these allegations the USOC set up an independent inquiry to investigate. At the time of writing the inquiry had not completed its report.[3] Both the IOC and sponsors have a clear interest in securing record-breaking performances: an interest that conflicts with detecting use of performance enhancing drugs. Yet, so long as the IOC provides substantial funding for

---

3 "US Accused of Drugs Cover Up", *The Times*, 6 March 2001, at 18.

WADA, it is unlikely that the IOC will cede control of that organisation to others. Continuing reform to the structure and operation of the IOC itself may affect the operations of WADA.

Sanctions and Restraint of Trade

This issue has yet to be resolved. As long as athletes retain recourse to domestic courts, there will be the possibility of sanctions being determined to be in restraint of trade. Indeed, this is probably the biggest fear of the International Federations, and affects their willingness to impose meaningful sanctions.

As the restraint of trade argument depends on whether a ban is justified on grounds of public policy, one must take into account evolving attitudes toward justifiable restraints. At the time of writing the European Commission is considering enacting legislation to overturn a decision of the European Court of Justice protecting the freedom of movement of athletes within Europe. In the case of *Union Royale Belge des Societes de Football Association ASBL v Bosman* [4] the Court found that a transfer fee payable by a French club to a Belgian club following the transfer of Jean-Marc Bosman illegally impaired Bosman's freedom of movement and was therefore in breach of Article 48 of the EC Treaty (dealing with freedom of movement of labour). In the aftermath of this decision, concern has been expressed that its effect has been to boost the market price for players on transfer, particularly given the fact that many football clubs have become public companies with greater resources available to purchase players. In March 2001, UEFA agreed to place restrictions on the free transfer system and movement of players. However, at the time of writing these changes to ameliorate the Bosman rule have not been agreed by the player associations and legislated for.

Many have expressed concern that the majority of clubs are unable to compete effectively for available talent. This concern has led to debate about whether freedom of movement is sufficiently important when weighed against the effect that its guarantee has had on parity within the professional leagues. Were similar concerns to be expressed regarding doping rules, it may be that the prospect of legal challenge based on restraint of trade may be reduced (as the public interest in promoting drug free sport may justify more punitive sanctions).

---

4 ECJ Case C-415/93, [1995] I, 4921.

Consent to Drug Testing

As the range of substances on the banned list increases, and with the advent of blood testing of athletes, the question of the consent of the athlete to testing arises.

As things stand, the athlete cannot be tested without consent. Consent to drug testing is required as a condition of participation in a sporting event. However, and especially given the fact that test results are archived, it is virtually inevitable that there will be a challenge based on lack of genuine consent having been given.

One solution to this difficulty may be an athlete-driven move to introduction of voluntary testing. In its initial meeting, WADA indicated (in its proposed agenda) that it was considering introducing the concept of an anti-doping "passport". Interestingly enough, this proposition is the brainchild of one of the members of the WADA board representing the athletes. In theory, an athlete-driven move to introduce such a passport, backed up by voluntary testing, may overcome this potential difficulty.

Finally, we would be remiss if we were to omit mention of the role that technology will have to play in the future. In the lead up to the Sydney Games there were concerted efforts to introduce testing for rEPO and Human Growth Hormone, based on a combination of blood and urine testing. Arguably, the tests are not yet accurate enough to be infallible and therefore are likely to be challenged. Similarly, we will continue to observe the technological game of cat and mouse between the testing authorities and those determined to confuse them.

One positive development that has emerged since the Sydney Games is the willingness of the IOC to ensure that where an athlete is stripped of a medal those who ought to have been awarded the medal during the Games will have their medals conferred ceremonially. An American weightlifter was given his gold medal at a public ceremony in New York, complete with national anthems and the presence of IOC Vice-President, Anita Defranz on November 16, more than a month after the closing ceremony.

As the work of WADA continues, the tests become more sophisticated and the rewards for athletes continue to grow, it is likely that this event will be repeated in the future.

LIST OF ABBREVIATIONS

ADR	Alternative Dispute Resolution
AFL	Australian Football League
ANOC	Association of National Olympic Committees
ANZSLA	Australian New Zealand Sports Law Association
AOC	Australian Olympic Committee
ARL	Australian Rugby League
ASC	Australian Sports Commission
ASDA	Australian Sports Drug Agency
AWIF	Winter Olympic International Federations
CAS	Court of Arbitration for Sport
FIFA	Federation International Football Association
FINA	Federation Internationale de Natation Amateur
FIS	International Skiing Federation
IAAF	International Amateur Athletics Federation
ICAS	International Council of Arbitration for Sport
IF	International Federation or International Sport Federation
IOC	International Olympic Committee
NBL	National Basketball League
NF	National Federation
NOC	National Olympic Committee
NRL	National Rugby League
NSL	National Soccer League
NSDC	National Sports Dispute Centre
NWBL	National Womens Basketball League
rEPO	Recombinant Erythropoietin
SOIF	Summer Olympic International Federations
UCI	International Cycling Union
UN	United Nations
UNESCO	United Nations Education Scientific and Cultural Organisation
USOC	United States Olympic Committee
WADA	World Anti-Doping Authority
WHO	World Health Organisation

INDEX

—A—

Abbott v Sullivan, 116
Adamson v New South Wales Rugby League Pty Ltd, 130
Administrative Appeals Tribunal, 42, 84, 110
ADR. *See* Alternative Dispute Resolution
AFL. *See* Australian Football League
AIS. *See* Australian Institute of Sport
Alcohol, 30, 31, 35, 56, 59, 68, 69
Alternative Dispute Resolution, 88, 89
Amphetamines, 20, 29, 31, 35, 46, 142
Angela Raguz v Rebecca Sullivan, 93, 94
Angela Raguz v Rebecca Sullivan, 94
Anti-Doping Convention, 19, 81
Anti-doping passport, 150
AOC. *See* Australian Olympic Committee
Arbeit, Ekkart, 4
Arbitration, 7, 19, 73, 80, 86, 88, 90, 91, 92, 93, 94, 95, 96, 97, 98, 99, 100, 111, 114, 135
ASC. *See* Australian Sports Commission
ASDA. *See* Australian Sports Drug Agency
Asthmatics, 6
Athletics Australia, 4, 36, 37, 71, 72, 73, 74, 111
Doping Control Tribunal, 36, 73, 111
Attorney-General's Department, 20
Australia and New Zealand Sports Law Association, 100
Australian Cycling Federation Inc, 104
Australian Football League, 5, 10, 11, 24, 25, 43, 107, 124, 125, 143
Australian Government Analytical Laboratory, 33
Australian Institute of Sport, 21, 39, 40, 49, 108
Australian Jockey Club, 143
Australian Olympic Committee, 5, 12, 16, 20, 23, 25, 40, 41, 51, 52, 62, 65, 67, 74, 75, 92, 93, 100, 111, 112
Membership Agreement for Athletes, 93
Australian Professional Cycling Council, 7, 19, 24, 104, 105, 126, 127

Australian Rules Football, 5
Australian Sports Commission, 5, 10, 11, 16, 19, 20, 21, 22, 23, 25, 39, 40, 41, 42, 43, 65, 67, 68, 74, 75, 100, 104, 105, 108, 113, 115, 127, 128, 132, 139
Australian Sports Commission Act 1989 (Cth), 20
Australian Sports Drug Agency, 5, 10, 18, 19, 20, 22, 23, 28, 30, 33, 34, 40, 41, 42, 57, 65, 66, 68, 69, 74, 75, 76, 82, 83, 84, 104, 105, 106, 107, 108, 110, 112, 113, 114, 122, 124, 132, 133, 134, 137, 139, 140, 141, 142
Australian Sports Drug Agency Act 1990 (Cth), 20, 42, 141
Australian Sports Drug Testing Laboratory, 33
Australian Sports Medicine Federation, 39
Australian Weightlifting Federation, 115

—B—

Baseball, 5, 91
Basketball Australia, 24
Beetson v Humphries, 131
Bias, Len, 143
Briginshaw v Briginshaw, 109
British Athletics Federation, 70
Buckley v Tutty, 130, 131

—C—

Caffeine, 40, 115, 137
Canadian Anti-Doping Authority, 19, 68, 104, 105
Canadian Centre for Ethics in Sport, 20, 135
Canadian Skiing Federation, 12
Canadian Snowboarding Federation, 12
Cannabis, 6, 59
Capobianco, Dean, 36, 37, 66, 71, 72, 73, 74, 111, 112
Carrol v Mijovich, 132
CAS. *See* Court of Arbitration for Sport
Charles, Justin, 5
Chinese swimmers, 4, 34

153

Chlorprenaline, 35
Chronic fatigue syndrome, 10, 124
Civil liberties concerns, 131
Clembuterol, 6
Clenbuterol, 68, 108, 123
Cocaine, 30, 35, 49, 135, 141, 142, 143
Commercial Arbitration legislation, 90, 93, 94
Commonwealth Games, 32
Conflict of interest, 147
Consent, 92, 93, 94, 98, 115, 138, 139, 140, 141, 145, 150
Court of Arbitration for Sport, 6, 12, 13, 14, 55, 71, 88, 91, 92, 93, 94, 97, 98, 99, 100, 122, 123, 124, 145, 146, 147, 148
Cricket, 28, 129, 130, 131
Customs (Prohibited Imports) Regulations, 60
Cycling, 29, 31, 36, 126, 127, 146

—D—

Damages, 71, 87, 91, 92, 104, 105, 109, 138, 139
Davies, Andrew, 6, 108, 123
Defamation, 87, 105
Defence of automatism, 123, 135
Defence of honest and reasonable mistake, 116, 117, 119, 120, 121
Department of Employment Education Training and Youth Affairs, 20
Department of Health, 20
Department of Justice, 20
Department of the Environment, Sport and Territories, 18
Dextro proproxephrine, 122
Diuretics, 32, 35
Donike, Professor Manfred, 66, 67
Drugs
Inadvertent ingestion, 38, 113, 114, 121, 123, 137, 148
Mandatory testing, 4, 5, 56, 131, 136, 137
Passive inhaling, 113, 137
Recreational use, 59, 142, 143, 146
Testing, 3, 4, 6, 22, 31, 32, 34, 67, 75, 82, 86, 122, 139, 148
Therapeutic use, 10, 11, 42, 75, 79, 113, 124, 125, 146, 148
Trafficking, 20, 77, 113

Drugs in Sport Handbook, 83
Dubin, Justice Charles, 34, 62

—E—

Edwards, Paul, 125
Ellicott QC, Robert, 19, 36, 37, 71, 72, 73, 105, 111
Employer liability, 58
Ephedrine, 35, 122
EPO. *See* Recombinant Erythropoietin
Evidence, 5, 29, 37, 48, 53, 56, 57, 59, 70, 72, 73, 74, 86, 87, 89, 91, 95, 99, 103, 105, 106, 109, 110, 111, 115, 117, 118, 129, 132, 136

—F—

Federation Internationale de Football Association, 15
Federation Internationale de Natation Amateur, 55, 67, 68, 69, 122, 124
Field, Craig, 49, 140
FIFA. *See* Federation International Football Association
FINA. *See* Federation Internationale de Natation Amateur
FIS. *See* International Skiing Federation
Football, 10, 15, 28, 55, 58, 88, 143, 146, 149
Freedom of movement, 149

—G—

Gasser v Stinson, 125, 126
German Athletics Association, 67
Government, 4, 5, 8, 14, 15, 16, 18, 21, 23, 24, 41, 55, 56, 77, 78, 80, 106, 107, 119, 132
Greig v Insole, 130, 131
Gymnastics, 122

—H—

Hall, Carey, 126
Haper v Racing Penalties Appeal Tribunal *of Western Australia,* 118, 119, 120
He Kaw Teh v The Queen, 116, 117, 118, 121
Heroin, 30, 135, 142

154

—I—

ICAS. *See* International Council of Arbitration for Sport
IF. *See* International Federation
Industrial Relations Act 1996 (NSW), 140
Intent, 7, 61, 68, 103, 113, 114, 116, 120, 121, 137, 148
International Amateur Athletics Federation, 34, 36, 37, 66, 67, 68, 69, 70, 71, 72, 73, 74, 75, 86, 87, 88, 93, 104, 105, 106, 109, 111, 112, 113, 114, 126, 137
Arbitration Panel, 68, 111, 112
International Athletic Congress of Paris, 14
International Council of Arbitration for Sport, 97, 98, 99, 100
International Covenant of Civil and Political Rights, 132
International Cycling Union, 24, 29, 126, 127, 146
International Federations, 10, 12, 13, 15, 16, 23, 73, 76, 91, 146, 147
International Inter-governmental Consultative Group on Anti-Doping, 81
International Narcotics Board, 14
International Olympic Committee, 6, 10, 11, 12, 13, 14, 15, 16, 17, 25, 31, 32, 33, 34, 35, 36, 37, 38, 39, 40, 41, 42, 46, 48, 49, 51, 52, 54, 59, 63, 66, 67, 69, 70, 71, 74, 75, 76, 78, 82, 86, 91, 97, 98, 104, 112, 114, 122, 123, 137, 142, 145, 146, 148, 149, 150
Medical Code, 6, 10, 12, 25, 35, 36, 37, 38, 51, 52, 70, 74, 75, 76, 112
Medical Commission, 31, 32, 35, 36, 37, 38, 39, 42, 49, 59, 112, 123, 142
International Ski Federation, 6
International Standard for Doping Control, 80
IOC. *See* International Olympic Committee

—J—

Jensen, Knut, 30, 31
Johnson, Ben, 33, 56, 62
Joyner, Florence Griffith, 2
Judicial review, 95
Judo Federation of Australia, 94
Jurisdiction, 2, 9, 12, 13, 18, 66, 86, 87, 88, 91, 92, 94, 97, 98, 99, 104, 121, 138

—K—

Kelly, Ros, 41
Kioa v West, 107
Krabbe, Katrin, 67

—L—

Lamaze, Eric, 123, 134, 135, 146
Laumann, Silken, 6, 121, 122, 124
Laycock, Ron, 115
Legal representation, right to, 110
Liljenvall, Hans-Gunnar, 31
Litigation, 5, 88, 89, 90, 91, 96, 97, 139
Lost earnings, 126
Lynch, Andrew, 10, 124

—M—

Mahon v Air New Zealand, 109
Mandatory drug testing, 65
Marijuana, 6, 11, 12, 13, 49, 56, 59, 113, 114, 134, 135, 137, 142, 143
Maynard v Racing Penalties Appeal Tribunal of Western Australia, 116, 117, 118, 119, 120, 122
McCaffrey, General Barry, 47
Mediation, 89, 90, 96, 100, 101
Modahl, Dianne, 66, 69, 70, 71, 72, 106
Multilateral Agreement in the Unification of Actions in the Struggle Against Doping in Sport, 19
Murdoch, Rupert, 5

—N—

Nagano Organising Committee, 13
Nandrolone, 23, 114
Narcotic analgesics, 31, 35
National Basketball League, 24, 25
National Drug Strategic Plan, 20
National Olympic Committees, 14, 16, 76, 97, 98
National Programme of Drugs in Sport, 39
National Rugby League, 3, 4, 5, 9, 11, 17, 18, 22, 24, 25, 49
National Soccer League, 17
National Sports Dispute Centre, 100, 101
Nationale d'Education Physique, 30

Natural justice, 95, 107, 108, 110, 111, 118, 120
NOC. *See* National Olympic Committees
Nordenfelt v Maxim Nordenfelt Guns and Ammunition Co Ltd, 128
NRL. *See* National Rugby League
NSDC. *See* National Sports Dispute Centre

—O—

OECD. *See* Organisation for Economic Cooperation and Development
Organisation for Economic Cooperation and Development, 132
O'Davis, Robbie, 9
Oceania Registry, 100
Olympic Charter, 11, 14, 15, 16, 37, 50, 75, 92
Olympic Games, 6, 12, 14, 15, 16, 17, 27, 28, 29, 30, 31, 32, 33, 36, 45, 48, 50, 51, 55, 56, 62, 67, 71, 76, 77, 82, 86, 87, 91, 93, 100, 122, 135, 147
Olympic Movement, 13, 14, 15, 16, 48, 75, 88, 123
Olympic sports, 11, 16, 17, 62, 83

—P—

Pate, Stephen, 126
Penalties, 4, 5, 6, 7, 11, 16, 17, 20, 42, 50, 61, 73, 85, 88, 103, 128, 129, 130, 135, 136, 143, 147
Privacy Act 1988 (Cth), 132, 133
Procedural fairness, 103, 107, 109
Prosecution, 4, 61, 136, 139
Pseudoephedrine, 6, 121

—R—

Raducan, Andrea, 122, 123, 124, 146
Raguz v Sullivan, 145
Rebagliati, Ross, 6, 11, 12, 24, 49, 142
rEPO. *See* Recombinant Erythropoietin
Recombinant Erythropoietin, 9, 35, 36, 45, 77, 150
Register of Notifiable Events, 42, 84
Restraint of trade, 7, 57, 91, 103, 125, 126, 127, 128, 129, 131, 141, 142, 143, 145, 149
Reynolds v IAAF, 109

Reynolds, Harry, 85, 86, 87, 88, 93, 104, 105, 109, 126
Richardson, Mark, 114, 115
Riley, Samantha, 6, 120, 122, 146
Robertson, Bill, 7, 23, 127
Rogers, Don, 143
Rugby League, 49, 58, 59, 134, 135, 140, 141, 143

—S—

Samaranch, Juan Antonio, 34, 47
Sanctions, 6, 12, 21, 23, 25, 35, 37, 57, 59, 65, 66, 68, 76, 77, 79, 80, 81, 106, 114, 116, 124, 128, 136, 137, 138, 146, 149
Saxton, Andrew, 6, 108, 123
Scott v Avery clauses, 93, 94
Simpson, Tommy, 31
Smith-de Bruin, Michelle, 68
Snowboarding, 12, 49
Soccer, 15, 16, 17, 29, 88
Sorby v Commonwealth, 136
South African Athletics Association, 67
Sponsorship, 22, 58, 87, 99, 115, 126
Standing Committee on Environment, Recreation and the Arts, 31, 38, 40, 56, 59
Stanozolol, 19, 35, 36, 37, 71, 73, 104, 105, 108, 111, 115
Steroids, 2, 3, 5, 10, 11, 23, 25, 29, 30, 32, 35, 36, 46, 53, 54, 56, 57, 59, 67, 71, 86, 109, 111, 117, 123, 124, 125, 126, 127, 137
Stimulants, 6, 31, 35, 40, 142
Strict liability, 114, 115, 116, 120, 121, 122
Superleague, 5
Suspension, 11, 42, 49, 52, 66, 68, 69, 85, 86, 87, 88, 104, 105, 106, 109, 115, 125, 126, 127, 128, 134, 141, 143

—T—

Testosterone, 32, 35, 46, 70, 71, 106
Tobacco, 30, 58, 59
Tour de France, 4, 31, 36
Trespass to the person, 138
Tribunals, 43, 71, 89, 99, 101, 109

—U—

UCI. *See* International Cycling Union
UEFA. *See* Union des Associations Europeennes de Football
Union des Associations Europeennes de Football, 149
UNESCO. *See* United Nations Education Scientific and Cultural Organisation
Union Royale Belge des Societes de Football Association ASBL v Bosman, 149
United Nations, 14
United Nations Education Scientific and Cultural Organisation, 14
United States Olympic Committee, 20, 27, 86, 148
Urinalysis, 35, 106, 113, 136, 137, 138
USOC. *See* United States Olympic Committee

—V—

Vicarious liability, 58
Victorian Institute of Sport, 23
Vinnicombe, Martin, 19, 68, 104, 105, 106, 108, 112, 113, 126
Voy, Robert, 54

—W—

WADA. *See* World Anti-Doping Authority.
Watson, Alex, 38, 40, 115, 137
WHO. *See* World Health Organisation
Winter Olympic Games, 6, 142
Woods, Tiger, 147
World Anti-Doping Authority, 12, 13, 39, 76, 77, 78, 81, 82, 145, 148, 149, 150
World Conference on Doping in Sport, 13, 49, 146, 148
World Health Organisation, 14
World records, 2, 46, 48
World Swimming Championships, 122

HOW TO SURVIVE A
Miscarriage

a guide for women, their partners, friends and families

Karin Holmes

Copyright © 2017

All rights reserved. This book or any portion thereof may not be reproduced or used in any manner whatsoever without the express written permission of the author except for the use of brief quotations in a book review.

Printed in Australia. First Printing 2017
ISBN: 978-0-6481476-1-9

White Light Publishing House, Hillside, VIC, Australia 3037

www.whitelightpublishing.com.au

White Light
PUBLISHING HOUSE

To Michael – my rock, my angel, my everything.

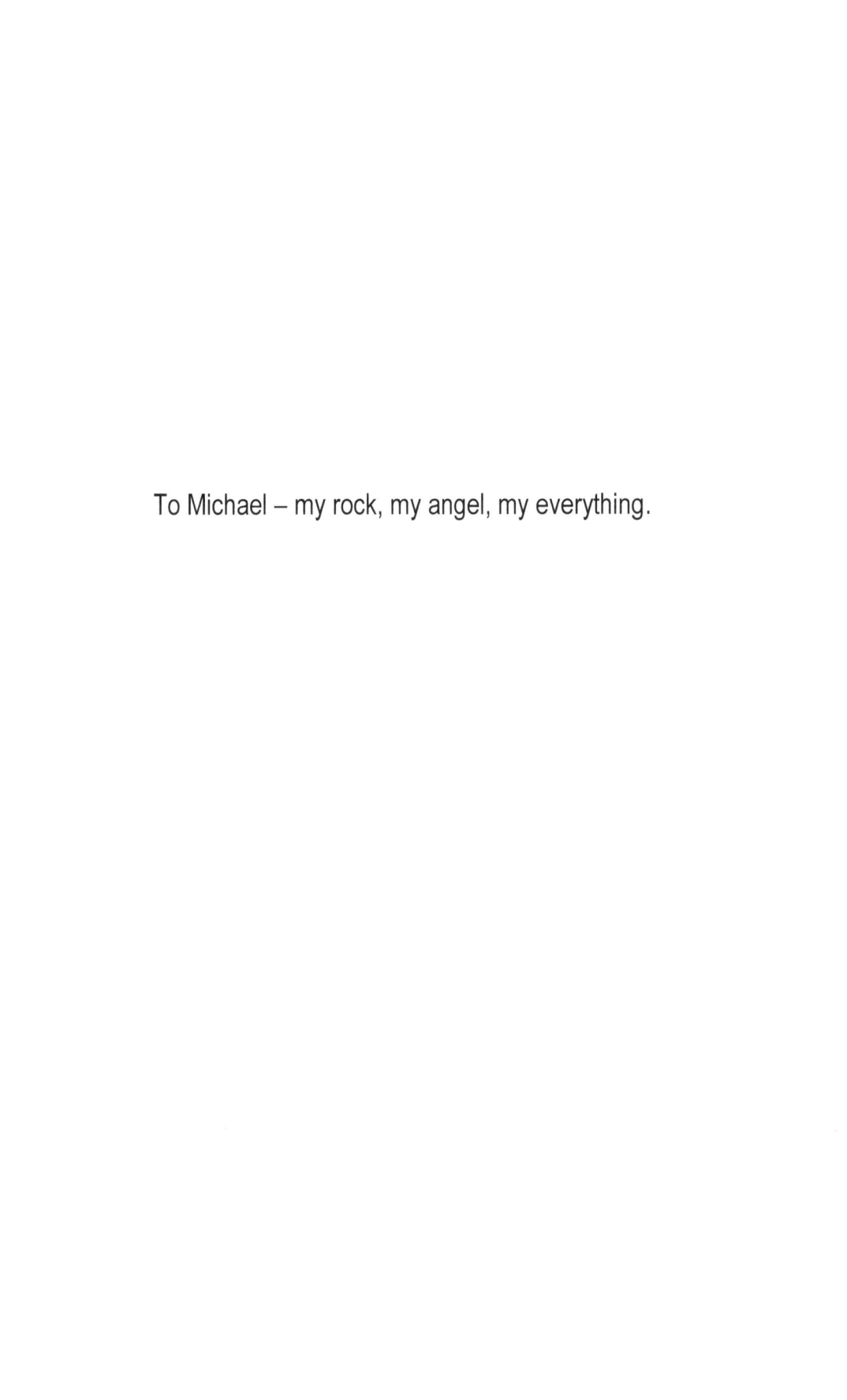

Contents

Introduction	7
Grieving 101 – The stages of your grieving process	9
Coping with loss: strategies to help yourself	17
Rituals	29
Dates to remember	37
Advice for friends and family	45
Advice for Dads/Partners	65
What's the big deal? Dealing with indifference	81
Acceptance – what is that?	89
Trying again and getting through this new pregnancy	99
Miscarriage – the dreaded term and what's behind it	111
What to expect from your body afterwards	119
Rediscover your body	123
Ode to your courage	131
Useful links	135

Grief fills the room up of my absent child,
Lies in his bed, walks up and down with me,
Puts on his pretty looks, repeats his words,
Stuffs out his vacant garment with his form;
Then, have I reason to be fond of grief?
Fare you well; had you such a loss as I
I could give better comfort than you do.

The life and death of King John, William Shakespeare

Introduction

Having a child – a wish millions of couples have. It is a powerful wish that brings great joy, love, happiness and challenges into people's lives.

In today's modern times most of us know lots about pregnancy, how to eat right, how to exercise to stay healthy during those nine months, where to go to buy baby clothes and furniture or what books to read to prepare for this life changing event. It is an event that is widely celebrated and connected with lots of positive feelings. However, it is also general knowledge that a lot of women lose their baby in the first three months of their pregnancy or even long after that.

But it stops there. The attitude towards miscarriage is very flippant. Doctors, family and friends know about it and those who have never experienced such a traumatic event brush it off when they talk to you. Yes, it is very common to have a miscarriage - but it is a big deal to survive one. The emotional trauma that comes with it is huge, the grieving of the event painful and the effects on the woman and her partner are shattering. The fact that most people think it is common doesn't make this tragedy any less terrible. Who has ever stopped and thought about the emotional ups and downs a woman and her partner go through after a miscarriage, about their deep sadness and confusion?

Society's ignorance and lack of interest make this suffering a quiet one. And a lonely one. That in itself is a struggle and needs ways of dealing with it.

I did it by writing about it and as I was reliving my ordeal a few things became apparent. One thing hit me very hard: The only people who took our pain seriously were people who either went through the same thing or something similar. Most of the time people's responses were dismissive and disrespectful. It started with the good old fashioned 'It is very common, it happens to a lot of women' comment to a lovely 'It wasn't the first, it won't be the last'. I was not only hurt by these mindless comments, I was outraged. No one has the right to belittle or minimise a woman's pain that she feels after suffering a miscarriage. It felt as if my pain wasn't legitimate for society and as if I wasn't supposed to struggle after this event.

I am not prepared to accept that. Miscarriage is a traumatic experience that comes with a lot of pain, soul searching and tears. It was hard and still is. I decided to write this guide because the pain so many women go through is legitimate and I hope I can help some of you to go through this tough journey ahead.

This guide is aimed at women who have suffered a miscarriage until week 20 and are struck by pain, grief and deep sadness. I hope you can take some advice and encouragement out of this book. It aims to offer help in this extremely upsetting situation and to help you get through your pain. The chapters can be read in order or you can pick one to start with. In this time of turmoil, do whatever is right for you.

A fair chunk of the book is dedicated to those around a grieving woman – her partner, family and friends. They all play a crucial role in her recovery but not all of them might be aware of it.

If you know someone who just suffered a miscarriage and you don't know how to react but would like to help then this book is also for you. It provides you with helpful guidance on what to do and what to avoid, as the last thing we need is another woman hurt by mindless comments and disinterest.

Grieving 101

The stages of your grieving process

So, here we are. The one thing you have probably never considered, happened: you lost your baby. One day, it was all good and the next you find that your tiny, precious, perfect baby is no more.

It feels like your whole world has come to a complete stop in a matter of seconds and darkness descended and put its heavy cloak around you, weighing you down so badly that you struggle to breathe. You are lost for words and in shock, with emptiness inside that is so vast, it could swallow up the entire planet. Feelings of joy and excitement are replaced with numbness and confusion and most likely, you had no or very little warning signs that this tragic event was about to happen to you. Yet, here we are and everything is upside down; you are in turmoil and nothing makes sense. Also, where do all these extremely strong emotions come from? They are taking over, they threaten to drown you, and you feel like you are sinking fast.

First of all: *breathe*. Take a deep breath, and then a few more. You have just lost your baby. It is normal to feel all these emotions and to struggle through the hours of the day. Most likely, a lot of questions pop up in your head: Did I do something wrong? Why me? Why did this happen?

The first few hours, days and weeks after your loss are a fragile and confusing time. Be gentle with yourself and let those tears flow. You might not realise it just yet, but all this emotional turmoil is the beginning of your grieving process and your new journey ahead. Yes, there is a grieving process after a miscarriage.

A lot of people with their "no big deal" attitude are probably not aware of that and those close to you might have the same impression. But, miscarriage is a form of death. The life that was growing inside of you is no more. You haven't met the little being; you don't have many memories, but that doesn't make it any easier to deal with the loss and the difficult emotions that come with it. Grief overcomes you instantly and enters your life with an incredible force. Your journey has been altered abruptly and you are thrown down a path you know nothing about and you didn't expect to go down either.

Yet, here you are and you will wonder what lies ahead of you and where this new path will lead you. It sure as hell is confusing and the future that looked so bright just yesterday is now a black, thick fog where you can see a way in, but not a way out. This might be your very first encounter with grief or maybe the two of you have met before, but not with such harshness and cruelty. Either way, grief is here to stay for a while to come, and your journey forward will only happen with it alongside it.

You might wonder what a grieving journey actually is, and what it entails. A straight answer is not possible as your journey through loss and grief is unique, so no one can tell you where your path will take you. However, there are a few similarities most grieving journeys share and it will be good for you to be familiar with them. That way, you can check in and see where you are at when times are extra confusing or hard. The reason might not always be obvious or clear, but sometimes a tough week can be better understood by remembering the stages of grief that all baby loss survivors go through. In this chapter, you will be introduced to the stages of grief and their characteristics. The description of grief can never be complete as it is so unique to everyone. You may experience all symptoms of the stages or you may miss most, but that is not the point.

The following explanations shall be a guide for you to turn to if you look for an explanation or reasoning for your current mood. They may be able to provide you with some clarity or a starting point to get an idea about what is going on. So, let's look at these grief stages a bit more closely.

A lot of research has gone into grief and grieving, and professionals who have dealt with loss and death extensively have developed different models for grief. Elisabeth Kübler-Ross, a Swiss-American psychiatrist, who was a pioneer in near-death studies and dedicated her life to research in to death and the grief associated with it, has developed a model of five stages (commonly known as Kübler-Ross model). Admittedly, she worked with adults who were close to death so it is not the same situation you are in right now. However, the stages of grief that are described in her model do apply to your situation.

The Kübler-Ross model entails denial, anger, bargaining, depression and acceptance. Other models include seven stages and I chose to follow that model, as it seems to be more detailed and often more fitting to grief experienced after the death of a baby. The seven stages are: Shock and denial, pain and guilt, anger and bargaining, depression, turn for the better, reconstructing and reassembling your life. Then, at last, there is acceptance. But let's start at the beginning.

Denial and shock
Denial and shock often help us to get through the worst part of the grieving process. Something awful just hit us full blast and we don't know how to deal with it. So, pretending it hasn't happened is only natural. We all know just too well that facing the awful new reality will cause a lot of pain, heartache and bottomless sadness. Of course, we don't feel like going through that, therefore we deny. It is no different after a miscarriage. One moment you were full of happiness, maybe struggling to believe that such a gift was bestowed upon you, and bam! The next moment it is gone, just like that and you are left with no answers, but a lot of questions. Your emotions probably can't keep up which leads to feeling numb, disorientated and lost. This is shock taking over but it has a limited life span and won't last forever. Reality will creep in – and that is when denial kicks in. You won't believe what is going on, you feel the pain rising inside you, starting from your heart, filling your body up, seemingly taking over every cell of your body. You start to realise that things are about to get real and the pain associated with it will take you for a hefty ride.

At first, you will direct your energy to fighting all of that. You are not ready to face the facts and so shortly after your devastating loss, this is very understandable. We can't go ahead with our lives straight away as if nothing happened and no one should expect you to either.

Please note though - when you catch yourself saying "I am okay", or "I feel fine", make a mental note to yourself that you have started the grieving process. Not that this is great news, but it is important. You have just taken the first step out of the horror that is dominating you at the moment – even if you start with denying your experience. It won't get better straight away, but you are on the right path. It is hard to say what you are going to get out of this stage, as everyone is different. Some might spend a day in that phase; others months. There is no road sign that is going to pop up to indicate, 'You are now entering stage two of your grieving process'. The borderlines between the stages are fluid anyway so who's to say you will be done and dusted within a month or two? Just know that it is okay to take your time. It is your life, your body, and your health we are talking about, so don't rush if you are not ready. If you are looking for signs that your process is moving along, then they are definitely around and will become apparent to you.

You will notice that your denial starts to fade. You start to think, "Wow, this is really happening", and you might wish you weren't in this situation right now. The numbness starts to ease; the raw emotions are coming back. Reality looks rather grim and it might feel as if your life has been shattered into a million pieces – what a gut wrenching feeling that is. The most important thing right now is not to hold back. You have started your new journey and are in the process of working through this immense pain.

This leads us to the second stage of grief – **pain & guilt**. You will have started off with denying everything but you will realise sooner or later that there are a lot of emotions inside of you and they are strong, scary and most of all raw. The pain hits you full on for the first time. To make matters worse, a new companion joins in – guilt. Often women feel guilty after a miscarriage and blame themselves for it. Your body has somewhat failed you because it wasn't able to carry this child. These thoughts and the guilt associated with it are, unfortunately, very common and incredibly poisonous. The trick of course is to move past them because those thoughts can be highly destructive and we want to stay clear of that. This won't be easy and we will to come back to the whole 'my body failed me' thing later as well.

Let's focus on the guilt first. Women can feel that they have failed their baby most of all, their partners and themselves, and feel guilty for all of it. They look back over the weeks of pregnancy and find things they think they shouldn't have done and feel guilty for it. You might have thoughts like the following: Should I have stopped working? Why was I so active? I should have slowed down! Why was I drinking coffee? The list goes on and on; it can and will drive you crazy if you don't stop. Guilt is part of your journey and it is a hard part to master. In this stage of the grieving process the question 'why' will come up – a lot. Why me? You will say or think sentences that start with 'I should have', 'Could I have done?', 'had I done this or that my pregnancy would go ahead'... but there are no answers to any of these questions. All it does is make you angry beyond belief. You blame yourself, you feel guilty for it and then you feel guilty some more. While we can't help to wrack our brains, trying to find an answer to this madness, this is a dangerous situation to be in. Your thoughts are driving you crazy, literally. This is when you have to stop yourself and make a choice: Do you want to be trapped in this negative whirlwind of thoughts and emotions that make you feel worse, or do you want to step away from it?

This won't be easy, as you have to consciously stop those powerful thoughts. They will keep popping up, as our mind likes to play tricks on us. Instead, tell yourself this: You did nothing wrong. There is nothing wrong with you.

Naturally, this will create a new wave of pain as you start to realise how helpless we are in a situation like this. True, we did nothing wrong, but why the hell did it happen? A question like this indicates that the next stage of your grieving process is coming your way.

Anger and bargaining. You might already be going through the motions and you feel incredibly sad, empty and exhausted. On top of this, your anger will start to show. Questions such as, 'why me?' or 'why now?' will become increasingly difficult to deal with as there are no answers to them. We feel like we are left outside in the rain, all alone and just so helpless. There is nothing we can do, even though we want to, and that is an awful feeling to have. It makes us down right angry.

Anger is a powerful emotion and while we might not like it, anger belongs to our journey and us at this stage. In today's times where strong emotions seem so inappropriate in a heavily controlled world, it can be hard to express anger. Don't get me wrong, this emotion can be destructive and lead to a lot of heartache but as mentioned, it is part of the journey right now – it won't have to stay with you for the rest of time. The key to dealing with anger lies in expressing it in a way so nobody gets hurt, and you can still release this powerful feeling. If you don't, it will eat you up and that is definitely not a solution. We will talk about options to express strong emotions in another chapter (see coping with loss – strategies to help yourself).

The second part of this stage, bargaining, is a result of our anger as we desperately try to make sense of our situation and restore some order.

Bargaining can be strong with some women or not happen at all. If it does happen, it is characterised by phrases such as 'I would', or 'If only I could'. Thoughts like this would have appeared already during the second stage of grief, but it is now that they become dominant and very intense. You will notice that you put a lot of energy into thinking up scenarios such as, 'I would give my new stuff back if only I could get my pregnancy back', or 'I'd give all my money if I could...'

As you go along doing this you will have noticed that you moved towards a rather dark place. Your thoughts are negative, sad, upsetting and cause you a lot of pain. These thoughts often create a downward spiral that pick up speed at a terrifying pace. It is normal to feel helpless to the 'if only' thoughts. They represent your yearning for a better time when things were great and you felt happy. We want that back and we are ready to give anything to get it. But life doesn't work that way.

It never moves backwards and what we realise now is that our loss is definite. It won't change. What we treasured most is gone and its happiness along with it. While it sounds simple, this feels like the world's end. This is a life-shattering realisation to make and it will lead you to the next difficult stage in your grieving process.

Depression. Unfortunately, the upward turn is not yet in sight and instead, darkness is around the corner. It is not going to be easy because you will be at a stage in your journey where you fully realise what has happened: You were pregnant, most likely excited about it and the whole new life ahead of you, but it is no more. This is a very depressing thought that brings on a new wave of sadness; not to mention the loneliness. It is incredible, it is deep, long, dark, daunting and an absolute energy killer.

So, you already know you have another hurdle in front of you. This stage is so hard and yet so important to go through. It is the moment where it gets worse before it gets better and of course, that is not the sort of news you would like to hear right now. The loneliness just swept over you, filled you up, starting with your heart and soul and there isn't a clear way out. Two things here: First, it will get better. Yes, it will. Second, while these moments absolutely suck, there is also a lot of power involved here. This is your pain and you can take control and release it in a way that is good for you (without hurting others). Suggestions will follow in the chapter Rituals. You can't see the path right now because darkness is around you. But know that it is there, and you will find it and walk away from this stage. It is up to you how this will happen. Be aware that depression is an incredibly tough opponent. It is highly likely that you will need help to combat it. There are different ways you can do this. At this stage of your grieving process, a doctor's visit might be a good idea to discuss your mental health and if you need medication or not. This is a very sensitive issue, accompanied by taboos, which makes it even harder to talk about. Some people will tell you all the evil things about anti-depressants; others will praise their benefits.

As you are vulnerable right now, it is crucial that you talk to the right people about it. If you opt to go on medication, have a talk with your doctor and make sure all of your questions are answered.

Remember though, anti-depressants are not candy and can't be popped mindlessly. They won't fix the problem, but often they will ease your struggle a bit and help you regain some much-needed energy. Everyone is different though and medication is not suitable for everyone. More than anything, depression needs to be recognised and it needs to be addressed. That is your only option. Denying it will cause a lot of damage and will prevent you from getting better.

As you tackle stage four, which is a real challenge as we just worked out, you are also nearing stage five, and there is finally some good news: **The upward turn** has started! It probably won't be that you wake up one day and feel so much better (although it is not impossible). More likely, you will notice suddenly during your daily routine that you have somewhat adjusted to your new reality and that you feel better about it than you have in a long time. You might stop in your day and realise that you notice the sun is shining, that you feel energy in your body and that your mind is no longer occupied with intense grief, but little things, such as what to put on the next shopping list. You might have missed the few first signs of this, which is absolutely okay. Just know that you have achieved a major win and that you are walking away from the sadness, the darkness, the anger, guilt and pain on much steadier feet now. You may be moving slowly, but your pace is regular and will lead you to your next stage.

Things will look a bit different from now on! Darkness and depression are fading away as you enter stage six: **Reconstruction and working through**. You will notice that you are more functional again with your mind no longer a whirlpool of thoughts about why, how, what the hell, and the like. You are able to acknowledge what happened and start to look for a life in your new reality. The thoughts about this reality are not as painful as they used to be and you start to feel that you can do this. The sadness is still around, but all of a sudden, it seems manageable. At times, it will almost feel like a background emotion. You know it is there (how can you not?) but the sun is shining and you feel like you want to get out and enjoy it – and that is exactly what you should be doing.

It might be wise to remember at this point that we are looking at a grief model and that means lots of theory about something very life changing. In theory, yes, we do reconstruct our lives and are working through issues and challenges. In reality, this phase can take time. Be gentle with yourself as you adjust to your new life after loss. Theories don't come with timelines – we all set our own pace as we rebuild our lives.

The same goes for the last stage of our grief model: **Acceptance**. You will learn to manage to live with what has happened, even though it is not easy. You come face to face with reality and it is not a comfortable look. But at the same time, you look forward to your future and might start to plan things again. You will feel like good times can be part of your life and that the heavy cloud around is not as thick anymore. Your energy comes back and you breathe easier as there is no longer a heavy burden dragging you down. However, reaching a place of acceptance can be tricky and we will be looking at how to go through this phase as well as the others more closely in coming chapters.

Coping with Loss

Learning about the stages of grief and getting an idea of what your journey might look like as time goes by will need a bit of digesting. This is no easy ride, no matter if you go through all stages or can skip one. If you feel overwhelmed or even a bit freaked out, then that is very understandable and also normal. The journey through loss and grief *is* a lot to take in but there is also some good news – there are many ways you can deal with your grief and emotions. When you start out on your grief journey, the term 'coping' might not be part of your vocabulary yet, and thinking about trying to deal with your loss might not even be part of your thinking and being yet. But, it will come.

We all have to find our own unique way to cope and manage life after loss.
In this chapter, I want to introduce some coping strategies many members of the baby loss community have found helpful. Hopefully there will be a few that will ring true for you and can help you on your journey. Every loss is unique and so is every journey; hence every coping strategy chosen. One coping strategy might work for some, but not for others. If you find some that don't appeal, then that is fine. You move on and keep searching as there are plenty of others. There are also many others you might think of as you go along. Whatever feels right for you – do it. This is not about doing it the right way, but doing it *your* way so you have something that helps you get through the difficult times ahead.

Start writing. It can be incredibly hard to grasp and understand your grief. The pain might be so strong that you are quite literally choking and are unable to say a word, yet you have the urge to voice your turmoil somehow. It is very important for your healing that the storm inside you gets an outlet of some kind – either because you wish to share it with family and friends, or want it off your chest. Either way, writing about your emotions or letting them spill onto paper can be a very good coping strategy. If you are unsure where to start, don't worry. It is not about writing outstanding poetry or putting together an award-winning novel. If you feel that writing down whatever is in your mind will help you, then do it. You don't need a distinct starting or ending point – if a few incoherent words are coming out, then that is fine. They will become more coherent as you write on. Maybe what you write down the first few times won't make any sense at all – that doesn't matter. You are not writing for an audience, you are writing for yourself, first and foremost. If you want others to read what you wrote – great! If not, lock your writing away, tear it up or erase it, and no one will be the wiser other than you.

Writing is a coping strategy with many benefits, as you will hopefully discover as you keep practicing. It will get your emotions and thoughts out of your head, which will provide relief. You will be surprised how you suddenly feel a little bit of that very heavy and dark cloud around you has gone and lifted after you've poured your heart and soul onto paper. Sometimes, you will even find that writing something down helps you put some structure into the chaos that might be raging on.

It won't always be easy – actually, most of the time it will be very emotional, but in a funny way, the tears that will flow have a cleansing and healing effect and you will find you return to pen and paper (or keyboard and computer screen) regularly to help you cope with your loss.

Of course, there are no limits as to what you write and the style you choose. Some women started to write poems, others wrote several letters to their babies or to themselves, or kept writing in their pregnancy journal that they had started, or set up their own blog (see below as well). The important thing to remember is – do what feels right for you. If you struggle to put your emotions into spoken words you might be surprised how well you can put them into written ones. One major advantage of writing about your loss is that you feel less vulnerable. It is just you and your pen, and no one else. If something comes out a bit crooked or not well put, you can erase it and start again. No one will say to you, "Oh, you shouldn't say that" or "I don't understand what you mean", and you won't have to explain yourself or get upset because someone doesn't get you. Paper is very, very patient and never judges. So, if you want to give yourself a break from all the thoughts tumbling around in your head – start writing.

You will find that on some days you can do it for an hour or so, and on others you have to stop after ten minutes. That is absolutely fine. It is not about how much you write or how often, but that you write. Every little bit that you do will help you to heal and that is all that matters.

If you are unsure where to start or are looking for inspiration, check out other parents' blogs. Quite a few have started their own (as mentioned previously) to share their story with their family, friends and the world. Blogs are an open space ready to be filled with anything you want to put there – an article, a picture or a video. It is sort of an online journal that you share with those who are truly interested in your journey. There are no rules as to how many times you should put up a post. It can be once a week or once a month – whenever you are ready to share another bit, the blog is ready for you to put it out there. Many support organisations have a list of blogs that can be accessed, so check out their websites (there's a list at the end of this book) to get started.

Grab a paintbrush. If any form of writing is not for you, then don't worry. The arts are plentiful and offer other strategies such as painting. You can put whatever you want on to that empty canvas in front of you. Your emotions will guide your paintbrush and let you choose your colours. One day you might paint something in one go, at other times you might end up working on a piece for several weeks. It doesn't matter how long it takes – all that matters is that you are doing it, and that you've found a way that helps you cope with the storm inside you. This goes for anything related to the arts, of course. If you prefer to sketch, draw or use charcoal, then go for it. Don't restrict yourself to just one surface either; draw or sketch onto paper, sand or anything else you find suitable. It doesn't have to be a lasting piece of art if you don't want it to be. As long as it has helped you make some sense of your emotions and what you are going through, then that is all that matters.

Another very healing activity is **scrapbooking**. If you've never tried it before, now would be a good time to immerse yourself into this world even though it might sound a bit weird to start with. The options are endless and your creativity is your guide. Women who turned to scrapbooking after their loss report that it gave their minds a rest, as they had to focus solely on one thing. That is exactly the aim with our coping strategies: we need to find something that helps us focus so these emotions and thoughts which threaten to overwhelm us constantly are kept at bay. Especially in the beginning; they are too raw and too deep to confront head on, but they bubble up anyway, which is why we need to address them and learn how to live with them. But, to achieve that is always very hard and a gentle start to it all is best. That is why an activity like scrapbooking is just the thing to deal with your loss in a way that allows you to set the pace. And best of all, just like writing, there are no limits or rules as to how your finished product should look – it is all up to you, and no one else.

Be outside. A lot of the time we feel like we want to hole ourselves up inside the house - preferably under the covers of our bed - and stay there until all eternity. And sometimes that is exactly what we need to do to shut out the world and its annoying noises. Peace and quiet are hard to find these days and it is what we crave most when we are exhausted by the emotional rollercoaster we are on right now. However, don't stay under the covers for too long. It will help you get through some days but on others, a walk on the beach, an early morning stroll through the forest or a swim in the pool are much better strategies to calm your mind.

Of course, this includes almost any type of physical exercise. Going for a run or hitting the gym (if you are up for being amongst people) can be very healing activities as they help us release some of our emotions. If you have always been someone who deals with life's stresses and challenges by physical exercise then don't stop now. Be mindful of your body though, and respect the trauma it has gone through. Start off lightly and build up slowly. The last things you need now are physical injuries and more pain in general.

When we talk of the outdoors, it doesn't necessarily mean you have to wander deep into a jungle or go bush for two days in a row. Such environments can of course help us to reconnect with nature – something we all desperately need in today's world of technology and cyber space. However, not all of us are in a position to break out the tent and set up shop near a lonely beach. Being outside also means simply leaving your house. A stroll along suburban streets can be just as beneficial as breathing in air on top of a mountain.

When we are in the midst of our grief, we sometimes need to take small steps that will help us move forward a little bit. If you have been cooped up in your house for weeks on end because you just couldn't face the outside world, then leaving your house is a big thing to do. If you make it to your mailbox and back, then that is a great start! It might sound funny that being outside can help us cope, but it really does. It shows us what we are capable of, despite our pain, and what we can do, despite the darkness inside.

As always, with any coping strategy, remember to take it easy and slowly if you want to give this one a try. You will have to find something that works for you – maybe find a special spot you can go to every now and then to think things over. Or, maybe a quick walk around the block is all it takes to shift the emotions and thoughts away from the darkness towards the light.

Whatever way you choose, remember that you set the pace. If you make it up the local hill in the nature reserve one day, but just into your yard the next, then that is just fine. You are on a path to healing and this should never be a competition or race. It is all about you and what helps you cope with your new life after loss.

Have a chat. A traumatic event like a miscarriage often leaves us lost for words. The pain is simply too much and so how can we describe to anyone what we feel when there is an emotional tornado raging within us? We have all been there and it is indeed very hard to say anything because quite often our own emotions silence us and keep us from reaching out. Nevertheless, talking to somebody about your loss can be a very therapeutic strategy when you are ready for it.

Some of you might find straight away that talking about it is the only way to help you cope. Others might take a few months before they are ready to open up. There is no right or wrong, and definitely not a better or worse time to start talking. Just make sure you are talking to someone you fully trust, who will take you seriously, and is committed to helping you. That may be your best friend, your partner or your mum – or a professional. You might want to join a group and talk about your experience with people who have been through the same or something similar. Once again, there is no right or wrong way. As long as you feel safe and comfortable with the group of people or the person you are talking to, you are on a good path towards recovery.

In today's modern times, more and more support is available online. Quite a few women find help and comfort in closed Facebook groups or by groups hosted by support services such as Sands (miscarriage, stillbirth and newborn death support), Bears of Hope and others. It is one thing to talk to someone about your pain that is very close to you, but it is somewhat special to have a chat to someone who went through something similar. A lot of women said that sharing their story with others who also suffered a loss like theirs was the most helpful to them. Some even grew that close that they kept in touch and helped each other through subsequent pregnancies and losses years after they met online. Help online is instantly available to you when you need it and provides you with a certain level of anonymity, which can often help you to share your thoughts and emotions, as you feel less exposed. You don't have to tell your whole life story, but can dive straight into what is bothering you and you get answers and support back straight away.

On the other hand, sitting in front of your computer can also increase your feeling of being lonely. The help is there, yet no one is around or near you to give you a hug or a cuddle. Best you give the online groups a try and see if it works for your or not. You might find friends in real life through those groups as you discover one or two people that live close to you. If that happens – great! If not, try and use the online groups as part of your coping strategy, but also access other people to have a chat to. The last thing you want is to feel more isolated, so if the online chat is not working, tune into the world around you instead. A lot of professional support groups offer support via phone as well, or group meetings so there is another avenue you can check out if you feel comfortable.

If you choose a group setting, just be mindful of your own emotions and mental health state. You are still quite fragile, so take a time out if you feel like talking about your loss or helping others with theirs, is getting too much for you. You need to look after *yourself* first and foremost. Once you are past the worst, you might be able to help others, but right now, stay away from anything that might overwhelm you and gather your strength before you venture out again. Many members of the baby loss community are very understanding, caring and patient people and they will welcome you back with open arms if you take a break. We all understand that sometimes we just have to be alone for a little bit and deal with our thoughts and emotions on our own.

Partner up. More often than not, you will turn to your partner for help with coping. That is fair enough considering they have been with you from the beginning of this. Talking to your partner will provide you with a lot of support, guidance and reassurance. But be aware that it only should ever be that: a help to cope.

You might have noticed that you are walking a fine line here. While talking to your partner helps you come to terms with what happened, it often unearths very raw emotions again so they can expect a few blasts of your anger coming their way. While I am sure they understand, there is a strict limit to this. Accusing each other of things and hurling nasty words at one another just won't cut it. It will make you both feel worse and, in the worst case, you might even drift apart from each other, which is most likely, not the thing you are after.

Watch yourself closely. Do you feel another bout of anger coming on? Are you consciously looking for your partner? Are you already thinking about mean things to say to them? Stop right there. Yes, your anger needs to be let out but you are on the road to misery right now. Take a step back and breathe deeply. Is this really what you want to do? Don't get me wrong – we have all looked for a fight and found it. The yelling and screaming might seem enticing – but they are really not.

Anger is part of our grieving process and a powerful companion that can be stubborn and is often hard to shake. It is understandable that we want to scream it all out and our partners are often the only ones available to hear it all. In moments like these, it is important to look for another outlet so the anger gets out, but no one is being hurt in the process. Your partner might be your emotional punching bag in these hard times, but how about punching the living daylights out of your sofa cushions? It will provide relief for you and keeps you and your partner safe from harm (just make sure the cushions are surrounded by other cushions – otherwise you might end up hitting the floor accidentally. Ouch!)

You could also go for a run or write everything down (in big, angry letters if needed) or find something else that will help you get the anger out. It is really worth it as you will be able to calm down and spare yourself and your partner a lot of pain. Also, you will (and should) be feeling very proud of yourself because you just gave the anger monster a real hard kick in the gut and it went down!

If anger is a constant companion of yours (which happens a lot) then maybe the following tip is also for you. If you have people in your life that you can fully trust with your struggle and can talk to, ask them for some practical help. Tell them to remind you that there is nothing wrong with you, and that you haven't done anything wrong. This is so easy to forget, as we tend to wrack ourselves with guilt – and where there is guilt, anger is never far.

So, if you can, and if you feel strong enough, give your loved ones a few pointers so they can step in and stop you if you are on the downward spiral again, and all these negative thoughts and emotions are coming back. Soothing words and gestures can often prevent another outbreak of anger, so if you 'coach' the people around you a little bit, they will react to you quicker and will be able to help you much better. It just has to be a quick grab of a pillow, getting their running shoes ready, or something similar. We are not looking for big gestures, but small and meaningful ones. When it comes to anger, we deal with it one outburst at a time, until it gets weaker and eventually vanishes.

Pray. In moments of deep turmoil, you might find comfort in praying. We all look for a bit of peace in times of upheaval, and praying could be a solution to this. Now, if you have never been religious and find it weird to talk to someone that we don't even know exists, consider this: There are many forms of praying and you don't have to be down on your knees reciting bible verses quietly for half an hour to do so.

Prayers can be more like a meditation session where you focus your thoughts on to one thing and while doing so, you become calm and collected. So, if you are after some peace and quiet, you can give praying a try. Some people may find an answer while praying, but don't count on it. The existence of God is a tricky subject, and at this point in life it is not about philosophical discussions or about whether or not our universe is guided by a bearded man, or no one at all. The simple truth of our darkest moment is that we look for a way out. And quite often when we lay in the mud, too weak to get up and not strong enough to stop the tears from flowing, having faith that one day, things will be better, is the only thing that keeps us alive. Having faith (however freaking hard it is being tested right now) often leads to having hope – hope that one day we will be happy again; that one day we might have that baby in our arms; one day where we will look back and realise we just made it through one of life's toughest challenges. Faith might just be a tiny speck to begin with, but it will grow, accompanied by hope, positive feelings and our strength. Hang on to it because faith and hope that things will get better, will become reality one day. Hope, as funny as it is and however hard to grasp, is the lifeline many people are looking for.

What our life after our loss will look like, no one knows. We all rebuild it on the ashes of our previous life that was not filled with grief and emptiness. So, when I say things will get better, that is true – but it is entirely up to you to shape that future and make it how you want it to be. And because that is easily a lifelong journey - retreating, gathering and collecting your thoughts - praying might be just the coping strategy that will keep you going in the long term.

Get reading. This might not work for everybody, but a few women have said that gathering as much knowledge as they can about what happened has helped them come to terms with their loss. This can indeed be very helpful. We do live in times where a lot of facts are accessible and where the medical world likes to share its new (and old) discoveries with the world. This is great at first sight and as much knowledge as possible should be easily available to the world.

For members of the baby loss community, this is a bittersweet opportunity, though. The medical world is ever changing as professionals keep discovering and learning new facts about the human body. When it comes to why babies die, there are still few answers available.

To this day, many women will never know why a miscarriage happened or why their baby was born sleeping. If you are looking for answers in scientific facts then your search can become extremely frustrating and disheartening very quickly. Quite often, the answers are just not there. We all hunger for an answer, we all want to know what the hell went wrong, but some of us will never know. To accept that is a whole different ball game and a tough part of your journey. If you want to embark on a quest to find answers, you should go ahead and see where it takes you. Keep the possibility that there won't be any answers in mind. It will be hard to do, because we all want to leave this 'not knowing' behind; we want to feed our fact-thirsty and logic-craving mind. This can be a good starting point and the craziness of our minds can be great motivation to try this path of finding answers by gathering knowledge.

As you get your facts together or dig deep to find an answer, you might notice that you are finding things – but not the ones you were looking for originally. You might be surprised what other answers you will come across on your quest for knowledge – for questions you weren't even sure you had. This is why an open mind is so important when you dive into the world of facts. We sometimes end up learning an awful lot, and mainly about ourselves. You might notice that certain parts of your journey annoy you more than you like, or that there are suddenly new paths opening up for dealing with your grief that you didn't think were for you. If that happens – wonderful! As you know by now, dealing with grief and learning to step back into life after your loss is all about taking one step at a time, and seeing where it takes you.

Get connected. When you suffer a miscarriage, you enter a whole new community that you probably didn't know existed. It is a fairly large one, but still a silent one, as we are pressured into being quiet about our loss so we won't upset the fragile balance between shallowness and awareness in our society. However, once you are a member of the baby loss community, you will find so, so much support in this community.

Of course, you don't have to reach out at all; it is entirely up to you, but help is available. Many other women who suffered a loss such as you, understand the depth of the darkness you are struggling through and they know that loneliness has just taken over your life. They sure as hell get it when you tell them you don't think you will ever feel whole again because a part of your heart and soul died with your baby. And, maybe best of all, they can give you hope again. When you share your journey with other members form the baby loss community, they will stick with you in your dark times and show you the way up. They can guide you towards those positive feelings you think you will never feel again: happiness, hope, something to look forward to and live for.

For once, the internet is on your side as it is home to quite a few baby loss support groups with their website and services. There are groups available locally in your area or those that work internationally – the internet (and mainly social media) make this possible. Check out the links section at the end of this book to learn about certain groups and their services and to see how you can get connected.

Forgive yourself. Did we just enter the weird sphere or what? Sort of. Is forgiving yourself even a coping strategy? You might think that it is a bit out there and if we are honest, really stupid. Such thoughts are very understandable because seriously, we are all not very good at forgiving, and these days it is only practiced by gurus, hippies and other people cut off from the grid, right? Well, those people have something ahead of us: inner peace.

The thing with forgiving is that we actually do more for ourselves than the other person when we do it. As soon as we release all these negative feelings such as anger or even hatred, we are set free. We are able to move on and leave others behind, and we can enter into a phase of our lives that is filled with more happiness and positivity, and excludes negative people that suck out all our energy. In today's world, we think if we forgive someone they will be off the hook, hence we don't do it because they don't deserve that. In truth though, we deserve to be happy and surrounded by people that add value to our life and enrich it. So, by letting all the haters and naysayers go, you make room for yourself to be much better off.

Now, imagine if the person you are fighting so hard against and are determined to never ever forgive is yourself. We all know how exhausting that battle is. The tricky thing with our loss is that we often will never get an answer as to why it happened, as mentioned before. So, we are left with an emptiness that keeps nagging at us because as humans, we want answers so we can understand!

As we don't get that and struggle with that fact, we keep looking for answers and causes and we turn to ourselves. We blame ourselves; we hate our body for failing at this task, the one that should have brought so much happiness to our lives. What we hoped for so much, did not happen. Over time, we build up all these negative thoughts and feelings because we are looking for a culprit for the root cause of all of our unhappiness and struggles. And where does the whole forgiving yourself part come in again? Right here, at that moment when you think of yourself negatively; when you blame yourself for your loss or when you think there is nothing you can get right, ever. Take a breather and remind yourself over and over again that you haven't done anything wrong to lose your baby. And you better stick to this routine, too.

It is the first step to forgive yourself for your own harshness and criticism, and will end up helping you feel much better. You deserve it. You are a battler and a fighter, but it is now time to lay down the weapons and rest. You have come so far and have done so well, so give yourself this gift of releasing yourself of any blame, guilt and shame. Coping with loss will become a little easier once we are no longer fighting ourselves. The energy you gain from allowing yourself to be at peace will be most useful to continue your grief journey.

Rituals

As time goes on, you might get to a point where you feel the urge to keep the memory of your angel alive. For some, this can be very straightforward and will feel like the right thing to do. Others might be unsure because their loss was so early in the pregnancy and they don't have any pictures or other memorabilia that remind them physically of their precious baby. It doesn't help that we are not all encouraged to remember a baby that died in the first three months of pregnancy, so it is very understandable if you feel like you are not supposed to keep your baby's memory alive. The fact is though, it doesn't matter if you have a few things or nothing at all; if you wish to remember your baby then that is exactly what you should do. Yes, some babies' lives were terribly short but that shouldn't stop anyone from honouring and remembering them.

Choosing and performing a ritual can provide a lot of healing even if it opens up old wounds or exposes all the raw emotions we carry around with us. The best thing about performing a ritual is that it is up to you what you want to do and when you want to do it. Some parents might feel the need to do something shortly after their loss, while others are not ready until a few years later. That is absolutely fine - a ritual makes no sense when you are not ready, so don't pressure yourself and think you 'have' to do it. You don't have to do anything at all.

Our journeys through our losses are so individual, there is no set of rules you have to follow. Some parents feel the strong need to incorporate a ritual into their journey; others don't feel comfortable with that. There is no right or wrong. We all do things to make sure we will never forget our babies, and that is the only thing that counts.

If you want to pick a ritual but you not sure what you want to do, here are a few suggestions. It is not a complete list, and you don't have to pick anything if you are not happy with it. Let the suggestion be a guide for you on your way to find something unique that works for you. It might be that you come up with something different altogether, and that would be wonderful.

Pick a name. The issue with early pregnancy loss is that we often don't know what we were expecting – a boy or a girl? That shouldn't stop you from naming your little angel if you feel it is something that will help you. You can even pick one name each, of course. This is not about wrecking your head with what sex your baby might have been, but about making your loss more real. In the medical world (and in the minds of so many in society) your baby wasn't really a baby, but a collection of cells. The loss of a pea-sized baby might feel somewhat unreal to you. So, naming the baby can help change those feelings– you are now talking about a little person and not something abstract like a growth of cells or a foetus. Quite often, picking a name is the first thing parents (and especially mothers) do after their loss. It is a very emotional thing to do that can unearth some powerful reactions. Naming your baby soon after your loss might get tears flowing that you might have tucked away somewhere deep in your heart. After all, it is suddenly not only about losing a baby, but losing Hugh, Lisa or June, and this comes with the pain of losing someone we have loved so fiercely from the moment we knew of his or her existence. Picking a name as a ritual is very powerful and bittersweet at the same time. Nothing will honour your baby more than giving it a name and keep its memory alive.

At the same time, there is also nothing that makes us realise how finite death is and that our precious, tiny babies are no longer with us. Do not hesitate to pick a name though – the benefits of it outweigh any short-term emotional setbacks. In years to come, you will always think of your baby with the name you chose and not just think of 'it' or 'the baby', which will make it easier for you and others to understand the importance of remembering their short lives.

Write. We have talked about writing already and its healing qualities. When you are looking for a ritual to help you deal with your loss, writing comes into play again. Many of us feel the need to record our stories and keep all the memories we have alive. Writing is one tool that can help us achieve this. As we established earlier, when you write, it is entirely up to you what you write about and how much you write at any one time.

This time around, it is no different. It can be an intimate journal about you and your pregnancy that you want your angel to know about. You could tell him or her in a letter how much you miss them and how life is without them here, or how you imagined life would be like with them and how it makes you and your partner feel; knowing that it will never become a reality. If you feel angry or upset, feel free to write a rant against the universe or God, or whoever, for making you go through this. Often, feelings are still abstract and bizarre to us even though we can feel them clearly. Writing them down and seeing them in front of us can help to better understand what it is we are dealing with.

And don't worry, the letter or the journal doesn't have to make sense. You are not sending it off to anyone, so you can jump from one topic to another, mid-sentence if you feel like it. This sort of writing is really to let out anything that crosses your mind at that very moment. If it is rows of swear words – so be it. Remember, it is a ritual, so you are not only remembering your baby, but you are also releasing what is weighing you down and what fogs up your thinking right now. Of course, writing one letter won't be the end of the grieving process but it can be a very powerful ritual to help you through the process. You might notice that writing has become a fixed part of your life and is something you return to often – perhaps you started writing every day or maybe you sit down to write on special occasions, such as an anniversary or any other day that is significant to your loss. Once you have a collection of written letters or journal entries, it is up to you what you choose to do with them. You can keep them or destroy them. You will know what is right when the time comes. Until then, keep doing what you are comfortable with, and what helps you to learn how to live with your loss.

Light a candle. This is a very symbolic ritual and one that a lot of mourning parents use. There is something about igniting a small light in the dark that helps us feel calm, and in a space where we can remember our little angels. The flame might be small, but it will help lighten a whole room and reach our hearts, which is why so many of us feel drawn to perform this ritual. You can light a candle whenever it feels best for you – maybe you have a set day of the week that feels right for you. Perhaps there is a day that you connect specifically with the loss of your baby. You probably remember the day (and time) it was when you suffered your loss, so why not acknowledge it by lighting a candle? It doesn't have to stop there, and you can replace a candle with something that might fit you and your family better. Some families have bought a special lantern that reminds them of their angel and they light it regularly in memory of their little one. Either way, what is important is that lighting a candle is a conscious act to stop whatever you were doing and focus on yourself and your little one. It can be your special time where you shut out the world and spend time either reflecting, meditating or just being quiet.

Make jewelry. When we experience a loss such as ours, we often long to have something in our hands; something that we can hold on to, touch and look at, while we think of our angel. Quite a few women have either bought jewelry (such as a charm bracelet or a special necklace) or made it themselves and wear it every day. It can be soothing to touch your bracelet while you either talk about your little one, or think of them. Quite a few mums in our community have a small angel charm on their bracelet or on their necklace but it doesn't have to stop there, of course. If you feel buying or making jewelry would be helpful to you, then there are once more, no boundaries as to what your special piece should look like. If you would rather have a heart charm than an angel – go for it. It is about remembering your precious baby, so wear what you connect with the most and what helps you remember them best.

Create a memory box. Unfortunately, the loss of a baby can happen at any time during pregnancy. A lot of hospitals now create memory boxes for parents that have suffered a stillbirth, where they put in photos, blankets, hospital bracelets, clothes and other things that were unique to the baby. For a lot of mums, this is crucially important in their healing process. It contains very precious and delicate memories of their angel; it will always be there and it can be opened whenever a mum is ready to look at it. The benefits of a memory box are plentiful. A big plus is that they don't have a set form, and can be created by anyone and at any time. If you had bought some little booties or onesies for your baby, then these items can go into your memory box if you feel like creating a special space to keep your memories of your angel – no matter how long or short he or she has been with you. Such a box could also be a place where you can store your letters that you are writing to help cope with your loss.

Basically, anything baby-related can go into the box and it will give you that one special place you can go to when you want to remember your baby. This box can stay closed if your emotions feel too raw; it can remain unopened indefinitely, or looked through frequently. It won't matter because the box will always be there, and it keeps your memories safe for you.

Release. If you suffered a loss very early on in your pregnancy it creates a special kind of emptiness inside, as you are not quite sure what you lost. You knew there was a tiny person growing inside of you; the size of a pea or a jellybean. It was still so small, but it was real! You may not have felt those kicks or hiccups, but that doesn't make it any less of a baby. Either way, in many grief journeys there will come a point where people would like to physically release part of their pain and send their goodbyes into the wind, sun and stars.

If you lost your baby early on, you might feel unsure about this urge because you possibly lack something that is tangible - like a coffin or an urn that you can see being sent off. Fortunately though, goodbye rituals are, like so many other rituals, adaptable and quickly changed so they suit your needs. Perhaps on special days you can plant a tree, buy flowers or visit a place that is close to your heart to spend a few moments in silence. It doesn't have to be something extraordinary; just something that feels right to you. Whatever you pick, it will be in spirit of releasing parts of your pain and it will be another step on your path towards healing.

Plant. Another ritual that will provide long lasting memories can be done right on your front step. A few survivors have turned to their gardens and planted either a fruit or any other tree, or a rosebush in memory of their little angel. The act of gardening itself can be very healing and it has short-term and long-term benefits. If you decide to plant something in memory of your baby, the actual act will help you focus on just your precious one, and shut out the world for that moment as you dig up the garden bed, prepare the soil and engross yourself in gardening. Once your rosebush or tree (or any other plant you like) is in the soil, you can watch it grow, and it will provide you with this special place that is just for you and your baby. The healing qualities of this ritual are really quite plentiful, as it is not only the physical act of looking after the plant that will give you purpose, but also seeing the result of it – the big tree in the backyard or the rosebush at your door, that you can turn to whenever you need.

Get a tattoo. This ritual is very popular amongst parents that have lost a child, and rightly so. Nothing stays with you forever and as permanently as a tattoo. The best thing about it is that you can get whatever is right for you inked into your skin. Some women pick a butterfly, others the name they had in mind for their baby, some might get a tiny foot- or handprints tattooed, or a little angel. As usual, there are no limits, so if you want to go big, go big. Cover as much or as little of your body as you like. Just be aware that tattoos are hard to get rid of, so have a think about a motif, picture or writing for a little while before you go ahead with it. Once you have found the perfect fit, the tattoo will be a beautiful reminder of your little one that you can carry with you on your skin, wherever you go.

Speak of them. The life you have lost might have been a very brief one, but it was a life, nonetheless, and it is a life that is worth remembering and celebrating. To speak of them as a ritual can be about reflecting on your experience and acknowledging that it has happened; that your baby has been with you and always will be, even if no one else will remember him or her. To speak of your baby is a good antidote against the pressure you might be feeling to be quiet about your loss, so you won't upset anyone. You can fight this pressure with this ritual, and give yourself the opportunity to heal.

To speak of your bub and dedicate a moment to them will also mean you allow your grief journey to happen, and to take you towards a new path and a new life after your loss. If you choose this ritual, then it doesn't mean you have to gather a large crowd first, or to put it on to your Facebook status (even though you are more than welcome to do so). Speak about your baby in a way and to people that you feel comfortable with. Be as quiet or outspoken as you like, as long as you feel positive energy coming from it.

Remember, this ritual is supposed to help you, so don't waste your time trying to educate someone who lacks the emotional maturity. Neither is this moment appropriate to fight society's ignorance and misunderstanding of miscarriage. That might come later, but right now, this will only upset and hurt you, so stay clear of the nay sayers. To speak of your baby could be as simple as saying their name out loud to yourself every now and then. It is entirely up to you what and when you would like to say something. It is your journey and your path towards healing, so perform this ritual when you are ready, and in a way that suits you and your baby.

Help out. It might seem strange when you are in the middle of your darkest time to think of others, how they are coping with their loss and how helping them can be a healing ritual to you. At times, this is incredibly hard or even impossible to imagine, as you are facing your own tidal wave of emotions that keeps crushing down on you. In moments like this, it is most important to focus on you and to get yourself better first. Once you have found some firmer ground to stand on and you feel ready to hear other people's stories, then another possible ritual can become open to you. A few women reported that they started helping out at SANDS, for example. That will always be a challenging activity as you will be confronted with the pain of others, but it can also help you come to terms with your loss, knowing that there is a whole community out there (unfortunately) dealing with a similar tragedy and that you are not alone.

By helping others, you can help yourself, as it can give you a sense of purpose which is very important in times where you are not sure if there is a point to much in life. Helping others is of course, a very noble thing to do, but it is not everyone's cup of tea. If you do decide to give this ritual a try, allow yourself to always check in and ask yourself, "Can I handle this or is it getting too much? Do I need to take a break?" If you answer questions like this with a yes, then that is fine. When we decide to help others, we can only do so if we are able to look after ourselves first. And, every helper will tell you that every now and then, they need a time out to regroup and reenergise. So, don't ever feel bad if you started helping, but need a break mid-way. There is only ever so much we can take on, and if the load becomes too heavy, it is time to stop – either for a while or permanently - to look for another ritual that will help you heal.

Get involved. Have you always wanted to do something good, or support a charity close to your heart, but didn't quite know how? Now could be a time to do just that in honour of your baby. There are many ways to go about it. If you are into exercise and a physical challenge, you can choose either a national event or something local to participate in, and raise money that you will donate to a charity in your baby's name. Some angel mums go all in and take part in tough mudder; others take it a bit slower and enter their local fun run.

But, it doesn't have to be anything so physical, of course. If you are more of an arts and crafts person, then you could use this talent of yours to donate to charity and to remember your little one. It could be that you either sew or make clothing items and donate them in your baby's name, or you could create a quilt that represents you and your baby's journey and then possibly pass that on. It doesn't have to be a grand gesture, but if you get involved with a charity as a ritual, then this can provide you with healing on many levels – most of all for yourself, but you will also help out someone else that is in a vulnerable position and will appreciate your kindness very much.

These are just a few examples of rituals you can perform if you found one that appeals to you. Of course, there are so many more ways to express your grief and to celebrate a ritual. If you want to walk on top of a hill and scream out your pain, then do it. If you just want to stand on top of it and release your thoughts, then do that too. The purpose of such rituals as described, is to help you deal and maybe even understand your loss a bit better. They can provide much needed time to reflect and remember your angel. You won't be at the end of your journey, but at least you will have made another important step in the right direction, which is why picking and performing a ritual is an important and powerful part of almost any grief journey.

Dates to Remember

The journey through grief is a curious thing. It can take you through lots of ups and downs, surprise you with unexpected turns of events and will rarely be a smooth, straight forward path.

Throughout your journey, you will come across a few milestones that will forever stick out and cannot be erased or ignored. I am talking about special dates throughout the year that will have a place in your life from now on, like your baby's due date and anniversaries. As these days will be difficult to get through, the ritual and coping strategies you picked will become important once more. They will provide you with the support you need to make your way through those days. Your journey through and with grief is a constant flow, so rituals might change as they will have served their purpose or you just don't feel like doing the same thing year after year. As time goes by, you will notice what works for you. You might stick to the same ritual or you might do something different every year – you will be your own best guide.

As every loss is unique, everyone will have special dates that are significant to their loss and you are encouraged to remember them as the years go by. Keeping the memory of your baby alive will help you cope with your new life after loss a lot better. Some dates are almost universal though, and very important to all of us.

The following is a collection of dates that many baby loss community members find crucial to remember and to prepare for as well as we are all able, depending on where we are at in our grief journeys.

The due date: It is highly likely that you would have known your due date as you either had worked it out yourself, or a doctor calculated it for you. It doesn't matter that the due date is ever only an estimate. It is a real date and it matters to you. It seems like there is a now a permanent imprint in your heart and soul with that date, and it won't let you forget the day is coming up when the time is near. It comes with a wave of different thoughts such as, "I would have a baby by now, if only", or if it is a second or any other anniversary after that, "my child would be xx years now". While these thoughts are difficult and trigger a lot of emotions, it is absolutely okay to have them. They will never leave you and as time goes by, you will learn to manage them. Also, and this is most important, by having these thoughts you recognise and acknowledge their short life. You give it meaning and importance, and what better gift could you give to your little angel than remembering him until the end of days?

Let the tears flow and give your grief room in your life, no matter if it is the first time around or twenty years later. You can return to your ritual and coping strategies that you have found useful, or you can choose something new. Nothing is set in stone when it comes to remembering our little ones.

You might find that one year you are doing quite well and then the next year you struggle. It will always depend on your circumstances and where you are at in life. But, because it is your loss and only yours, it is up to you as to how you will approach it, and you will find a way each time that will be right for you. Once the first 'due date' has passed, this day often becomes the birthday of your little angel. Yes, technically, it doesn't have one, but that doesn't matter now. Our little one would almost be five now, and every year so far on his due date, we buy a birthday cake for him and light a candle for him.

You don't have to think of the due date as the birthday of your child in the future but you can, of course. If you are more comfortable to keep referring to it as the due date, then that is more than fine. You do what feels right for you, because that is the only way you will find some healing.

The anniversary. When we talk of the anniversary here, we mean the day you lost your baby. This one is the traumatic one, and you can't escape it. It will make its presence known days or even weeks before, when the thoughts about that day might creep back in or become stronger than usual. Quite likely, the very first one will also be your hardest one. Of course, some time will have passed and lots of things might have happened in the meantime. But, emotions have a funny way of showing themselves and it could be that they sweep over you and bury you under them on that day. As you know by now, the emotions associated with miscarriage are far deeper than anything else and they have a strength and depth that is hard to understand sometimes.

Once more, you are in charge as to what to make of the day. Will it be a special one or will you try to have as normal a day as possible? You will have to do whatever feels most helpful for you. Like the due date, you can stick to a particular ritual and repeat it every year, or you can play it by ear and plan something different whenever that time of year is approaching again. If you feel like going to the beach one year, but want to take a holiday the next, then go ahead and do it. If you want to busy yourself with lots and lots of work on the day so you won't have much time thinking, then go ahead and do it. Quite often, it is all about getting through the day and hoping it will pass quickly. None of us like to remember those awful and dark days where we lost something so precious and it was out of our control to stop it. Unfortunately, the memories are etched deep into our hearts and come to the surface, especially on days like this. It will hurt, no doubt about it. So, if you can't get out of bed that day, then don't. You have been through a lot, and remembering and reliving a loss is one of the hardest things in life. If we could skip the day, we all would.

In some years that will be a strong urge, and in others it will be a lot more manageable. Life is constantly changing and flowing, so one year is not like the next year, and the same goes for your emotions. Certain milestones might be harder and therefore, the anniversary will be more intense, too. As we have learned by now, pain will be your constant companion and it really doesn't matter how long ago you lost your child. The 21st anniversary might be especially hard as we tend to celebrate that birthday in our children's lives as a milestone, and your angel's 21st will be no different. It is not much, but it is something. By then, you will know what works and you will be able to commemorate the day in a way that is right for you and your family to make sure that, after all this time, your little angel will never be forgotten.

There are a few other days throughout the year that might not be specially connected to your loss at first sight, but can have quite an impact on you anyway.

Christmas time, for example. The festive season is very hard to get through for many members of the baby loss community. It reminds us of everything we don't have, but wish for so badly: A happy family of our own. Often, family gatherings don't help with that, either. Chances are high that there is at least one family member who is either pregnant or has just had a baby, or you get those family members that are incredibly insensitive and don't get why you are upset. Both of them are hard to deal with.

If you are lucky, you will have an understanding family who will either try and keep a baby away from you, or distract the unhelpful family member so they won't hurt you with their thoughtless words and comments. As is often the case though, families are a rather funny and complex group of people that don't have a lot in common. It can be quite possible that you will experience a very stressful Christmas time because you are either being forced into pretending you are fine, or playing along with the festivity program. In the worst case, you get to told to be quiet as no one wants to hear sad stories at Christmas and really, why would you bring up something as small as a miscarriage and dampen the Christmas spirit? The short answer to this is: stuff 'em. Celebrate your own Christmas. There are many ways to do that. The following ideas are of course, also suitable for those among you that *do* have supportive family. Tell them about your ideas and they might be more than happy to help you make Christmas peaceful for you – now, as well as in the following years if you need it.

Christmas is, for many of us, all about family, and there are ways you can include your angel into your family celebrations. What symbolises Christmas more than a well decorated Christmas tree? And right there, are a few ways to make your angel part of your celebrations.

Create your own Christmas bauble. For this, you don't have to be very crafty either. It could be as simple as writing your angel's name (or any word related to your angel that means something to you) on a large bauble and hang it on the tree. Once more, you can do whatever you are comfortable with. Use lots and lots of glitter if you want to, have a few baubles dedicated to your angel, have one with a photo in it – do what feels right for you.

If baubles are not quite the thing for you, then worry not. The good thing about a Christmas tree is that they are mostly quite large and need a lot of decorative things to look good. Create something else instead that can go on to the tree - a woolen angel, a star, a leaf or a heart. It should be something that carries a lot of meaning to you and will light up your Christmas a little bit. You don't have to create something on your own, of course. Buy an ornament or a decorative item and place it on your tree. It is all about including this special family member that isn't here with you physically, into your Christmas celebrations. Something from a nice shop can carry just as much meaning as anything you create yourself.

If making things is not your forte at all, and shopping at Christmas time seems too hard to endure, then don't worry about it. You can remember your angel by lighting a special candle, playing a song that means a lot to you, or writing something such as a poem for your baby. This, you could do in the lead up to Christmas, or on the day itself. Again, it needs to feel right for you and you will know if the activity you pick is the right one to include your angel into your Christmas. Listen to yourself, talk to your partner about it and do what you feel will help you get through these festivities with less of a broken heart.

That time of the month. There is another time during the year that might be a challenge to get through and unlike Christmas, it is not necessarily a time you can actively do a lot about. I am talking about your monthly visitor, your period. Many women find them hard to deal with, especially shortly after the loss, but also later on in their grief journey (for practical advice on what to expect from your first period after your loss, see chapter 11 'what to expect from your body afterwards'). It is a tough one because nothing shows us any clearer that we are no longer pregnant than a period.

Mother Nature can be quite cruel. She picks up where she left off, no matter if we are emotionally ready or not. The cycle of life starts again. In a way, that is a good thing because it will also give us the option to try again and see if we can conceive our much-anticipated rainbow baby[1].

---

[1] A Rainbow Baby is the understanding that the beauty of a rainbow does not negate the ravages of the storm. When a rainbow appears, it doesn't mean the storm never happened or that the family is not still dealing with its aftermath. What it means is that something beautiful and full of light has appeared in the midst of the darkness and clouds. Storm clouds may still hover but the rainbow provides a counterbalance of colour, energy and hope.

But, before we get to that point, having your period sucks. As you can't stop your body from doing what comes naturally, focus on your emotional and mental health instead. Be gentle with yourself during these days. Allow yourself to be upset, but don't be too harsh with yourself. Do something that will help you feel better – anything really that will lift your spirits a bit and leave your heart a little less heavy. Indulge in a good book, make some 'me' time available if you can during the day, go and have some retail therapy. Acknowledge that these days are difficult, but don't let them drag you down. Grieve and mourn for your baby actively during your period. People will tell you to get over it, of course, but let's not listen to them. Write a letter instead to your baby and tell him or her how much you miss them. Tell them you wished they were still here with you and that you hope they are okay, wherever they are. Or, do anything else that feels right to you and that will make your pain more visible. The emotions that we carry around with us are often abstract and hard to pin down, which make them very draining to endure. Focus on getting them out so you can examine them with some distance.

Most importantly when getting through your period, give yourself time. Don't pressure yourself into thinking that you have to be fine a month or two after your loss. If your period is painful for you emotionally, allow it to happen. Dealing with your period is often uncomfortable enough, and now it is even worse as we not only deal with physical discomfort, but crazy hormones and emotions, too. Take one day at a time and remember that this period won't last forever. It will probably take a few periods until you have a firmer grip on things, and know what works for you and how you can get through these days of the month a bit easier. But, you will get there. You will find your way, and the tools to manage this time of the month until it becomes less painful to go through.

Mother's Day. Once a year, we all turn our attention to our mums for a day and say thank you for the outstanding and incredibly hard work they did and are still doing for us. It is a day of happy celebration, love hearts and laughter - and a very painful and sad one for many women. Those of us who have lost babies are excluded from this joyful occasion. Are we even allowed to celebrate this day when our babies are in heaven? Does this make us mothers? Yes, it does.

Mother's Day is a huge deal for many of us, but it is also a very hard day for so many reasons: It brings up painful memories and sad thoughts, such as what could have been, had our babies lived. But, it doesn't stop there. While there is no open and compassionate discussion about this, Mother's Day is only for mums with living children. This is an unwritten rule of our lives. And it is one reason - if not the most important - why this day is so dreaded by many members of the baby loss community. We don't count on that day and neither do our babies. What a horrible feeling that is! Luckily, some wonderful members of our community have created a day just for us: A week before official Mother's Day is Bereaved Mother's Day, where you are invited to celebrate your life as a mum and where you are encouraged to share your story and pain, and honour your special baby in heaven. Unlike the official day, Bereaved Mother's Day is often a quiet occasion, but if you choose to participate, you can create a day after your own liking. You can celebrate by having a traditional Mother's Day with brunch, flowers, chocolate and the like, or you can go to a place that is special to you to remember your angel baby. You can spend the day alone or in loving company, you can prepare presents or you can leave it. This day is for you. Make of it what you feel comfortable with, and don't let anyone tell you otherwise. It is not a competition and it is not about pleasing others. It is a day for remembering, healing and honouring you as a mum who survived the loss of your baby.

Advice
for friends & family

As mentioned in earlier chapters, the loneliness that follows a miscarriage is profound. The question is, though: do we have to go through it alone? Not really, and preferably, there should be lots of support around you. More often than not though, you are met with disinterest, misunderstanding and carelessness, which is not a very good environment to be in, if we are honest. Reality can be quite harsh in times of need, as you find yourself alone all of sudden, when you were just surrounded by so many people a moment ago. You need to look around and see who is left standing at your side.

A good starting point could be your partner, as this is their experience as much as it is yours. I remember that my husband was always the closest to understanding me, as he was right there with me all the time. Of course, it wasn't easy for him at all either. He copped it quite badly and I do feel for him. He carried me through the darkest parts, pulled me away from the few cliffs I was standing on; ready to jump and die. We shared our loneliness together, as there wasn't really anyone else out there that cared about our pain.

My heart felt heavy and empty at the same time, and life passed me by through a grey haze. My loneliness went unnoticed. It is the logical consequence of a death, because the pain of it is contagious and could hurt others, so people around will try not to be too close so they don't have to deal with your pain.

Many women who experienced a miscarriage (or a stillbirth, for that matter) tell similar stories, unfortunately. Most people around them didn't know what to say or they were compassionate at the time, but then it faded quickly. Even worse, quite a few women reported that people around them started to feel uncomfortable when they mentioned their loss after a while, as though they were given a time limit for their grief and were not supposed to mention anything after that time had passed. If you are someone who has a friend or family member who just suffered a miscarriage, and you are truly interested in helping, then check out this chapter carefully. As this situation will be quite likely very new to you, there are a few traps and potential issues that could set off a bomb, rather than provide help and support.

The first and maybe most important step is to stop looking at the situation your way. Try and see through the eyes of your friend or family member before you react. For example, as just mentioned, many angel mums experienced pressure to not talk about their loss after a certain time, because others weren't all that interested in it. Know this: Simply because you, as a bystander, would like to forget about it, doesn't mean the woman going through her darkest time will do just the same. Or, to repeat what a surviving mum said very poignantly: "Grief lasts longer than sympathy. A lot of people don't understand that some things cannot be buried or forgotten". That hits the nail on the head. As the loved ones and other people important to the grieving couple, you can't also expect your friend or sister to just return to normal because it has been two months since her miscarriage.

Make no mistake, this situation is difficult for you too, because you weren't given any preparation time to react properly to this devastating event. It is not like we live in a society that acknowledges death in general and approaches it as a matter that is okay to talk about. Considering so many of us work so hard to stay young forever, who wants to talk about death or the fact that no life lasts forever?

An angel mum told me that people know how to offer condolences, but they don't know how to help someone cope long-term. And that is quite true. We often don't know how to react when someone is suffering a loss, and our natural reaction these days is to get away from it and to leave the grieving person behind. Or, we do a half-hearted job; sending a card and flowers, and feel we have done our duty. We often then don't realise that we hurt the person in need, and made her feel more isolated, even if that wasn't our intention. So, the question is – what can you do in this situation as a person from the outside?

The answer is simple: A lot.

Of course, it won't always be easy for you as you enter a minefield of emotions, and you might get hit quite hard every now and then. But, not to worry. This is new for you, and you will learn and grow as time goes on. You don't have to come up with some grand gesture to show that you care, so relax and take a deep breath. You are not required to provide a solution for an unsolvable problem, but to give support.

Let's start with the most common potential trap that needs to be avoided at all times – your choice of words. In today's times, we are all masters of throwing around shallow sentences, of not listening properly and especially of not caring all that much what sort of damage our words can cause. We all fall back into the habit of repeating clichés easily and constantly, and they are a no-go right now.
It is so hard when a person mourns their loss and people respond to it by saying something meaningless. I have talked to many women and there is definitely one thing we all have in common: We all have a sentence that we heard so much, that was meant to help us feel better, that we absolutely hate to hear. So, if you want to stay clear of those and not inflict further pain, here is a list of responses to avoid at all times:

- It is very common
- It wasn't meant to be
- It is nature's way
- Everything happens for a reason
- Get over it
- You're young, you can have another
- I know exactly how you feel
- Focus on your children that you already have
- Heaven needed another angel

As you might have noticed, I just listed the most common sentences people use when they try to comfort a woman who suffered a miscarriage. The 'everything happens for a reason' is an all-time favourite – and one of the worst things to say. And, that goes for all of the phrases we all so often use. You might just feel robbed of your go-to phrase – don't all the new age people insist that everything happens for a reason? Don't we just have to wait and see, for it all to make sense? This is indeed a popular belief, and if it is one you like for yourself, then that is just fine.

But, when it comes to the death of a baby, 'everything happens for a reason' is an insult. The other phrases are not much better, so they need to go – don't say them if you want to comfort someone from the baby loss community.

The question is though, why we end up going back to these hollow phrases. Part of it might be because we just don't know how to react to loss. Death in general is not a widely discussed topic, and even less so when it comes to babies. As humans, we are supposed to give birth to life, not death. But see, simply because we are 'supposed' to do something, doesn't mean we all get to do it. And when it comes to losing a baby, being the outsider who does things differently than the rest is neither great nor recommended.

All of a sudden, we are part of a weird club that seems to be shipped off to some lonely island that resides in the middle of society but with a seemingly unbreakable wall around it. We are gone from the limelight, death has been silenced once more and people can keep talking about reality TV and smartphones. Now, those are lovely and easy topics! But not death – that is never easy to talk about. Yet, here we are. Someone you know and love just lost a baby. We all fall into reaction mode where we need to say something, don't know what and really, we'd rather not talk about it. So, out come those shallow phrases that cause more grief and are not helpful for the healing process.

Comforting someone after a loss is a major challenge at the best of times, but gets even bigger when it is a loss where the outside world has never met the deceased. To top it off, we as a society tend to like bigger and better. A baby who died in the first trimester of pregnancy is not big - it is tiny. But it is still a huge loss to mum and dad. With that in mind, ask yourself, why would a bereaved mother find comfort in the thought that losing her baby happened for a reason? That being here with empty arms was for a reason? She just lost her most precious thing in the world, but it was for a reason? She lost her baby, not her job! This will never make sense; it will always hurt so much, and even if it happened for a reason, that doesn't help us heal. We are not looking for reasons right now; we are missing our babies terribly. So, focus on that, rather than blurting out empty phrases.

Another reason as to why these phrases hurt so much and need to be erased from our vocabulary, is because they belittle the woman's pain and it can't really get worse than that. Yes, miscarriages are very common. Technically, every woman should have one, according to the numbers. But, as life is just so fair and excellent, it will hit certain women more than once, while others will never know what a horrible experience hides behind the word miscarriage (a general word of advice here – stay away from number crunching and telling her that she is one in four is not a good idea right now, either. We are talking about humans, people. Caring mums and dads, and not cold numbers. Now is not the time to show off any math or research skills you may have).

It can't be stressed enough, that the baby might have been tiny, but the loss is not small, little, benign, tiny or not worth mentioning. It is huge, and therefore we need to choose words that describe the deep impact of such a loss, and not the meaningless phrases of our 'do I have to care about this?' – repertoire.

We all need to remember how powerful words are – now, more than ever. We live in an age where everyone has easy access to information and the internet is an easy platform to share opinions. That is great, but the dark side of it is that we tend to get more and more careless with our words. We've probably all been part of a forum where someone said something and then got a bashing for it (cursed be the internet troll). That in itself, is despicable and a worrying sign of the world we live in. But what is worse, is we tend to take this behavior into the real world where we just say something, but don't really care what it causes in others; possibly thinking life also has a delete button so you can erase your words if needed. Here's the kicker though – words still hurt, and always will. For example, if you say you know how we feel if you have never been through a miscarriage is disaster, times ten. Truth is – you *don't* know how we feel. Simple as that. Yet, in our 'blah blah' mentality, we say something mindlessly, thinking it will do.

Grief and loss are so powerful, deep and complex, that they are hard to understand in just one minute. A grief and loss journey is unique, every time. This is the part we need to remember; this is the time where we need to dig deep and come up with something genuine. It is the time, above all, where common phrases like the ones listed, have no place – not ever. This is the time of intense sadness, depression and struggle. If any of these phrases come to your mind, keep them to yourself. Give a hug instead. It is way more powerful and healing than you might imagine – for both of you.

This is only a quick breather though before we do get to the point where something needs to be said. Quite possibly you are now more than ever, unsure what to say if the 'fall back' phrases are off the table now. Suddenly this whole loss thing has become a landmine, hasn't it? That is true as so many words can set off chain reactions of negative feelings and thoughts, and set off a downward spiral towards darkness. When we try and comfort someone who experienced such a complex loss like a tiny baby they always loved but never met, we will experience our own flood of emotions. We might feel insecure, scared and plain uncomfortable, yet it is time to react and step up. At this point, it is best to go back to basics. Remind yourself that you are not expected to be some wise person who has all the answers to life's challenges and puzzles. An "I am so sorry for your loss, I just don't know what to say", can do wonders, because it is the truth and it is coming from your heart. You expressed your sorrow and leveled with the person in front of you. She is lost for words and so are you. But you are together now, spending time together and that is what matters.

So many women would have loved for people to just be there – it is not always about words. Sometimes it is just about not being alone on this roller-coaster ride of emotions and dealing with this big, empty gap in your heart and soul on your own. So, rather than thinking about what to say, think about what to do. Doing the grocery shopping, for example, or putting a casserole in the fridge, will do more wonders right now than any sophisticated phrase about grief and loss.

Now that we've addressed the challenge of what to say, there are also heaps of things you can do to help your loved one dealing with this terrible tragedy as time goes on. Immediate help right after the miscarriage is crucial, but also logical. The tragedy happened, and we react to it. It might be that you are not sure how to react, so the following suggestions provide you with some starting points.

Be a friend. It sounds simple, but it is not. As we know now, many women who have experienced a miscarriage report feeling very alone afterwards, because their environment wasn't very understanding, caring or sensitive about the pain the woman was going through. So, rather than risking being hurt again by some smart-arse comment, we all started to be quiet. We'd rather said nothing, than being hurt again in a situation where we are already so vulnerable.

So, as you can see, times like the ones described are possibly your time to shine. You can break through the silence and loneliness by being sensitive, alert and truly committed to being a friend. As mentioned above, you can help by cooking for them or going to the shops to get a few items. These things are extremely helpful at a time where any task put in front of your friend seems like a mountain too high to climb. In times of grief and raw feelings, the person suffering often lives in a haze and doesn't really worry about trivial, yet important things such as food.

It may be that your friend has gone without proper food for a couple of days and hasn't probably noticed that, either. She is consumed and overwhelmed by her loss, and can't think straight right now. It might even be that she values her own life very little, so not eating seems to fit the bill. When you lose a baby, life becomes meaningless and it is a struggle to get back to a mindset where you will think life is good again.

One small thing that helps to get some energy back is a meal cooked with love. So, get cracking and prepare something you can bring over. Make sure your friend will have a bite or two before you leave, so you will be sure the fueling up process has taken place! Focus on creating feel-good food that she will like. And if there is a lot of chocolate involved in it – even better. An aching soul needs all the sweetness it can get on the long way to recovery.

In this early stage of her journey, we shouldn't expect anything of her and give her room to find her pace for her journey. Of course, it can be difficult to approach the subject, because you want to give the right kind of help and not just do something that won't make any positive difference to her.

You will have to choose your words carefully, and that means in this case: be honest and clear about what you think you can offer for help. Things like, "Let me know if you need anything", can be tricky. Your friend has just lost her baby and doesn't know anything other than her pain. She probably doesn't know what she needs right in this moment. Instead, say things like, "I am going to put some things in your fridge for you to eat later", or "I will call you this afternoon at 3. Is that ok?" She can work with statements like this, and doesn't have to think about what she actually needs. She won't know that for a while to come, so be a guide for her in these dark times and help her through with a gentle and clear approach.

A word here on expectations: That is a silly thing to have right now. Every one of us grieves differently, so we can't expect people around us to do it our way, or how we think dealing with death is appropriate. For example, it is very important to get out of the house eventually, but she needs to do that when she is ready.

Of course, encourage her to get moving or encourage her to do something good for herself in a way that suits her. Every woman is different; her feelings to this sucker of an event are unique, so the response to it is also one of a kind.

Considering you have known her as your friend, you might have a hunch as to how to address this. Has she never been much of a talker? Does she try to avoid talking about private feelings whenever possible? If so, talking is probably not your favoured approach. In a situation like this, the most important thing is your presence as a friend. Don't give up, keep coming back, check in on her, and sit with her in silence. Be aware though, that progress might take a while. A while could be a month or a year, or more. If you are not willing to do this, be honest and back out. Do not come up with lovely sentences such as "It has been a couple of months now, you should feel better". Remember – there is no time limit on grief! And our compassion needs to keep up; it can't just take a holiday or disappear permanently.

Also, this: the word, 'should' is not a good one to use for a quite a while now. It indicates lecturing, shows your impatience or not understanding the situation, and puts pressure on someone who already has enough on his or her plate. So no, 'you should' sentences in the near future, okay? This will require some conscious word choice on your part, but you will be fine. Instead of saying, "you should", make a question out of it; use this chance to enquire how your friend is doing. For example, you could say, "It has been a couple of months now, how are you feeling today?" That way, you leave out any hidden accusations, but also show that you are still interested; even if some time has passed since the event.

Start talking. If your friend is indeed, generally known as someone who likes to talk, initiate a conversation. In the beginning, these more than likely won't be long. Talking about your deepest pain and sadness is incredibly draining, so not many of us will enjoy diving into it headfirst to dissect our struggle. Most importantly, watch how your friend is behaving. If she gets more and more distressed, break it off and leave it for a while, unless she insists on getting it all out. If your friend is not up for talking, stop and tell her, "I see that you are not up for talking and that is fine. I just want you to know that I love you very much and I care about you, so I will keep asking how you are". Of course, you can shorten that speech to suit your needs, as long as she gets the gist of it: You *really* care and want to be there for her.

One talk will hardly fix everything, though - be mindful of that. You will be required as a listener many more times - sometimes for hours on end, sometimes for ten minutes. It is possible that in these situations, you will feel quite unsure how to react best. You want to help, but don't want to be too pushy, and most of all, you don't want to hurt her. That is absolutely fine, because putting pressure on her to talk about things is definitely not the way to go – at any time during her journey. Honesty is the key here. Admit that you don't know what to do, but that you would love to help. That way, you make it clear that you are serious and that is already quite something.

Another thing to consider for friends, is: Should you give advice? Well, that depends. Do you have anything useful to say? Be warned that there is a potential trap right in front of you. I remember when I was recovering that a friend suggested I go and see a fertility doctor. Now, that was excellent advice, of course (insert sarcasm here). I lost my baby, I felt weird about my body even months afterwards, and now I am supposed to go to a doctor who might tell me there is something wrong with me? What great advice that was! I am still very upset about it because it was just so out of place, so inappropriate and insensitive. You might know a thing or two about miscarriages, and one of them might be that miscarriages can indeed be a sign of infertility or other problems when it comes to conceiving. But, who the hell told my 'friend' it was a good idea to discuss that with me? I felt enough guilt and anger already! So, when you talk to your friend, keep in mind that she just went through hell. The last thing she needs is to be told that there might be something wrong with her fertility. Give her time.

You might think having a thorough checkup will shed some light on why this has happened. It might, but it might also be pointless. Doctors do know a lot, but it is not that much, either. If the couple would like to know if they have a problem with fertility, then it should be up to them to decide when they want to address that. You as friend should stand on the sidelines and be alert. If your friends decide to go down that path, then there might be more pain waiting for them, so you might be required again at a later time as a friend. For the time being, just zip it and remove the words 'fertility doctor' from your vocabulary.

Be patient. Recovering from a miscarriage takes time, even if you might think it is not a big deal and the best thing to do is to get back on the horse and start trying again. Always keep in mind, if you haven't had a miscarriage you won't really know for sure what it is like to be left with all this pain. If you have been in the same boat as her, then still practice patience as her journey is different to yours. You may have been ready to move forward earlier than your friend. That is fine and is what it is. But for now, remember that you won't know how long it will take your friend, sister or cousin to recover. Unfortunately, many women experience the 'drop away' scenario. They are being left alone when they need people the most.

The shock after a miscarriage can last quite a long time and by the time women start to grieve, most people have disappeared. And, if she says something now, she only gets the "Is she *still* struggling with this?" look. So, if you are really committed to helping, stay put for as long as it takes. There is nothing worse than being left alone with pain, sadness and depression because everyone else is just too busy not caring. And you know better than that, don't you?

Be crafty. Not one for many words? That is okay, as there are other ways you can express your sadness towards your friend. Are you someone who is creative or thinks that being creative right now might be the best way to express what you are feeling, and could be a way to help your friend? If so, go right ahead.

You could create a special picture or put together a memory box. It could be one where you can put in a pair of tiny socks you might have bought for your friend's baby, sensible poems about loss, or maybe a figurine of an angel...the options are many. You know your friend best and will be able to figure out what could go into her special box. If you are not creative yourself, someone else will be able to help you out. You could have a special piece of jewelry created that you then give to your friend. It doesn't have to be something super expensive; a simple and thoughtful charm for a bracelet will be plenty. As long as your present is sensible and has healing qualities you can't go wrong.

Be sensible. There is one major thing you should be extra careful of, if your loved one just had a miscarriage: announcing your own pregnancy, if you are at that stage of your life. Of course, this is a great time for you and you should share the happy news! When it comes to sharing your news with your friend or family member who just had a loss, however, you will need to put a bit of thought into how to break the news to her.

Would it be a good idea to sit them down in a quiet place and tell them one on one? Or would it be better to send a letter so she can read it, think about it and then respond to you?

If you want to really help her, take the time and think about how to do this. Do it yourself though, and don't let her find out through someone else. Also, be prepared that she might not be happy for you straight away. That is not because she is a heartless person, but because she is just too filled up with sadness and grief, and there is no room for happy feelings at the moment. It could be that she will begrudge you your happiness. If that is the case, then back off a bit. She is not doing that out of spite, but because she is at a certain stage of her grieving process where seeing pregnant women or babies is extremely painful, and possibly something you weren't aware of. That has nothing to do with you, and you did nothing wrong. Just accept that she is going through this and once again – talk to her. Ask whether you should back off, or if she wants you to leave her alone.

Don't assume things, and then make a decision – discuss it. That way the two of you will find a way that works for both of you. If you have been asked to stay away for a bit, accept it. There are surely plenty of people who want to know all about your pregnancy and are happy to share their stories with you. Go and focus on them for a little bit. Keep an eye on your loved one, though. There will be a point where she is ready to participate, so it would be better to welcome her then with open arms. She will be forever grateful for your sensible approach to the whole thing, simply because the rest of the world doesn't think they need to consider the feelings of an angel mum when it comes to announcing their pregnancy news. This is an incredibly tricky moment for everyone involved – the ones with the joyous news beam with happiness, and so they should. They are in such a happy place, that nothing but happiness is on their mind. This is so wonderful and precious, and every couple wishing for children should be able to experience this state to the fullest. All we ask for though, is that you choose a time and place for it when there is a member of the baby loss community present. If your friend, sister or cousin knows about your pregnancy, but isn't that outgoing at the next gathering, then accept that. She is very quietly and deep down, happy for you. At this stage, she is just not able to express it to you in a way you might prefer. But, if you give her room and remain understanding, she will get there in her own time.

Be alert. If you are a friend that never has had a miscarriage, then you will always struggle to fully understand what is going on. But that is not the problem at all. If you are a compassionate person, you will have realised by now what a tragic event this is. And that is all you need. However, society built a few traps for you that you need to be mindful of.

What often happens with women who had a miscarriage and others that haven't, is that we get separated into 'us' and 'them'. *Them,* being the lucky ones who never suffered through this living hell and are blissfully unaware of what can happen if something goes so terribly wrong. There is a wide and deep gap right between you and your friend. Society obviously wants you to ignore your friend, and join the happy celebration of not being a member of that club. And the invitation is of course, quite tempting. On the one side, there is your friend who struggles through something so hard to comprehend, and on the other side awaits the happy train, where you talk about mostly happy things and you get excited about stuff.

Naturally, that side of the story is a very important one, and this is not about making women who never suffered a miscarriage feel bad. It is about being mindful that not all of us are that lucky, and that everyone around us is more than happy to forget exactly that. So, while we all understand that you will be drifting off to the fun side, be aware that the other side of things is still around, too. It is more than okay to go baby clothes shopping with another friend who is just plain excited about her happy news, and to share her joy and not think about darker things. Just remember that your other friend who just lost a baby is not part of that, probably doesn't want to be part of it, and more importantly, will struggle through a subsequent pregnancy because of her fear and her previous experience. Just don't judge her and don't fall into the trap of caring for her pain for only a limited amount of time. Grief and sadness have no expiry date.

Keep in mind that a sense of normality will not appear in your friend's life for a while, and that the whole pregnancy experience has forever changed for her, especially if she has lost her very first baby. Which is why it is so important for you to be alert around her. The vast majority of people will put the event aside and think no longer of it, and expect her to do the same. Well, as we know by now, that is not going to happen. What is even worse is that your friend is expected to be super happy and joyful if there is a new baby on the way. And you know, she will be, but more than likely she will also be frozen with fear. 99% of the people won't understand that and will have a rather flippant attitude towards it. They will say things like, "but you are past the first three months, so what is the problem now?" or "why are you scared?" Worse still, they her to get over herself and not carry on so much. One thing you, as an outsider might not be aware of: a new pregnancy is not three months of fear; it is nine months of fear.

Once you've experienced the death of a new life growing inside of you, there is no way of going back to being oblivious to the horrible things that can happen during a pregnancy. As a good friend, you need to acknowledge that fear and take it seriously. So, rather than going on and on about what to buy and how cute those onesies are, ask her instead, how she is feeling. Regularly. Insist on an honest answer and encourage her to express her fear. There is a good chance you might be the only one who will be doing that.

If you find the task a bit daunting from time to time, remember that you can switch sides for a breather and always go and talk to someone who has no idea about the ordeal that a pregnancy can be. As long as you cross back over to your friend to help her through her nine months, you are good. You will have worked out by now that things others thoroughly enjoy is very stressful for her. There will be a time where she has to get a move on and get organised. Don't push her though, and let her decide when she is ready for it. Even if that means after birth!

I have spoken to women who haven't bought a single thing until the baby was there because they were so afraid they would lose this one, and couldn't bear the thought of a made-up nursery that would end up being empty. So, that is another trap to avoid: Don't expect pure joy, as it might not happen, and accept it if fear is the dominating theme of your friend's pregnancy. If you are not sure what sort of issues your friend is encountering, find out. After all, you know her best and there are no guidebooks for any possible situation you might encounter. Listen to your heart and not your head, in order to avoid the mentioned traps and you will be fine. If you find it is getting a bit much and you are not sure how to handle it all, because you just don't seem to fully understand her, you might be the one that could direct your friend towards a more suitable support person. These can be found in support groups, or maybe that could be a professionally trained counsellor. Just be very sensible about it when you approach that topic. You bowing out of this one, doesn't necessarily mean you are no longer friends, but she needs to know that. Another loss right now would definitely not be a good idea.

Be proactive. The hard thing about surviving a miscarriage is that the world around us doesn't stop. It keeps turning, people go about their own business and eventually, your friend has to face that world again. That is a tough challenge on its own, and the path back to normal (whatever that is) is difficult. The last thing she needs is people asking silly questions that will upset her - and that is where you come in.

Returning to work can be made easier if the workmates are informed before your friend returns. Do you know her workplace well, by any chance? Is there anyone there that you could talk to and inform about what has happened, and ask her or him to instruct the immediate team on how to react upon her return? Stepping back into the world is a lot less daunting without having to answer the same questions over and over again. If people are respectful and wait for her to bring up the topic, rather than prodding her, then that would be a good start for the way back into daily life. So, if you could be the one to contact her office and get that coaching done – great! This could be done with a few lines in an email, or a chat on the phone. The key here is to allow her to get back into a routine and do regular things that are familiar.

Obviously, that doesn't help everyone, and your friend might struggle with the fact that no one is asking her how she is doing. In that case, discard the coaching of her workplace, focus on your friend duties and check up on her once that first day of work is over. This scenario can be adapted to many other situations in life, of course – for example, prepare her for her first time back with a certain circle of friends, attending her regular yoga class again after a longish absence from it, or going to her local baker where they know her well and will be curious why they haven't seen her in so long. After a woman loses a baby, she forgets about many things, as she is consumed by her grief, and the feeling of missing her baby dominates every minute of the day. We forget about the outside world, curious people and well-meaning acquaintances. This is why she will be eternally grateful that you paved the way for her any way you can – it will make these encounters so much easier to get through.

Remember. A couple of years have passed, and your friend seems to be back on track. That is great! No need for you to talk about things from the past, right? Well, not quite.

As we worked out earlier, it is never a good idea to push your friend to talk and pressure her to get over her loss, or to force her to talk when she is not up for it. However, that shouldn't stop you from asking every now and then how she is going. It doesn't have to be an in-depth conversation. By asking her how she is doing now, with some distance between her and her terrible loss, shows her that you have not forgotten about her little angel, and that you understand that there will always be a hole that can't be filled. The baby's life might have been incredibly short, but that doesn't mean it didn't have any value. The little peanut probably meant the world to his mum, so by asking your friend how she is now, after all these years, will show her that she is not the only one thinking about her little one, and the life that could have been.

One of the hardest things for women in our situation is that we constantly have to justify our grief and fight to be heard, when we are already tired from pushing through the darkness. Anyone who acknowledges our loss, takes it seriously, and stands with us when we look up to the sky to our angel's new home, is definitely one very special and treasured friend. Remembering also shows that your sympathy doesn't have an expiry date. When a loss is fresh and raw, everybody is on board with remembering and trying to help. But, as many grieving parents know, there is a time limit to this. At some stage, we expect the parents to return to normal and fit in with our life where we do not talk about the past, a loss or anything ugly like that. This attitude clashes with the sufferer's new reality where the loss is as present as it was on the first day, but they get reminded that nobody cares.

So, if you remember - even if it is not with many words - you help your friend on many levels. To know that someone doesn't put a timeframe on them, accepts them as they are, and still talk about their baby, will trigger so many positive and powerful emotions that will provide healing. And, it can be done with just a few words from you. How awesome is that?

The parent trap.
As good parents, we only ever want the best for our children and to keep them safe from harm. If we could, we would take their pain and bear it ourselves so we can make sure our children don't have to suffer through the ugly and dark parts life throws at us. So, when your daughter or your child's partner suffer a miscarriage, such thoughts come to a grinding halt because the opposite just happened: your child experienced one of the most heartbreaking life events ever, and there was nothing you could have done as a parent to prevent it. It feels like the clocks are set back to zero and while life goes on, it is a different life – for everyone involved, including you.

A traumatising event like a miscarriage can become a defining moment in your child's life, and yours as well – your relationship might change, your bond might develop further, or tear as you walk along this new road where you share the grief of losing a baby. Pain will come in many forms to you and your child, which makes the time from now so very important as you will be needed on many fronts; most likely all at once. Your daughter will be in desperate need of help or your son, as the partner, may need a shoulder to cry on when his partner is not looking. It is an incredibly hard time for them – very emotional, draining, exhausting and overwhelming.

As parents, we want to help and stop our children's suffering; preferably with one clap of our hands, if possible. Of course, things are never that easy in life, and this life changing event has brought up so many challenges at once. You might wonder, how to go on from here? There are indeed, a few dos and don'ts for parents. Our urge to nurture and protect, clashes with the stark reality of pain suffered and hearts broken by a death so early, we can barely comprehend what happened and why.

We want to say many things at once, yet the words escape us, and what we say seems empty and pointless before we even speak. To make matters even trickier, communicating with your child has never been more important and more difficult than now. This is not a situation where we can say, "you had to learn this lesson eventually" or, "that's life" and finish up with a nice chat and a bit of a lecture. We are far from that. It won't matter how old or young your child is when they experience something as devastating as a miscarriage; all they will want straight afterwards is mum and dad, a cuddle and kisses, and shared tears. At a time where they feel lost, they want their childhood security; back where mum and dad fixed everything because they seemed to know almost everything. We all know, no one can fix this presenting situation, and trying to do so won't help either. I am sure you have many questions, worries and concerns, and your thoughts are probably bundled up into one big whirlwind of confusion. If that is the case, take a deep breath and remember that right now, it is about being there. Just be there. It is not about fancy words or smart explanations you might have come up with, or explaining what you found while reading stuff on the internet. Your child needs you. Be there for them, tell them you love them very much and that is that, for the time being. You don't have to reinvent the world for them, or tell them everything will be okay (who knows what will happen) – rather, focus on this very moment; right now, in the present. For the moment, that is all you have, and the future is not yet important enough to think about.

A few words should be said about our attitudes and expectations as parents. The reality we face with our children after loss is hardly a nice one, and definitely one that makes life seem like a minefield; never knowing when we stepped on to another thing that will blow up in our faces. When it comes to a loss like a miscarriage, you need to remember that there is no quick fix. Gone are the days when you were able to put a band-aid on and your kid was ready to play again. This situation will take time – lots of time.

So, if you have been a mum who is known to be a problem fixer for everyone and everything (which is a great attribute to have), be aware that your skills for quick solutions will do nothing here. They are simply not made to tackle such a tragedy, and if you insist on trying them to solve your child's problems, both of you will be in a world of pain, and unnecessarily so. Being a mum often means that you are in control of the situation, because the problem presented to you by your child can be fixed (such as a bloody knee or the question of what to wear to the formal). We are used to the expectation that we can help and solve our child's problem.
But now... losing a baby so early has taken everything to a whole new level. You will notice that you require either a whole new set of skills, or need to adapt existing ones. This can be quite scary and confusing. We spent so many years being parents, addressing problems, fixing up issues and striving to tackle things as they come. We should all be well equipped to handle anything, right? No. Parenthood is an incredible journey; one that compares to nothing in this life. We learn every day with our children and from our children, and we do acquire an immense set of skills we never knew was even possible! The challenges were tough; sometimes unbearable, we were exhausted beyond mentioning, struggled through the early years where life often seemed more like a living hell than an enjoyable journey. We have been through so much with, and because of our children, so this is just another bump in the road, right? No. Losing a baby your child never met, but loved and loves so fiercely, is something so terrifying that there are no words (hence the pressure of so many to keep quiet when a sufferer speaks up).

As parents, we are all well used to words, and to communicating with our children. But now, things have changed, as there is a new and very powerful player on the field – grief. So, if I say you might need to acquire new skills or adapt existing ones, then it means that this might be your first time meeting grief in such a way. Or, it may be that you know about grief, but need to adapt your coping strategies because this loss might be all new for you. But fear not – as a parent, you learned resilience, developed strategies to keep your sanity, and stayed immensely flexible while adapting to your ever-changing child as they were growing up. This is good news! All these qualities will come in very handy right about now, as you walk beside your child while they try and make sense of life after loss. You might surprise yourself with your ability to tune into your child's emotions again, as you did when they were thirteen and heartbroken for the first time. Trust yourself on this! You can do this. Always remember though – keep it simple. No fixing up, no lectures, no pestering, just be there.

As mentioned previously, the right communication is incredibly crucial right now. Your own emotions and your need to deal with your grief will make this a big hurdle every now and then. People often mistake asking questions for talking. While they are easily part of a conversation, to your grieving child they can be treacherous. Questions such as, "Why is it that I have to call you all the time?", "Why are you not talking to me?" or "Why don't you go and do...?" might sound good to your ears, because you do mean well and you want to help! Your child's welfare is your number one priority and that is great. It means you are on the right track and that you are committed to helping your daughter or son.

However, how we mean things is not always how the other side perceives them. Asking anyone who is grieving the question why they are not doing something, sounds like an accusation. When we are in highly upsetting situations, we don't have the energy to defend or explain our actions, which is why it is best to avoid such questions from the start. The simple fact also is, that when we are in such emotional turmoil, many actions are hardly rational or well thought through. You might be well aware of the fact it is Wednesday, but that fact might elude your child completely. They might not even be aware that time is moving on around them, while they are stuck in that very moment they lost their precious baby.

Of course, their behavior is highly worrying to you and as parents we need to make sure our children are okay. But here, you might hit yet another roadblock – what is there to say, if asking questions is not really an option? Keep it simple. It might be better - especially in the early days - to say you are worried, you love them very much and leave it at that.

In the early stages of grief, words don't come easy, if ever. The numbness and shock make sure that we all struggle to form a straight thought, and express it. As your child travels along their grief journey, talking will become more important and you will be needed to listen and if asked, give advice. But, during the time right after the loss, actions will speak louder than words. Are there week-old dishes in the sink at your child's place? Is the fridge empty and you are not sure if she has eaten properly for a while? Such situations are just perfect for you to get stuck into. You know what you are doing and you are actively helping your child to get better – slowly but surely. Be careful though, and don't just barge in and start to take over. Announce you will be coming over and that you intend to do some housework. And remember: no lecturing about how the place looks or that they should get a grip and do it themselves. If someone is in the middle of depression, clean dishes are not even close to making it on the to do list. You might be surprised about how your child reacts to this tragedy. They might not handle it as well as you expected them to, and you need to acknowledge that.

But, look at this situation as a chance to reconnect with your child on a different level that you didn't know existed before. It might sound weird to you, but times of crisis can actually be a chance to bond again, if your relationship is strained or maybe not quite where you would like it to be. It will require a lot of patience on your part, and a commitment to not exploit your child's current vulnerability. So, no emotional blackmailing or showing off your hurt feelings. If that is on your mind, then bonding is really not for you right now. Instead, think of things you always wanted to say to your daughter or son, but never had the chance to. For example, share a similar experience that you never told them about. Or, you could use this time to start over new, by demonstrating that you are really there for them now, and you commit yourself to helping your child.

If all of this sounds like a lot – it is. As a parent, we are in this for the long haul; for better or worse. As mums and dads, you will be there, long after good friends or family members dropped out because they think after a couple of months, one should be over such an event.

You as the parent, will need to stick it out until the end, and be there when the upward turn kicks in. You'll also need to be there when things are back to a normal sort of lifestyle. Amongst this all, there is also the matter of your own grief that you have to address. The tragedy that just rocked your child's world, is also yours. Most parents love to become grandparents, and spend lots of time with their grandkids; watching them grow up. You had a glimpse of a part of your life that you might have been waiting for, and now it is no more. While your first priority must be to look after your child and care for them in any way you can, there comes a point where you have to look at yourself and your grief.

There are a few strategies that can help you deal with the loss. Read up on it in the chapters 'Coping with loss' and 'Rituals' to get some ideas. It might be important to you to perform a ritual with your child. This could be a lovely bonding experience and could provide healing for you both. Let your child call the shots, though. If they are not up for it then you will need to accept that. At any time, be aware that you are a bystander in this terrible situation, not the main act, and that there is a good chance you will have to deal with your grief quietly, as your child might not be up to listening to what this tragedy has done to you. At least, not straight away.

Rest assured, that your daughter or son knows how hard this is on you, but they are tangled up in their own grief. Just like your child's journey, yours will also take time. Healing won't occur overnight, and you need to take one step at a time, just like your child does. The similarities between your journeys can be a great asset to further strengthen your bond and relationship. Grief is highly complex and surprises us with many unexpected feelings and happenings. One of them can be that out of something so devastating as losing a baby, results in newly gained strength, compassion and love between you and your child. Be open to where the journey takes you. The ending is open and you do have some control over where your path is taking you. Remember to take small steps and keep it simple – you will find your way and your pace, and you and your child can head towards better times together.

Advice
for Dads and Partners

After a miscarriage, it is not only mum's world that comes crashing down. Dads and partners are going through the same, or at least similar, motions. Their hopes and dreams are no more, they are left with a broken heart and an aching soul, just like the mums, and they struggle to come to terms with what's happened. The only difference is: not many care. It is quite a cruel situation to be in.

Many people close to a couple who lost a baby through miscarriage know that dad is just as hurt, but our attention turns almost naturally to the woman. She was the one carrying the child, after all. As the signs of the traumatic event are so devastatingly obvious on her, dads or partners seem to blend in with the background around her, and don't get noticed much. To make matters even tougher, they are expected to be the strong one now, and carry her through her toughest challenge.

There is no doubt about it; the dads or partners are in for a rough ride. The challenge ahead is complex and presents itself in different layers. It comes with no instructions on how to tackle them best, or in what order. It is all at once, overwhelming and way too much, yet to keep going is the only option. The path ahead is full of potholes, bumps and obstacles – and that is only your journey as the dad or partner.

Right next to your road to healing is your partner, who will rely on you to guide her through this stark darkness, where the silence wears heavy and the feelings only feel numb for so long. Her journey is in many ways the same as yours, but in just as many ways, it is totally different. This makes the time ahead for you so much more exhausting, and let's not kid ourselves: as the partner, you are in a very difficult and very painful position. By now, you might have a vague idea of your own pain that you carry with you, but it gets pushed into the background immediately. Most likely, your partner's pain is the one that dominates the day, the hours, the weeks and every waking moment. At times, that is the only thing you will have energy or time for, as her pain threatens to eat her up. She will lean on you for support, energy, love and an embrace so strong she can stand on her own legs, even though it is you that bears her weight. This sounds insane and it is.

Grief does so many things to us, and it spares nothing. If you thought the emotions couldn't get any more intense, they will, and if you think she cut a corner, a boulder comes rolling her way to knock her back to where she was stuck for so long. Sound like too much? You know, it probably is. There are not enough words in the world to really describe what you are in for – every journey is unique, which makes your support role so incredibly challenging. Before you go into panic mode though, do two things – breathe. And remember this: Right now, it is not about fixing your partner's grief. No one can do that. We don't *fix* grief; especially not someone else's, and the best outcome we can hope for is to learn to live with it and to manage it. So, you don't have to think it all has to go away and that her world should be filled with pink hearts, white bunnies and fairy floss, packed away from real life. Instead, allow her to grieve; allow yourself to grieve. This might sound easy and often, it is.

A lot of time, grief happens and expresses itself in many different ways – crying is only one of them. There can be anger, frustration and depression that accompany grief on its journey. Sometimes they happen all at once, and the wave of dark emotions will roll over you as you try and comfort your partner. Other times, there is icy silence, a numbness that suddenly returns, and every move and every thought seems sluggish as if you can't get it together for even five minutes. Grief has many surprises in store for us who lost a baby. This means there are no rules when it comes to allowing yourself to grieve. This is you, this is your partner, and no one has walked in your shoes before, or ever will. While this might sound terrifying or hardly bearable, it really is an opportunity. This is your chance to walk your path at a pace that is comfortable for you and your partner, and to give emotions their space and time.

We all need to shape our grief and bundle it up into a package (or a few smaller packages) so we can carry it around with us, without it dragging us down 24/7. But, to get to that point, we are sometimes required to delve into our grief and explore it with all its rawness and insanity. As you do that, there are a few very important things to remember: 1) There is no 'right' solution, so don't try and look for it, but the one that suits you and your partner to walk towards healing. 2) As there is no guidebook or clear rules to follow, you should take it easy. Be gentle with yourself, and don't put unnecessary pressure on yourself. Right now, it is not about coming up with a perfect plan for healing or developing a magic wand to wish the problems far away. It is so much more important that you are there for each other, mourn your loss and take one step at a time. And, if it is small steps you take, then that is what you do. 3) This is not a race or competition. Once you've joined the club of grieving parents, the rules of the normal parenting world don't apply. We don't compare milestones of our children to others. Grief is not about that, nor should it be.

While what you go through is similar to what many others have experienced before you (which is great when you seek help from those who understand), your and your partner's pain is not comparable. It is not about who is ready to face life the quickest, or who has reached a certain level of peace in the shortest amount of time. People from the outside will of course, have their opinions about when you should be 'over it'. Let's forget about that one straight away.

By now, you will know that 'getting over it' doesn't exist in our world. Don't be blindsided by other people's ignorance. It will only suck the energy out of you, and energy is still so very precious right now. You and your partner's journey through grief has only just begun, and you need to focus on allowing the journey to happen. As mentioned, there is no set pace and any attempt to control it, will only make it harder. Try and accept that going through grief is suddenly a speedy process when you least expect it, and also one that will slow down and drag on so badly that you think every second is as long as an hour. You will get stuck, and you move forward again. This is very much the nature of grief - as in, it doesn't have one size that fits us all. Some couples might be doing quite well for the first few weeks or months after their loss, and then – bam! The journey comes to a sudden halt, just like that.

Others may struggle through almost every minute of the day at the beginning, before speed picks up and helps the days go by faster, and in less gray and black tones than at the beginning of the journey. *Take your time.* This can't be stressed enough. As this is your journey, you need to take your time. For you, as the partner, this is especially important. Up until now, you will have carried two loads of grief; yours and your partner's, and chances are, you will be doing that a little while longer. So, take your time.

Your energy is precious, and we don't want it to run out because you tried to get everything fixed and her sorted in three months' time. Take one step at a time. It might be a really big step; it might be a step so small, you weren't even sure you took it. Another time, you might feel quite certain that you are both just walking in circles, talking about the same thing, the same emotion over and over again, and ten times more because it has such a strong grip on you. That is okay. To allow ourselves to heal means to keep going, in no set direction. Walking around in a circle might be entirely unhelpful when you try to find a place you need to get to but with grief, it is part of the way. It might even be needed to find clarity about something we didn't even know needed sorting out. So, remember – *take your time.* Move forward, inch-by-inch, meter-by-meter and eventually, in leaps and bounds. It is not about having an end goal that needs to be reached at all costs. You and your partner's journey to the new 'normal' after loss is a work in progress, with you doing almost most of the work.

You both walk on unsteady feet at the moment, still shaken to the core by your loss. Of course, you can't see the path in front of you, or the light at the end of the tunnel. Again, that is fine. Things will reveal themselves when we are ready for it. Besides, we don't know at this stage what will be at the light at the end of the tunnel. It is, of course, a life full of opportunities and a life you and your partner have the power to shape. But for now, we won't focus on what will be. For now, focus on each other and get each other through – one day at a time. It is not always about the abstract side of a loss that you need to deal with. There are a few practical things you can do to help her.

Depending on the stage of the pregnancy and how she has lost the baby, it will shape her journey from now on. You will surely agree that having to give birth to an eighteen-week-old baby (which is still considered a miscarriage) is one of the most horrible experiences your partner will ever have to go through. The whole idea of giving birth and going through labour, is to have a healthy and living baby by the end of it.

But, that has been denied to you and your partner. So, she had to deal with the pain, the labour, and the extremely deep emotions for a devastating result – a baby that has gone way too quickly and early. If your partner has lost your baby very early on, it comes with an experience that is so painful, that there are simply no words for it. The worst thing to ever discover as a pregnant woman, is blood in her underwear or in the toilet. More often than not, it means that life is fading away, slipping through our hands, and there is no way we can stop this.

A large number of women lose their baby at home; feeling every painful cramp, often alone with their incredible fear and terror. Other women need to go to emergency because their body is not able to terminate the pregnancy by itself, and an operation is necessary. There is nothing worse than lying on the operating table knowing that when you wake up your baby won't be with you anymore.

These awful experiences result in medical needs that have to be addressed, such as the bleeding afterwards. You can help her by making sure there are enough pads in the house, by keeping an eye on the bleeding, and if it doesn't improve, call the doctor or take her back to hospital. She will be weakened by her ordeal so much that physical side effects of it are the last thing on her mind. Yet they need to be taken care of, so her health won't get any worse. Practical help like the one just mentioned, might seem odd and somewhat cold and distant. Who cares about bleeding when her heart and yours just have been shattered into a thousand pieces? It seems too cruel, but if you look out for her now for such small and maybe silly things, her health will benefit in the long term.

Sometimes we have to remind ourselves of exactly that – the bigger picture, the future, the time when things will be better. You both might not think they start now, but by offering such help as mentioned, however insignificant it might seem now, you paved the way towards recovery and the many beautiful things to come once you both will be on steadier feet again.

Coming back to the present situation, you also need to make sure that she is eating something to recover her strength. Sit with her and have a meal together, even if it is not a big one. Make sure she changes out of her pajamas or trackies after a few days, so they won't get all grubby on her because she just couldn't be bothered getting dressed properly. If you have to go back to work, which is unfortunately quite often the case, call her regularly to see how she is doing. Organise for people to come over and spend some time with her, if you have such a support network available. If not, you might need to chat to your boss and see if you can get any time off, depending on what you do and how busy work is. More often than not though, men are required to do this insane balancing act between going about their daily routine (such as work) and dealing with an emotional catastrophe at home. This will be very taxing on you, no doubt about it. It is not only that you have to deal with so many things at once (and we haven't addressed your pain yet!) it is also very sudden and unexpected. You went from being a very happy couple, to a very unhappy one.

As we found out earlier, this experience will test your relationship and the outcomes can vary. A miscarriage will change you, and it will change your woman even more. Just don't give up when you hit the first rock. You never know what is around the corner. There could be sunlight, or there could be more clouds. That doesn't matter, though. Take each day as it comes and don't think of tomorrow. It is right now that you have to deal with, and it is right now where your partner needs you.

At any point on your grief journey after a rough patch, you both might be wondering whether the world post-miscarriage, will always be this bleak for you as a couple. There is no simple answer to this, as every journey takes its own path, has its unique bends and bumps and hills to climb. All journeys do have one thing in common – it is what you make of it. Many couples struggle through the darkest times of their lives, but come out the other end with often the same conclusion: This tragic event strengthened their relationship, they are now stronger than ever and bonded in a way they didn't realise until later. Those couples can lean on each other like never before, and they understand each other in a way no one else can, because they have been through the worst and they have survived – together. Of course, getting there meant a couple experienced a few heavy and dark hours, clashes and maybe even fights. That is not necessarily a bad thing. If you are able to stick together, these experiences will make you stronger and you will look at each other in a way you have never done before. Unfortunately, where there is a bright side, there is also a dark side. The bleakness of the early days might not change; it is possible for it to turn into a thick fog where a way out is just nowhere to be seen.

Losing a baby might bring a whole other level of pain for couples – a split, a divorce, a breakup. This is an incredibly tough situation when you realise grief has torn you apart, and the new normal you need to find will be without your partner. You both would have given your all, but a future together is not always the outcome of fighting through the troubles. This is a sad and heartbreaking fact of losing a child. For the time being though, this scenario is far away for you two, so don't worry about things that haven't happened yet. The end of your journey is unknown at this stage and that is okay. You will have to take one step at a time as mentioned – together, as well as alone.

If I say alone, I mean the time when you do get around to deal with your own grief, after the madness that is carrying yours and your partner's grief on your shoulders. There *needs* to be a time where things are all about you. We might forget about ourselves quickly when we are caught up in watching our loved one suffering, and we'd rather focus on getting them better, first. That is a very special trait and an important one, but also one that you have to put on the backburner eventually. There has to be a time where you ask yourself: How do I cope with *my* grief? Do I have any tools available to help me deal with my emotions? Do I think I am prepared for the rocky road ahead?

When we first meet grief, it is not only very draining, but also unpleasantly surprising. We don't know how to handle it because chances are high that we had never encountered this type of grief and loss before. When you and your partner were trying for a baby, the chances were probably even higher that you didn't consider the end result would be death, instead of a new life. So, if you realise that you are unsure if you are actually equipped and ready to deal with your grief, then that is normal. When we meet grief for the first time, we embark on a lifelong journey that has a few huge learning curves in store for us; some them are thrown at us straight away; some appear later in life. If you recall the chapter 'Grief 101', you might remember that we all go through stages of grief. How long these stages last is different for every one of us. Remember though, grieving and finding a way to manage it, is not a race or competition. It is your own unique journey and you have to find your path as you go along; sometimes one tiny step at a time.

But, let's focus on whether or not you think you have the necessary tools to deal with your own grief. It might be possible that you learned a few strategies unknowingly, by helping your partner. That would be great! If not, then that is fine, too and let's start now. It is not about developing some fancy techniques the world hasn't heard of yet. Quite often when it comes to our grief journeys, a good starting point is knowing what NOT to do.

For example, pretending nothing happened and going about your life as normal, or refusing to talk about it – these are not useful tools to have, to deal with grief. Instead, these should be warning signs. It will simply *not* do, and will put a lot of unnecessary pressure on you, your partner and your relationship. The hard truth is, we can't uphold something that no longer exists. Your life, pre-loss, has gone and is no more. The death of your baby is like a cut in your life – there was a before, and there is now an after, and you don't know how it looks. It is very possible that your life after your loss will be quite similar after a while to the life you had previously. Or, it might be entirely different because we just don't know what grief unleashes and brings to the surface in all of us. Only time will tell where your path will take you.

For now, we know that losing a baby is simply life shattering, and it needs to be acknowledged, recognised and dealt with. You might be wondering - how should you take a first step on to this unknown road? Perhaps, by simply telling yourself that it is not going to be light and fluffy, or a very enjoyable ride, but one you are on, nonetheless. What you will realise pretty quickly after a miscarriage, is that people around you show their true colours – most of them unintentionally, but they still do. In your case, as the partner, reality often looks more somber than your partner's.

People around you will focus on your partner first and foremost, and if you are lucky, one or two might ask how you are feeling and then move on to other things. The partner's pain is not something many people consider or think about, which may leave you in a very lonely place at a time where you need support. This will cost you some energy, but you need to take an inventory of your mates and see who will be up for the challenge to help you through this. As time and energy are precious, don't waste any time on the duds, as they are obviously not worth it. Even if it is your best friend, or the person you thought was your best friend. Confront them later, and tell them how disappointed you are (which is your right, by the way). But right now, look for someone else that can help you. Approach that person and have a chat. It doesn't have to be about the serious stuff the whole time – this is more about getting away from the tragedy for a little bit to either recharge your batteries, or to just clear your head and think about something else for a change.

Do you have family members that are capable of dealing with something like this? Don't talk to the ones with issues – they will make your pain worse. Reaching out to family now can hold many healing opportunities, as long as you pick the ones to talk to wisely. If you know your dad is not one to be able to deal with emotions, leave him out, or don't bother with your mum if you realise that she is not able to give you the comfort you need.

Unfortunately, this is a time of hard choices for you. But you need to get better, so therefore you need to pick people that can help you. Now is not the time to play the usual family games if you have those established, or to try and please people. People need to help *you,* and there will be a few around that are happy to do just that. It just might take some time to find them, and here again, grief can have a few surprises in store for us. You might find that someone is helping you who you least expected to. Don't wonder, but enjoy, and be thankful that they are there for you. If you have one or two good souls around you, then you are in a good starting position to walk the path ahead of you.

Of course, talking to others will help you along the way immensely, but it is not the only coping strategy you can add to your arsenal. Every now and then you will feel like you need to get away for a bit, and rightly so. All of a sudden, your life has turned into a series of heavy emotions rolling over you, so it is only normal wanting to take a step back from it all. Your sanity depends on it as well.

Do you have a hobby that you enjoy, such as playing footy or tinkering around in your shed? If yes, very good. These things will be able to provide you with much needed distraction and will give you a chance to recharge. You need this time to yourself and you are entitled to it – as long as it is well planned. I know, it sounds like as soon as something good is on its way, the negativity is already there, trying hard to put an end to all the good things you had in mind. Well, no, not quite. But let's not beat around the bush here - the emotional storm at home is still raging in full force, and that can be very tiresome.

The temptation will be huge for you to turn to your hobby and be consumed by it. Of course, it would be heaps more fun to spend hours in the shed on your own rather than dealing with a miscarriage and a partner in tears who's battling depression. The urge to escape the dark side of this experience is only normal, and very understandable. That is why the time to yourself is so precious and important, and we don't argue it. All it needs is a timer to it, so it won't take too long, but also isn't too short, either. Use your hobby as a distraction, but go about it consciously. Enjoy it and gather up strength, but be aware that you will have to go back to the real world, where the sun isn't shining yet. The same goes for your work. Staying longer at the office, or taking on another job so you have to work weekends as well, could seem like the golden ticket right now. Well, it is not. Your partner is lonely and isolated enough as it is right now, so don't join the crowd of careless people. Working long hours does look tempting as an escape route, and might be one you travel along with for a little bit. But remember how we said that grief throws us a few surprises along the way? Not all of them are pleasant; some can be pretty nasty if we allow them to be. Grief has no clear shape and it can be moulded into many things – a big force at the forefront of our thoughts, where it happily settles in. Or, it can be squished at the very back of your brain; struggling to get by, as your mind is filled with so many other things. It doesn't matter though, if it is tucked away or being ignored – it will always find a way to become more prominent, or even dominant again.

Grief needs to be dealt with – it is the only way it will settle back down again, and find its place amongst your emotions. Denying it is normal, ignoring it is understandable, but not addressing it is treacherous. Grief will come back around and bite you in the arse when you least expect it – it is just that nice. But always put things into perspective – don't feel bad about getting stuck into work or a hobby (there is enough guilt going around in your home, as it is). We have all been there; especially when we went through our denial phase while grieving.

The death of your baby is one tough and massive challenge for you. It tests you to no end, and seems a bit much most of the time. It is not only your partner that is expected to act a certain way in situations like these; it is you as well. The whole 'boys don't cry' nonsense is still firmly implanted in society, and so many of us think that like mindless zombies. Even better, if you do cry as a man, those zombies also have the audacity to judge you. But, just like your woman, you have to put yourself first (yes, eventually, you will have to do that, and before it is too late!) and do what is right for you. If it is all getting too much, ask for help. Don't play the proud man who can sort himself out. Easier said than done? Certainly. Many a woman looks at her man after their loss and worries herself sick about him. She can see that he struggles, but he closes up shop whenever she starts talking about the subject, or urges him to go and get help. She will ask around for a book, or anything that might help him because she knows he is close to breaking point, but not changing course. There is nothing worse than seeing the one that just saved you, deteriorate right in front of your eyes. And if we are honest, it is probably not pride that holds you back, but fear. Fear of what might come once those gates are opened; fear of how other people will react when you show your vulnerable side; fear that you might not be able to recover. My dear man, you are human and these feelings and thoughts are part of the process. There is clearly nothing wrong with you.

The journey through grief is more than once, an uphill battle. We are confronted with something we haven't experienced before, and we are lost in these moments because the way out is hidden somewhere, and we don't have a bloody clue how to get better. Coping strategies and mechanism from our earlier life just don't cut it. You will realise that you need to change something – in the middle of the storm when you are exhausted from everything, and you long for some peace and quiet. It is then that you have to gather up your strength and explore new ways and ideas on how to get out of this mess, and feel better.

A thought should be spared about professional help. It is available and you can access many services anonymously, so no one else other than you and the therapist know. Of course, the challenge is how to find a good therapist. That is not really a topic that you can bring up easily and solely rely on word of mouth – no one will tell you lightly or easily that they have seen a therapist; let alone tell you if he or she was any good. There is really only one guiding point you can stick to, if you like: if you ring up to make an appointment somewhere, inquire if the therapist has experience in the field of miscarriage; either personally, or by having treated others before. If you have picked someone, but the two of you just haven't clicked, don't keep on going. You need help now, and if the person sitting opposite you can't provide that, then don't waste energy. Rather, keep looking for someone who you feel comfortable with, and you think you can work with.

There is always the possibility of calling support groups for help, such as SANDS or Lifeline. The phone can give you some comfort as well – it is anonymous, but you are connected to another human being who is committed to helping you. The same goes for online support groups. They give you the chance to get something off your chest, but in a safe environment, because everyone there will have experienced a loss and will understand you better than most people in the world. Online groups also provide a certain amount of anonymity, because you can leave if it gets too much, or you can just log out for the day and return later.

Above all, be honest with yourself. Don't deny feelings that come to the surface, such as anger, or maybe guilt. Those two are very common and very stubborn companions during this challenging time. Were you not super excited about the news of becoming a dad? Did you have doubts about parenthood and how it would affect your life? Did you ever consider running away from it all? If so, you are not alone with this. Many a man (even ones in committed relationships) thought about getting the hell out, before the little one arrived. We are not going to discuss if that is a good thing or not right now, because we are going to focus on the guilt.

Do you feel guilty for having had those thoughts; do you think they were responsible for everything going down the drain, because you weren't 100% there for your partner? Such thoughts are normal, as they are part of your grieving process, but they are hard to handle, nonetheless. The challenge will be to accept that you had them, and to realise that they had nothing to do with what happened. This is not your fault, as it is also not hers. Anyone with half a brain thinks about the massive changes ahead when they find out their partner is pregnant. There is no need to feel guilty about a human reaction like this. The same goes for anger. What a powerful emotion that is! And, one that needs to be dealt with, because bottling it up inside is a really bad option. With this emotion, comes another task, which is to accept that it might never quite go away. Anger can flare up any minute; even years after an event.

It is now about managing this emotion, and there is quite a lot you can do to let go of that anger. Very effective strategies point towards sport, where you can run, box, row, push or swim out your emotions. It has to be a deliberate act though, where you focus on the anger and visualise how it leaves you as you punch, kick or push through your exercise. There are however, many other strategies available that can provide healing for you. Check out other suggestions in the chapter 'Coping with loss' or 'Rituals' if you are unsure where to get started. On your journey through grief, you will have noticed that one person is never far from your side – your partner. Just like she turned to you for support and help, you should now turn to her. You know each other, you enjoy each other's company in happy times, and now is an even better time to huddle up close and weather the storm together – you might have had this experience already, when you helped her through her darkest moments.

So many people surround us, yet the ones that truly understand us are few. This was the case when your partner struggled, and it is quite likely the case for you now. So, turn to your partner and work your way through the next hurdle together. This won't always be easy, because you both deal with powerful emotions and dark thoughts. Yet, herein lies your strength – you know all too well what the other one is going through, because you experience it as well. Of course, everyone feels emotions differently, and maybe not as strong. But you get the gist of what is going on, and that is knowledge that no one else is likely to have around you.

In the middle of it all, it might seem funny, but it is often very important for women to see their partner's grief. It shows her that you are in it just as deep as she is. Sharing your pain can be very powerful and helpful to her. You are not shutting her out; you are letting her in, and you allow her to see a side of you that is mostly hidden away. While this could be seen as a risk (which is understandable), you should remember that it will be a growing experience for both of you. It will make you stronger when you see each other's pain, and actually talk about it. You might not believe it, but she wants to hear your fears and wants to know if you are dreading a specific date, or if you have thoughts that freak you out. After a miscarriage, we are often so caught up in ourselves, we don't realise that there is fog all around us that threatens to swallow our partner. Suddenly, we are all alone and wonder how we got there. Wasn't it just yesterday that you shared something beautiful together?

Drifting apart is the greatest danger you will face after such a traumatic event, and while some distance will arise; don't let it become part of your daily life. Go and search for your partner again, because she will be your ally, greatest support and help right now. Of course, there will be fights and the feeling your partner doesn't understand you, but more importantly, there will be heaps more times where you know exactly what is going on. This is something incredibly precious right now, and something you will come to cherish and rely on as time goes by. It sounds ridiculous at the moment, but this very trying time will make you so much stronger – both individually, and as a couple.

On your journey through grief as a couple, there are two more subjects you will have to address, that will keep their own challenges in store for you. Number one is sex. It could be that you think sex might be a good way to release stress and tension. You are of course, not wrong there, but in the current situation this could be a touchy subject. It will depend on your previous sex life and how active you have been. Was sex always your go-to thing to help deal with stress? Has she ever been on the same page as you when it came to that? If so, then maybe sex is the way to go for you two. However, there are a few things you need to be aware of before you get going. Don't get into it straight away – her body needs a recovery period from the shock it just suffered. You might want to check out the chapter: 'What to expect from your body afterwards' to learn what is currently going on with her.

If you'd like to have sex to try for another baby, it is recommended that you wait until your partner has had at least one normal period, so keep that in mind. When it comes to trying again, a few chats about it will be best, as trying for another pregnancy will offer its own challenges (check out chapter 'Trying again' for more info). However, sex in your current situation doesn't have to be about conceiving at all. It can just be about stress release, being intimate with each other, and enjoying each other.

In fact, being intimate doesn't always have to lead to sex, therefore your partner and you might be able to reconnect on a deeper level by enjoying private moments, without the actual act of sex. It is really up to you. Just talk about it first, and then see where it leads you. Rediscovering each other as sex partners at this time can be very healing, and also help make your relationship even stronger. Number two on this list is no less confronting. As we deal with our grief and find our way slowly, we know that many nasty surprises await us. It could be that you suddenly feel emotions you never thought you would have, think about issues that you know are not healthy, yet you do it anyway. We can't help it, as the desperation about not knowing why we lost our little ones can drive us nearly nuts. We want to blame someone or something so we know this or that caused all our turmoil and pain. When we look around for someone to blame, one person will come into our firing line first: your partner. This is quite tempting, but it is just oh so wrong. Don't go down that path. If you do, a whole new world of pain will open up. This is a very tricky situation to be in, and it's not one you can get out of easily. Simple advice is: Don't do it.

Don't tell her she failed you, because the only thing she is supposed to do is to carry that baby and she failed. Don't tell her it's all her fault that she lost your baby. Stop and breathe if such thoughts cross your mind. Imagine what they will do to her if they are ever said out loud. How devastated, humiliated and crushed she will feel if you, the closest person to her, would say such nasty things. Stop the blame. It has no part in your life, or hers. It is poison and causes destruction that can't be fixed.

Of course, if such thoughts occur, they need to be dealt with properly, so they are gone once and for all, and won't come back. The strategies suggested earlier to address your grief could be helpful here as well. You need to find an outlet that will help you clear your head, and will enable you to move away from such dark thoughts. It could be that you need to write them down to get them out of your system, or you might need to talk to a mate about it, or even a professional. But above all, remember: This is nobody's fault. Not yours, not hers, no ones.

You loved this baby just as much as her and that is the one thing to remember – love, and not blame. Love has led to this little life; love will lead you to more happiness. Blame on the other hand, will send you into a downward spiral quicker than you can say 'stop this' and will fill your life with emptiness, despair and no hope. Of course, to deal with this step is very hard and will take time. But shaking off the blame is worth it. You have come so far; now don't throw yourself out of the race, so close to the finish line. Once you've learnt how to live with such a terrible loss, a new chapter in your life and hers will begin, and you sure as hell wouldn't want to miss that, right?

What's the big deal?
Dealing with Indifference

We put a lot of our attention on those around us, and how they can best support us. It is incredibly important to have a good support network around you – not only to get through the hardest part of grief, but also to have people to fall back on when the rest of the world is being indifferent, careless and just not that interested in being kind to people recovering from loss, and finding their way into life again.

When it comes to losing a baby early in pregnancy, it appears everyone around you has an opinion (however uninformed they may be) and feels not only very entitled to sharing it without asking, but most people also think they are actually doing something good.

We all know by now, that they are neither helpful, nor entitled to any opinion about your loss, but we also know, it won't stop them from talking some more. And just when you feel you are ready to say something for once, you get the silent treatment of the worst kind. All of a sudden, there is this enormous pressure from everyone around you to be quiet, to not talk about your miscarriage, to hide away your feelings and struggle. The time after such a loss like ours is difficult on so many levels. It is not only that you have to come to terms with your loss and learn to live with it, but you also have to 'fit in' to regular, normal life after yours has been turned upside down. In a way, returning to 'normal' life is a good thing, because routine often provides a surprising amount of sanity.

At the same time, it is also impossible to return to your 'normal' life – nothing is the same anymore, you are not the same person anymore, life makes little sense at the moment, yet it goes on, all around you. So how to go on now? Sadly, there is not a set path that you can follow, or a recommended approach. The heartbreaking loss of babies is still taboo in our society – it is something we just don't talk about. And that is unfair, silly and highly inappropriate. It is easier said, than done, that you should stand up and say out loud what you want people to know, and how you think they should react to your loss.

During our journey, we will all come to a point where we will be saying things out loud, and we have to. The world needs to know about our babies, because they were real, they were here and most of all, they were and always will be loved! It is up to you in which way you would like to say it out loud. It can be that you say your baby's name out loud before you got to bed, say it quietly during the day or on special occasions, or tell a whole crowd of friends.

Considering though, that society reacts very indifferently to our loss - especially if it was early on in the pregnancy - it is extremely hard to say anything, let alone out loud. Perhaps, keep that step in mind for later (also check out chapter Rituals, and how speaking of your baby can indeed help you). For now, there are a few things you can do, that can help you feel better when faced with all the terrible and thoughtless things people say to you (and just won't stop blabbering on about).

Get rid of it. Don't let the hurt eat you up. Talk to someone who understands – your partner, a close friend, or someone from the baby loss community. Simply because you are expected to be quiet, doesn't mean you have to be. Share your pain, share your anger about a silly comment you had to listen and respond to. It will make you feel so much better to get it off your chest. Whoever you talk to might not have an answer for you, but they will understand because they either know you very well, or have been through the same, and just know how it feels when you were knocked down to the ground by ignorance.

If you are reluctant to talk to someone face to face, there is always the online world available to you, with understanding people ready to listen to you. Choose wisely though, and try and find a forum or group that you feel comfortable with (SANDS for example, has a closed group on Facebook where bereaved mums and dads can meet and chat). Once you have found such a group, you will be amazed how comforted you will feel, being surrounded by people that just get you – without many explanations necessary.

Put it in a letter. It could be that you have serial offenders in your life that repeatedly come up with hideous things to say, thinking in all seriousness that they are helping you to move on! Those people are rather tricky and there is no point talking to them, because they don't understand one very important thing: For us, there is no such thing as 'moving on' - as in, we'll just 'forget what happened'. Yes, life goes on and eventually we will come out of our darkness, but we haven't moved on or 'gotten over it'. All we do is learn to manage our pain – some days, we are really good at it and some days, we are not.

We pick up our life but we 'move on' with a lot of pain hidden away in our hearts and souls. Don't waste any time trying to explain to a serial offender – they won't understand, it is that simple. Instead, write them a letter. Get everything on paper that you want to say to them – how upset you were about their stupid comment, how it feels to hear such terrible things, and what mindless idiots they are. Just write, and don't mind your manners for once, if it makes you feel better. The thing about writing such a letter is that you get it all out, but you don't send it off. It is not for their eyes, it is for yours.

Just like any writing you might have done previously to have a go at the universe for the unfairness of it all, repeat it now. If you like to use swearwords, then knock yourself out. It is your letter and if it feels good, then pepper your letter with a few good ones. Make sure though you destroy the letters after you are done. Release all the negative emotions surrounding them, and set yourself free.

Try and have a laugh. You might think this is a bit sarcastic? Maybe it is. At first, when the first few inappropriate comments are hurled at you, you won't laugh at all; you will cry. The first few are always a shock, and you have been completely unprepared to hear such nonsense in a time where you are very vulnerable and upset. But, as time goes by, you start to look for ways of how to cope with this very unpleasant occurrence. Friends of mine started giving out awards for the dumbest or most hurtful comment they heard. They would ring each other up and tell the other what they were told; by doctors, colleagues, so called friends, family and others. Of course, they would talk first about how it made them feel, and consoled each other. But, once they felt better, they made up fake awards and hypothetically handed them out to people: the most inconsiderate doctor, the worst family member, and so on. It put a smile on their face and that is a massive achievement in times of grief. It might not work for you, but maybe give it a try. Call the awards what you want – award for extraordinary douchebaggery, award for careless stupidity, or loser comment of the week! The idea is to realise that whoever said something to you is the person in the wrong, and *not* you. You have done nothing wrong, but you are the one that needs to feel better. So, do something that makes you laugh, if you can. Don't let the idiots around you spoil your newfound grip on life.

Be creative. If you've taken to writing, painting or any other creative way to deal with your loss, now might be another time to get that strategy going again. It is crucial that you get your anger, disappointment, hurt and tears out, so you can leave what has been said to you behind. If you feel that being creative is just the right thing for you now, then go for it. Just like earlier, your end product is for your eyes only if you wish. The activity you pick needs to help you and no one else.

Steel yourself. Of course, there are many other things you might think of that will help you deal with situations where you are cornered by an ignorant person, and the shock and pain prevented you from a good come back (if there are any). But, if we are honest, the best defence most of the time here is not a good offence. Far from it. If you take to responding every time, you will waste a lot of energy trying to educate someone who doesn't get the problem in the first place. It will be like telling a banana it is now a peach – absolutely pointless. So, don't waste your energy fighting windmills, and pick your fights wisely. No one says you have to be quiet all the time, and more than likely, you will have someone close to you that just keeps hurting you with comments or complete silence. Maybe your sister, mother-in-law or favourite aunt did not react the way you were hoping she would. If that is the case, give it a go, and give some back if you are up for it. People like that are most likely to learn something out of it, and it might make you feel better to get some of your disappointment off your chest. After all, simply because we are pressured into being silent after our losses, doesn't mean we have to take it all and say thank you at the end. Also, you have had enough mountains to climb and challenges to face, so a bit of attitude on your part can't hurt. Let them hear you roar!

As mentioned, for everyday life, two challenges remain with you: One, you need to learn how to live with your loss and rebuild your life after it, and two, most people won't care one bit what you have been through. It is so unfair. You have just experienced one of the most devastating things there possibly is, and the wound is so deep, you wonder how much more pain might come your way.

While you come to terms with that, only a few will give you a helping hand throughout. The thought that no one cares is incredibly hard to swallow. But it is one that will stick around. To this day, I wish someone other than my hubby and I would acknowledge our first baby; remember what we lost, and just ask how we are now. But, no such thing. We are just expected to get on with it, and the heartlessness of it all is tough to stomach. It hurts so much, it will threaten to eat you up. But don't let it come to that; it is simply not worth it. So, steel yourself for the world outside your door that only sees your surface, and doesn't really want to look any deeper. Most days you will be just fine, but on others, you will struggle. That is absolutely fine. Just look back on your journey and see how far you have come! Be proud of what you have achieved, and most importantly, know that your baby always has a place in your heart and soul from this day onwards.

There is nothing to be ashamed about and don't even start questioning if you are entitled to such thoughts. You are. It was your baby, you were his mummy, and if someone else thinks that is a load of rubbish, then so be it. Imagine how much they miss out on life because they have a heart of stone, and not one caring bone in their body.

You will have noticed that by now, many roadblocks appear in your way towards healing. They are literally never ending, and this one right here we have to talk about, has intense destructive power. I mentioned this one in the chapter 'Advice for Dads/partners' as well, because it can affect both sides, and if this roadblock occurs, it needs to be blown up quickly, otherwise it could end your journey instantly. I am talking about blame. That is a very human thing to do – if something goes wrong or is just not how we want it, we look around to blame someone or something. It is what we do. We blame the weather for a crap weekend, the traffic for being stressed and so on, and so forth. Part of this is normal and in most cases, it evaporates into thin air as soon as we are able to get it off our chest.

In your current situation, blame, however, is much more powerful. You might have come across it already because certain thoughts have gone through your mind.

Maybe you thought your partner's sperm is probably lame and there is something wrong with it. How else could this baby not survive? He *must* have lazy swimmers! Or perhaps, he lived so unhealthily, he must have damaged his precious cargo to the point where it wreaks havoc; rather than helping to create a tiny human. How useless is he?

If issues like that are part of your journey, stop right there. Literally, stop, take a breath and calm down. To blame the ones nearest and dearest to us seems like the easy way out – however, they are not perfect, and we knew that all along.

Well, nobody is perfect, and it's not about that, anyway. You are about to walk into one hell of a trap, and one you might get out of, but you will be alone afterwards. Yes, it happens that we want to blame our partner for something, but your situation is not one of these scenarios. What happened is not your fault and it is not his. No one is to blame. *No one* is to blame. Life post-miscarriage is incredibly fragile and we are vulnerable to such poisonous thoughts. We want explanations and we want to know who did this. But, don't give in to those thoughts. If you do and say them out loud, you will wake monsters that you didn't think existed. Imagine how he will feel when he is being told he didn't perform; that he is not good enough? After everything you have been through, don't throw in the towel now. You need each other now, more than ever. Don't push him away or even worse, send him away for good with such hateful comments. Blame will do that to us, if we let it. You have to remember that this is not your fault and not his, and that your precious little one was created out of love from both of you. Right now, focus on love, as it will save you and guide you towards a life that can be filled with happiness again. Blame will just destroy anything you might have, and ensure you will never get it back.

Naturally, with thoughts as strong as the ones just discussed, we need ways to deal with them, so we can rid ourselves of them and their negativity. You need to acknowledge such thoughts, and you need to find a way to get them out of your system – for good. As always, there isn't just the one strategy that fits the bill. Think about what will help you. Write it all down, talk about it, and run until you are too exhausted to think. Whatever works best for you, do it. Just make sure it is not self-destructive or will hurt anyone else. Give yourself time to deal with the issue at hand. You need to be in a calm state of mind to say goodbye to blame and its poisonous buddy thoughts. Turn to others in a similar situation, and ask them how they dealt with it. Seek support from people you trust and feel comfortable with. And, always remember how far you have come and how strong you have been. Yes, there is another and very massive roadblock in front of you, but it isn't the one that will defeat you. Smash through it and keep going, with your partner by your side. You deserve it.

Acceptance
What is that?

When we come across things in life that are unexpected (good or bad), we are taught that we have to accept them, in order to move on with life. That is how it works, right? This approach can work quite well in various situations in life – losing a baby is probably not one of them.

How can we ever accept that we lost something so precious and innocent, gone way too soon and with no explanation? Most likely, we will all have tried at one stage or another on our journey, to accept our terrible fate in an effort to 'move on' from it and to get back to a normal life – whatever that is. More often than not, this step though, is incredibly hard to conquer. The question 'Why?' or 'Why me? Why my baby?' will pop up constantly, and won't leave you alone. How can we ever accept that losing a baby - a tiny human at the very beginning of life - was not meant to live?

Can this be done? So many strong and conflicting emotions are tied to this step and stand in our way of finding a new life balance; where we are able to deal with our loss and still participate in the 'normal' life that goes on around us. Accepting our fate seems to be the only way to go, otherwise we will never be able to enjoy the brighter sides of life again, go to work and have those chitchats with others that are part of human daily interaction.

Once more, finding acceptance is a very personal journey and there isn't a right way or a wrong way (haven't we heard that a few times already?). You also might remember that 'acceptance' was part of the seven stages of grief, where it says that we will come to accept what has happened, and then go forwards calmer and happier. In reality, this is the outcome we all seek, but it can come with different names. Acceptance is just one of them, but there are others and we will have a look at how we can come to peace with our terrible loss.

When we look at accepting what has happened, it feels like we have to put a tick behind the event to indicate to the outside world that we are now done with it and won't ever talk of it again because, you know, we accepted it. That is terribly daunting and far from the truth. Closing the chapter of loss and leaving it behind is not how it works. 'Accepting' that our babies died seems exactly like that though – one thing crossed off the list, one test done, to never speak of it ever again.

As we all know, this is far from reality. While others would prefer we never speak of our loss ever again, we will always have the urge to do it so that we can heal. We will always remember our tiny ones – sometimes all the time, sometimes occasionally. But we will always know that something is missing – that little life that went too early and that we never got the chance to meet. Society might think it's a common event, but for us, it was life changing and can't be ignored or erased. Emotions and realisations like these make it hard to take this important step of acceptance. There is pressure connected to it; to do something we don't necessarily feel comfortable with.

So, what can we do instead of trying to find 'acceptance'? Integrate your loss in your life. It may sound weird, but we have heard the idea behind it before: It basically means consciously learning to live with our loss and making it part of our life, instead of trying to accept it. It takes the definite aspect of acceptance from it, and turns things on its head a bit. Rather than fighting every inch of the way to get to acceptance, we instead acknowledge the loss. It will always be remembered and it is now part of our new life, just like going to work is, or having a new hobby. We don't ignore the death of our little one, we are not silent about it, and we give it as much room in our new lives as we think is best.

Now, you might wonder how you are supposed to integrate your loss into your life. Once more (it sounds repetitive, doesn't it?), it is up to you. It doesn't necessarily mean that you have to do a grand gesture or perform a special ritual.

You can, of course, if it feels right to you and you notice it does help you come to terms with events. If you consciously integrate your loss into your new normal, then it does mean you celebrate your bub's birthday or anniversary and you prepare for it in whatever way is best for you.

As discussed in the chapter 'Rituals', one year you might feel like something a bit bigger, next year you want to spend a quiet and reflective day. All of this is fine and is part of integrating your loss. You are not denying it, you are not downplaying it, and you are making it what it is: your loss, which is now forever connected to you. This is not about making your life harder, though. It is just one possibility on how to learn to live again after your baby died.

The objective of integrating your loss into your life is that a certain weight is lifted off your shoulders, and you feel you can breathe a bit easier now most of the time. Also, by choosing to integrate your loss into your new normal, you will take control and decide how your loss will be part of your life – it can take up a lot of room or only little, or you can change your approach whenever you feel that what you are currently doing doesn't suit you any longer.

The main thing is that you are calling the shots and following your heart, rather than trying to fit into a concept that was made up by others.

Integrating your loss might of course, not be your cup of tea. It doesn't feel right to you? Fair enough. It is time we look at the 'traditional' model again and check out finding 'acceptance' a bit more in depth. We have heard about the downsides to it, but certainly, there are good points to it, too. If you want to give it a go, then go ahead. As you go along, you will find out for yourself if finding acceptance is the right thing for you, or if you like, to switch to integrating your loss into your life. If we want to try and accept what has happened, we first need to go back to the start when everything was so raw, and we refused to believe what just happened.

Everything was just painful and to have that as a constant part of our lives was definitely not an option. As a result, we hold on to everything that is connected to our loss and unfortunately, most of it is very negative – dark emotions, reactions that hurt us and others; a constant state of turmoil. When we refuse to acknowledge something so powerful as a loss, there are no happy times involved. Instead, our refusal to accept brings all of those negative feelings back up again (same goes for refusal to integrate your loss into your life, of course).

I know what I am talking about here, as I really took my time to come to terms with my miscarriage. I just absolutely and completely refused to accept what happened to me. I did not let it go, and it kept coming back to me. I kept having all these negative thoughts and every pregnant woman I saw seemed to cross my path just to tease me. It was awful. But still, I refused to let go. I was still angry at myself, at my body, at the whole world.

One day I came across a sentence that said, 'What we refuse to let go, will come back to us'. And how true is that? If we don't accept what has happened, the negative thoughts and emotions keep coming back, we start our downward journey again towards depression, self-doubt or even hatred, and end up feeling like total crap. Letting go and accepting is the only available solution here that will help you feel better. How you let go is up to you, and a few suggestions will follow. Let me just tell you first, how I managed to get some peace of mind for myself. I kept saying to myself 'I accept my miscarriage, I accept my miscarriage, I accept my miscarriage'. Not out loud, of course (society is not there yet for that kind of stuff). I kept repeating it in my head and a funny thing happened: It indeed lost its power. Suddenly, it seemed like a weight was taken away from me, I could breathe again and look at my life with a new perspective. It was quite amazing, because the tragedy suddenly seemed more manageable. Saying that sentence out loud enabled me to finally and fully grasp what had happened, and to acknowledge it. And, it was not like the full-on slap in the face that I expected.

So, the key to achieving acceptance is to tackle it in a way that takes the suspected power away from it. We need to turn the whole thing into something we feel we can grasp and acknowledge much better, because it is no longer this dark, overpowering and emotional mess. Achieving acceptance is all about regaining control over the situation and the feelings involved as best we can, and by actively deciding what this control looks like, and what we want to do with it.

Talking to yourself might not be your way of letting go and finding acceptance. There are other ways, and they are as individual as you are. Before we look into a few options as to how to approach the matter at hand, be aware of the following, though: finding acceptance can take a really long time. It might be years until you are in a place where you can say, "I remember this pain, but I choose now, not to go there'". We all have to learn to master the lessons life throws at us. Right now, it is more about making that ground under your feet steadier, stronger and more reliable, so you feel like your life is moving forward again, rather than going around in circles, or being caught in an endless loop of misery and chaos.

We need to make the mess more real; something that we can grasp and hold on to. Quite often it helps to try and make that mess visible. Saying something out loud can do that trick, but so can other things. What does the mess look like to you? If you are the visual type, pick up a pen, paintbrush or pencil and nail your ideas, thoughts and emotions down on to paper or a canvas. Then, take a step back and look at it. How does it feel now? Has that dark cloud started to lose its power? Is the term miscarriage a little less frightening to think about, or even say? If yes, then you have found a possible way to walk towards acceptance with big steps. It could be that you are done after one painting, or you might return to a fresh piece of paper or a canvas later on and tackle the whole issue once again. It doesn't matter if you do that on a daily basis or every couple of months. It is more important that you acknowledge the urge or wish to sort this mess out a bit, and do something that you know works for you. By doing that, you will soon notice that this darkness starts to shrink and that it loses its grip over you. You will be feeling more at ease, calmer and ready to come face to face with your tragedy, and accept that it happened.

Writing can have the same effect, if you feel comfortable with that, and have used it before to cope with your loss shortly after you lost your baby. Many people before us have found that once you have written something down, it loses its power over you because you can see it in black and white.

Writing something down can have a cleansing effect, but it can be draining as well, because quite often, the emotions literally flow out of you through your pen. Not to worry though, because just like with painting, you can put your pen down anytime and return to it later, because you don't want to feel tormented at this stage. You might wonder what you should write down. Well, pretty much anything that comes to mind. Some of it might end up being a poem; other parts will look more like a letter. Another attempt is sentence after sentence, with no particular order or sense. It is not about making sense at this stage; it is about regaining control, and if rambling on for a bit on paper helps you to get there, then that is just perfect. No one needs to see what you are writing down, if you don't want them to.

Like goodbye letters to your precious baby, you can burn what you have put on paper and release it that way. The good thing about trying this creative approach is that it gives you the possibility to do it anywhere, anytime; whenever you need it.

The path to acceptance (and the same goes with integration) will bring back some good companions of yours: emotions. Strong, powerful and still raw. While it probably felt good to hold on to anger sometimes (after all, that emotion can give you power and a drive to do something) there is no room for it in the letting go process. If anger is still part of your journey, now is a good time to come up with some creative anger management techniques.

As we said earlier, by painting or writing, that dark cloud crowding your space is literally coming off you, and is being transformed into something else. We have to do the same with anger, or any other strong emotion that can be highly destructive. You will need to do something that you feel comfortable with. This could be working with a professional to get anger under control, or you can find something in your house that has punching qualities, like a beanbag or a big pillow. Once more, try and punch the living shit out of it, focus your anger on that beanbag or pillow, and go nuts. Screaming while doing this is also helpful. It will exhaust you and calm you down so much, and the amount of anger or frustration you release is astounding. Weird approach to achieving acceptance, you might say? That is a good point, right there. You don't have to go all cave man, but you need to be aware that you are dealing with very strong and powerful emotions that have a great force behind them. That force has the potential to take over your life now, even more than ever before. You are so close to the end goal (acceptance), so they are roaring up again and will try to pull you down once more, because you are putting up one hell of a fight. If you don't deal with your emotions right now, they will eat you up and the worst thing will happen: The miscarriage will define you. It will take over your life, instead of being part of it. And, there is not much happiness around in that kind of life.

As you battle through this stage of your journey and are really close to the goal, you need to consider a few things. While cutting through the last bit of crap that is hanging around you, make sure you don't hurt any others around you; not your partner or your kids, if you already have any. By now, you know that lashing out at someone (most likely your partner) is part of the deal, and that you might fall back into old habits is only normal. However, if you feel like it is getting too much - get away. You have a right to your emotions; after all, it was and is your ordeal. But don't take it out on your closest loved ones; it is not their fault that you have to deal with all of this. Get focused and stay on target, to avoid causing negativity and darkness. Instead, let that new phase of your life begin in full.

Part of reaching acceptance is quite often, to relive your darkest hours in order to realise how far you have come. It might be that you will take a few steps back first, instead of going forward. Going backwards a bit is okay, and happens to all of us. The trick is to avoid as many triggers as possible, so you don't go back to hiding under your blanket or being silenced by depression again.

A very important trigger to look out for, is pregnant women and babies. What most people perceive as just wonderful, can be absolute torture for us. It is important to acknowledge that, if it happens to you. If you do find it hard to deal with women who are pregnant or have babies, there is only one thing to do - stay away from them. Even if they are your best friend or sister, or whatever. It will probably just hurt too much. Trying to be cool about it won't work, so don't waste any energy on that - it is literally not worth it. On your path to acceptance, jealousy might be a good companion of yours – so are feelings of injustice and unfairness.

Now it is more important than ever, to focus on yourself. Don't focus all your thoughts on others, and what wonderful lives they must have; considering they are pregnant or have a baby in their arms. Of course, it is fine for you to feel grumpy or angry about the unfairness of it all, and you are allowed to have a little pet hate about it, but it needs to stop there. By looking at other women and comparing yourself, you deny yourself your uniqueness, and you start to put yourself down. That is just not the way to go. You have your life, and it is only you who can live it. So, let's focus on that, rather than on the lives of others. It is not easy to get to that point. Our minds are ridiculously powerful and allow negative thoughts such as jealousy in easily, and they always have a real ball messing with us. And here again, life just has another challenge in store for us: We need to allow these not so pretty feelings to have their own place in our journey, but we have to control them, too. So, it is very understandable to feel jealous when you see a pregnant woman, or even be angry and think that someone is teasing you or playing with your feelings when they parade their big belly in front of you. How could you not feel this way after what has happened to you? But, as we established earlier, some of us have been chosen to go through the hell that is miscarriage, while others get spared, and that is not their fault either. Can we change that? I am afraid not.

If you are trying to change it, those negative emotions and dark thoughts will eat you up, and destroy any chance you have to lead a happy and fulfilling life. Be gentle with yourself and give it time. Your wounds are deep and don't heal quickly; even if we sometimes wish they would.

Also, remember that you don't have to grind your teeth and put on a brave face all the time. You can say no, and sometimes you have to, in order to protect yourself. If it is simply too much for you, ask pregnant friends or family members to give you a break. Maybe don't see them for a little while after you've explained what you are going through. If you are lucky, they will realise all of this by themselves, and won't bother you too much. But, in case they don't, you will need to gather up your strength and put a hold on the baby talk. Right now, it is not about pleasing others or doing the right thing by them. It is about what is right for you.

After all, you have come quite a long way. You recovered slowly, but you are not quite there yet. So, keep focusing on yourself a little bit more, and do what is right for you; even if that means not doing a complete shop because you couldn't bring up the courage to walk past the baby aisle in the supermarket. That is okay. You will walk past that aisle again in the future. But right now, it is about avoiding it, so go ahead and do just that. Quite often, acceptance is a step by step process and as it is your life, you determine which step you take, and when and how big that step will be. Unfortunately, as we live in a society that is programmed to like absolutely everything about babies (well, everything about healthy babies, anyway) it could be that a few people don't understand it when you ask for some space for yourself, or don't appreciate what you are doing. Obviously, that will hurt you, but better to take that lesson and learn from it right away. Those people can safely be deleted from your address book. They are simply not worth your time. Remember, this is only temporary. You will be in a place again where you can talk about babies and being pregnant. If there are people in your life that don't get that you need some time right now, then they are not worth your time.

By the way, talking about all baby related stuff would be a good indicator as to where you are at in reaching acceptance. You will notice that one day it won't bother you as much because you have learned to accept that this has happened to you. So, keep your energy focused on your inner development, because it will be your best and only guide you towards finding peace with this chapter of your life.

No matter which way you choose, acceptance or integration, one thing is clear: Permanent closure is not going to happen. Too deep is our pain; too strong are the memories, to ever forget what has happened. We can try (and we will, have all been there), but a loss this profound will not go away, even if we push it away for years on end. This is why it is so important to tackle this step head on and either find your way to integrate your loss in your life, or achieve acceptance. Both of these options will allow you to keep an active memory of this challenging time in your life, but one that is manageable and one that you can *choose* to access, rather than it dominating you and haunting you at every corner of your life.

Trying again
and getting through this new pregnancy

The following might feel like it is light years away when you first start to recover, but you will reach this point in your own time. It could start off with just a fleeting thought that becomes more regular, or it is something that is constantly on your mind: The thought and wish to start trying again.

This is a time filled with mixed emotions. You both want it, yet you might be scared to bits that the whole thing will repeat itself. And there isn't a certain way you should do it. There is no bullet proof way to conquer this challenge, there are a few things you can do to prepare yourself as best as you can.

For starters, lots of healthcare professionals give you general advice on what to do when you are pregnant, and how to look after yourself. It would be good to follow their advice and implement a healthy lifestyle, and cut out any vices that you may have, such as smoking or drinking alcohol (also check out the chapter 'Miscarriage – the dreaded term and what's behind it' for more health risk info).

The big question for many women is always: Has stress caused my miscarriage? There is little evidence that stress does cause a miscarriage. However, no one really knows and in some cases, doctors do strongly advise that women live as stress-free as possible, which sometimes means quitting a very challenging job and taking a step back, career-wise. Only your doctor can give you appropriate advice here, and it is strongly recommended that you listen to your trusted healthcare professional. Every regular Joe on the street will have their opinion about stress and miscarriage, and they are pretty much useless. It doesn't matter what everybody *thinks* you should do. If you are concerned about stress triggering a miscarriage, talk to the professionals and listen to their advice – it will provide you with much more peace of mind.

If you are considered to be low-risk, then many healthcare professionals will tell you that a little stress won't hurt your pregnancy. This may be true, but it will ultimately be up to you to decide if you are willing to put up with certain stresses in your life, or not. Some things we just can't avoid; others we can tackle straight away. Wouldn't we all just love to quit our jobs? But then, where does the money come in? This is often the most difficult point to consider and in reality, hardly anyone can afford to quit a job and avoid that psycho boss or the long hours at the office. In this case, it will be more about managing your stress and to try and reduce it as much as you can. It will be more about reducing hours or taking a step back from a stressful project. This way, you can still go to work without being exposed to too much stress.

Of course, this would all need to be discussed with your supervisor, and clear communication can solve a lot of problems. It will depend however, on your environment, and whether it will be appreciated that you share part of your journey and current situation. It will be worth a try though, because any stress that can be avoided, should be avoided.

A new pregnancy, especially in the very early stages, might also be the motivation to try new ways of coping with stress. Maybe you have never been the one to go for walks at lunch to clear your head a bit. Now might be a good time to do just that. It will get you out of the office, away from the stress triggers and it will be calming for you (as well as beneficial for your mental and physical health).

There are many forms of exercise that are good for you throughout pregnancy, and many of them, such as yoga or antenatal classes, will help manage any stress you may have in your life. The same goes for meditation if you want to give that a go. Or, you could indulge yourself a little bit and visit a naturopath, and get some help there for managing stress, as well for boosting your health during pregnancy. Of course, there are many other options for you to explore. Listening to relaxation music or any music that calms you can be built into your day quite easily, but with great effect. The important thing is to try them out, and see if anything works for you. Once you've found something that fits the bill, you will be going through pregnancy with a bit more peace of mind.

The possibility of a new pregnancy will also trigger a lot of emotions and most of them very powerful, like fear, anxiety, maybe even depression. We do live in a modern age, and medicine is well advanced, but when it comes to pregnancy, many things are out of our control, and doctors won't be able to help either. Many thoughts will rush through your head, such as, "would I be able to handle another loss?" or the famous, 'what if' questions. It is absolutely normal to have these thoughts – they just can't be avoided. So, take some time out right now, and reflect.

Where are you at when it comes to trying again? Do you feel pressured into having another child? Are you looking forward to having sex, or are you dreading it? Do you secretly hope there will be a period this month? Do you still struggle with seeing pregnant women, babies or anything 'baby-related', really? If yes, then that is absolutely fine. These are just indicators that you might not yet be ready to conceive again. You will notice over time, that these feelings, thoughts and reactions start to vanish. And one day, possibly out of the blue, you find yourself surrounded by baby stuff, and you are fine with it. That would be a clear sign that you have taken a crucial step in the trying again process.

But of course, there is no way that is right and the only way to go. Some women are ready to try again six weeks after a miscarriage; others require a year or more to be ready again. Each of the ways has its own challenges, but that is not important now. If you listen to yourself, what does your heart say? If you are ready again, the knowledge will come to you whenever that time may be.

Once again, here comes a built-in kicker for you: fear. There is a high chance it will be ever-present; especially if you have lost your very first pregnancy. It is an awful situation to be in. If you already have a child, you would know that it had worked once for you, so it might happen again (even though 100% is not available, unfortunately). But if you've never had a successful pregnancy, how the hell can you know that you are going to be alright? As there is no guarantee, and only one way forward, fear will be a constant companion for you for a little while.

As we know by now, the journey through a miscarriage is challenging enough as it is, and it might come back to haunt you when you are pregnant again. Just to be clear though: This *can* happen, but it doesn't mean it *will*. People are different after all, especially women, and that is a very good thing.

Remember, this is a new pregnancy. It is a different pregnancy. The clocks have been set back to zero. Yes, you did have a loss, but now circumstances are different, you are different, your body is too, so you can't really compare this pregnancy to the last one. This might be hard to read, especially when your mind races a million miles an hour, and is occupied with fear and terror. But, that is exactly why you need to remind yourself that things are different now.

This is a new pregnancy. This thought should become a bit of a mantra for you, as it can help you guide your way through the confusing, and sometimes upsetting emotions you will feel when you think about being pregnant again, or you've just found out that you are. Allow these strong emotions some room, though. They need to be dealt with so you can feel better about a new pregnancy. Many women in your situation reported that it really helped them to either get counseling, talk to other mums (online or face to face, but definitely only people you feel comfortable with, and you trust them enough to share your emotions) or, they joined a support group for subsequent pregnancies after a loss. There, they could chat with others in the same situation, and could get support from someone who knows what they were talking about.

Most importantly: acknowledge that you are afraid, but don't let it control you. Acknowledge that you have lost a previous pregnancy at this date, or in that week, or in general, but don't let it define your new pregnancy.

You have a great thing going on right now, so try and push the fear aside and focus on the joy of the moment. Visualise yourself with a healthy baby in your arms, and attract some positive and loving thoughts that way. You deserve it. Of course, it is very easy to write all of this. Doing it is a whole other matter. You will need courage, and you will need to force yourself to think about what happened honestly, and then shift your thoughts towards the present, that, at this stage, is looking very promising.

As usual though, there are a few roadblocks that could stand in your way. If we lived in a perfect world, we would fall pregnant straight away with no hassles and be on our way to having our own family. Reality, however, often paints a different picture and we are forced to exercise patience, over and over again. Don't get me wrong - if you start trying again, it might happen after the first few tries, or it might, as mentioned, take some time, and that is another challenge that needs addressing. The longer it takes, the more stressed you might get. You dread your time of the month, hope it won't happen, but when it does you are disappointed, sad, upset and probably angry. It is such a hard thing to go through. You are ready again, you are trying, but it is not happening, and you might wonder if there is something wrong with you or your partner. It is not a good feeling.

There is not really much you can do, either. At the end of the day though, it will take one ingredient that most of us all don't like: time. It can be exhausting and actually *is* exhausting, to try month, after month, after month. The solution to it: the right mindset. You have a choice. Either you look at each month as a new opportunity to get pregnant, or you think of it as yet another month where you have to go through the same scenario, yet again. That can be draining, stressful and puts a lot of pressure on you and your partner.

It is another tough challenge because in the back of your head, you might have to the thought of, "what if something is wrong?" There are appropriate doctors out there to assist you with this question, and it is a good idea to consult them. However, it is up to you when you want to do that. After all, you will need to be ready to hear both possibilities: either there is nothing wrong, or yes, there is something wrong, and it might not happen because of that. It will be good to set yourselves a time limit. Say, in two years' time for example, nothing has happened, go and see a doctor. Or, if nothing happens in the next two months, go and check out what is going on. There are obviously people out there who would tell you to go to a doctor straight away. Well, sure. But you know your body, and you also know if you are ready to face a potential grim reality.

Don't pressure yourself into something you are not comfortable with. But then, it also depends on the situation you are in. Perhaps you may need to rely on IVF to get pregnant? If so, there is a chance that you might not have a lot of time on your hands, and you need to take control of the situation as quickly as possible. If that is the case, then a good doctor on your side is very crucial. He or she should be able to give you advice on how much time there is left, if your body is ready to try again, or if you should wait a little bit longer. Women who have experienced a miscarriage after IVF treatment do report that they have to get cracking again soon, and don't feel they have time to fully grieve their loss. That is of course, one hell of a situation to be in and unfortunately, one that will require hard decisions. Will you go ahead with the treatment, despite recovering from your loss? How would you cope if you suffered the same fate again? Again, have a long and good chat to your doctor. You might require further treatment before you can start again, or you might be ready to go again. I spoke to one woman who lost her baby after IVF treatment, and she knew that time was scarce. She looked at getting another round of treatment as something really positive, and something to look forward to – she approached it with a positive mindset. Easier said than done, you say? You are exactly right.

When it comes to trying again, every woman is unique and has to deal with it her own way. One might be able to look at the next round of IVF treatment as something to look forward to; another might just feel faint and simply not be ready. You have had your unique experience, and this situation you are in now, is one in a million. Honesty comes into play once again. We know that time can be a very good healer, and not getting it is a risky business.

On the other hand, as we know now through our experience and our journeys, we are not dealing with something lighthearted and fluffy here. These situations are one of the most challenging in life; they require us to face a cruel truth, and difficult decisions have to be made. But, remember – you have come this far, you pulled through, and left darkness and depression behind you – you can take this next step!! And, you know no decision is right or wrong. If you can't face treatment six months after your loss, then that is fine. If you can, then that is great, too. What is that you want? Are you okay with the current situation, or would you like to change it? Answers to these questions will become clear to you, and you will be able to follow your path and continue your journey.

Once the pregnancy is confirmed.
By now you know the deal – your period is late, you might be noticing changes in your body already, and a trip to the pharmacy can't be avoided any longer. And when those two blue lines show up on your home pregnancy test, there is no more denying – you are pregnant again! Yay! Or nay? It will be highly likely that your reaction to your new pregnancy is incredibly mixed. You might be overjoyed and can't wait to tell your partner. Or, you might burst into tears and feel worried and anxious from the moment you find out. Emotions you thought you'd left behind come rushing back, and that can be quite scary when it happens. Also, you are aware of your own vulnerability because from that moment onwards, a

lot of things are out of your control. Will this baby live? We won't know until later. Is there anything you can do to prevent another miscarriage? Highly unlikely.

Out of my own experience, I feel honesty serves you best in this situation. Was I scared? Oh, hell yeah – shit scared, actually. I felt stressed and was worrying about every little twitch I felt in the first three months of my second pregnancy. Why am I cramping? Is this the beginning of the end again? I don't know how many times I was terrified to go through everything again. I dreaded going to the toilet, because I was horrified I might see blood in my undies. And, even after the first three months were over and we saw our baby bouncing around during the first scan, the joy was only short lived. Now that we knew that there was indeed a baby with tiny legs and arms and a healthy heartbeat, new worries were born. Will she or he continue to keep growing normally?

Five months into the pregnancy, I was absolutely exhausted. I suddenly realised how tense I was, and how worry and stress dominated my daily life. If you experience the same or similar things, then know that you are not alone. Many of us who went through a miscarriage and then conceived again, encountered the same thoughts, feelings and worries. We all were horrified that something would go wrong again, and we just longed for these nine months to be over, so the baby comes out and we can hold them in our arms; knowing for certain that they are here, healthy and alive.

To cut a long story short: it is completely normal to feel worried and anxious throughout your pregnancy. You might find it challenging though, to admit that to yourself, or even to those around you. Often, people don't understand why you would be worried. The first three months are over, so what is the big deal now? The big deal is that you know all too well what could go wrong, and you just don't want to go through that again. Also, while the first three months are very critical, people tend to forget that at any time in pregnancy, something can go wrong. Now, we don't live in a society that is particularly good with admitting hard truths. We are very good at denying them, and turning our heads the other way. And that is fine – to a point.

With a new pregnancy, you will be walking a fine line for nine months. Should you be worried about every little thing, or should you relax and not be such a worry wart? These are hard decisions to make, as your head will tell you to relax, and your heart will be frozen with fear. Naturally, it is very easy for people around you to tell you not to worry too much. They are right to some degree, as we still don't know what impact constant stress has on a pregnancy. You see, you can easily be trapped in a downward spiral of confusing emotions, where you just won't know what to do anymore, and how to think clearly. This happens to a lot of women, so try to not get too upset about it. Walking this fine line is now part of your journey, and you will get better at it as time goes by.

Remember, the most important thing is to take care of yourself, and in a way that is right for you. This is your body, your pregnancy and your baby. If you feel worried and anxious, be honest with yourself. You will make your life even harder if you don't admit those feelings. Take a step back and look at the situation: What is it that you want to do right now? Would you feel comfortable developing a plan for anything that could go wrong? If so, then do it. Women have reported that they felt better after answering 'what if' questions, such as "what do I do if this or that goes wrong?" It gave them a feeling of being prepared, so that horrible element of surprise was out of the picture.

So, if you feel better once you know what you would do if you discovered blood for example, then write it down and develop an action plan. Which hospital do you want to go to? Who should come with you? Who are you calling? In what order? This might sound weird to some women, and is not right for them. Fair enough – if this is not for you, something else will work. The most important thing is to be proactive. If you are frozen with fear, you will put yourself through a lot of suffering, and that is the thing we want to change.

A very important thing that many women mentioned, is to have a very good caregiver – one that supports you and acknowledges your fears. You will need someone with enough patience and understanding so that you can share your concerns, current state of mind, and anything else that is going on with you. It might be that you will only feel a bit calmer once you know you can have frequent visits to your obstetrician or midwife. If you found one that will be happy to book you in whenever you need it, and check the heartbeat of your bub whenever needed, then stick with them. If you were treated the first time around by the most insensitive and uncaring doctors, then you will want to look for a better one. If that is the case, have a listen around amongst your friends, or online in a mum's forum.

Ask other women whom they went to, and if they liked the treatment they received. The vast majority will be very honest, so you will get a feel if a particular doctor or midwife will be for you or not. Once you find someone, get an appointment and suss them out. If you don't feel comfortable, keep looking. Or, if you are in the care of midwives, ask to be seen by a different one. You will be spending a lot of time with that doctor or that midwife, so you need to feel comfortable and well supported. This is now a good time to think back a bit, work out what went wrong and what you would have liked to be different, when it comes to medical staff. Write a list if you think that might help, and make sure your new doctor or midwife ticks off the requirements you've written down. It is crucial to be vocal about what you want with this new pregnancy, and communicate that to your caregiver. There is no harm in giving that a shot. After all, doctors are not psychics; they need to be told what you expect out of your care. Once the doctor's sorted out and you are happy with your choice, you can address your other worries and how to deal with them. Have you considered writing your thoughts and worries down into a pregnancy journal of the special kind? It is not one where you would note down all the positive stuff that is going on, but what is going on in your head and heart. Writing the fears down can have a very calming effect. Once you see them spelled out in front of you, they tend to lose their scariness and you feel like you can handle them a lot better.

Or, you can get talking. As discussed, a good doctor will be your starting point with any medical worries you might have.

If you have a really good friend or in general, a good support person, lean on them and tell them what is going on. If that is not for you, then you will be able to find something else. It could be that people around you just don't understand what you are going through because they never experienced it, or they don't want to be confronted with something as challenging as worries related to an event that society dictates so clearly, has to be a happy one. Not to despair though – this is really a time where it should be all about you.

If you don't feel like talking to someone about the pregnancy, then don't. Even if the in-laws or your good friends from work pester you with questions. In your current situation, you are quite vulnerable, and there is absolutely no point sharing that with someone who won't understand. Stick to those you are comfortable with. If you are happier talking to your neighbour than a family member, then go ahead and talk to the neighbour. It is about what helps you to cope with the worries and fears of your new pregnancy. This is a time where you have to look after exactly one person: Yourself. No one else.

Now is not a time to try and please people – it is the time to comfort yourself and your partner, and focus on what works for you, and you only. You have been through hell, and here you are, back to square one. And, square one is not only scary; it is also a lonely place. You might ask yourself if you are supposed to be anxious or not, considering everyone else is so joyous, and you just had the umpteenth woman at work coming to you to share her pregnancy story. But for you, every day that has just started might be filled with new worries. Especially once you have passed week 20 to 24, and everyone will ask you if you've felt the baby yet. That can be a whole new level of stress. There is one thing you need to know about babies: they are so very different from each other. One might kick the living daylights out of their mum; others are very relaxed and don't move much. The third might be active, but rather small, plus the placenta is in the way, and softens any kicks and punches, so they don't get through to you.

So, there you have it – with people talking and asking questions (even though most of them are well-meant), there are a new set of worries just being made obvious to you. But, not to despair. The old trick of listening to yourself will help once more. A good doctor will tell you that you should not ever compare yourself to other women and their pregnancies. They are just all too different. The only time you should compare is if you've had a pregnancy, and a second or third, and then you can compare those, as they are yours and most accurate for you. So, you will have to practice a new and very important life skill: shut your ears to outsiders.

Of course, talking to your doctor should not be stopped, so ask him about baby's movements. It could be that you might need to wait for a while until you can clearly feel your little one, but that is okay. After all, the little thing has quite some growing to do over nine months, and won't fill out your uterus until the very end. Unfortunately, that will require a lot of patience from you in a time where you might be worried sick. A new pregnancy can teach us a few things that are important to learn, but come as hard lessons.

We need to let go a bit, and try not to control everything, because we can't. Of course, such a sentence would appear in a self-help book, you might think. Well, it does, and yes, it is easier said than done. In a time where we feel exposed and vulnerable, we need to learn to let go and just have faith? Yup, pretty much. The situation is just that tough.

The one thing we want the most, is most likely out of our hands: the arrival of our healthy baby. We can hope, we can pray, but the fate of this little one is in the hands of the gods. So, what else can we do but to try to stay positive, and take each day as it comes? It is incredibly difficult, but it can be done. Share your fears or struggle with being positive with someone you trust, such as your partner if you have one, or your family, who most likely will follow this pregnancy very closely. Don't do this alone, if you can help it. It is always easier to get through a day when you're struggling if someone else can take the burden of having faith for you, and can do it for you for a little bit. You will be back on track the next day.

Miscarriage

The dreaded term and what's behind it

When you suffer a miscarriage, you are not only left with deep emotional scars, but also with a lot of confusion when it comes to the physical side of things. As we have seen in previous chapters, the questions about whether there was anything we could have done to prevent it, or if there is something wrong with us, are inevitable and part of the process. They need to be dealt with, and we will all embark on a journey into the medical world to look for answers. We want to know why our loss occurred, so there must be something a doctor or scientist has found that will help us understand. Indeed, when it comes to purely physical questions or uncertainties, there are a few things the medical world can tell us, and that is what we look at in this chapter.

There are different forms of miscarriage that will be explained. We will have a closer look at known risk factors and what you can do to avoid or manage them; should they apply to you. Be mindful though, that none of the known information might apply to you. It is unfortunately still very common not to know exactly why our babies died, and we will be left with lots of maybes and possibilities, but no peace of mind. Also, it might be hard to see all these numbers and feel like you are just part of a statistic. To you, this baby meant the world – to the rest it's one number amongst many; counted and accounted for quickly.

Remember that we are now entering the world of science where cold, hard facts rule and emotions play only a small part. This is okay – we need science now, more than ever to help us understand the complex world we live in. But, it is hard sometimes, to deal with their approach when all you feel is that dark hole where a chunk of your heart has been taken out. Read this section slowly, and maybe not all at once. Give your emotions room to deal with what is written in black and white, and seems so cold. We want to hear and read the facts, but until we do, we won't know how we'll react to it. Please know that there is no magic formula that we can pop into a computer, so it gives us the exact answer we are looking for.

Let's start with the well-known knowledge (that was probably quoted to you at one stage or another by someone), which is the estimate that one in four women suffer a miscarriage on their journey to parenthood. The numbers are indeed high – experts speak of 55,000 miscarriages in Australia, per year. The major amount of these losses will occur in the first trimester, and research has shown that week six to eight seem to be the trickiest and most dangerous time for losing a baby. Why that is the case, remains unclear. But, those numbers shouldn't be taken as gospel – many losses are not counted as they have probably gone unnoticed. What we do know at this stage, is that there are different forms of miscarriages. So, chances are high that you can put a name to your loss and make it less vague that way.

If you suffer a **menstrual miscarriage**, it means your loss happened so early that you will actually have your normal period and not realise you were pregnant for a short time. It is highly likely it went unnoticed because your period happens around its normal time, with no unusual signs or symptoms. The only way to know would have been if you had taken a pregnancy test before your period started. This type of miscarriage is also referred to as a **chemical** or **biochemical pregnancy**.

A **subclinical miscarriage** means that a very short pregnancy has delayed your period for a week or two, but then your monthly visitor comes around anyway. This form can again, go undetected, as you might not notice anything different other than your period being late, and if that is something familiar to you, the thought of having suffered a miscarriage might never occur. This can often be the case for women who have an irregular cycle and a week or two off is happening regularly, and they therefore might think nothing of it.

Threatened miscarriage: This describes any bleeding from the vagina that occurs before week 20 of a pregnancy is completed. This one is a very scary one, as it can really go either way. Your body shows symptoms of a miscarriage, like the bleeding, but they can go away and you are likely to experience a healthy pregnancy afterwards. Bleeding is quite common during pregnancy and may happen for various reasons without having to expect the worst. This is one fact many of us learn the hard way when we are worried sick about blood on the toilet paper or in our undies. The sad side of this is though, that a large percentage of women who do bleed and have cramps will suffer a loss through miscarriage.

An **inevitable miscarriage** might occur after a threatened miscarriage or can happen without any warning. This type is also called **spontaneous miscarriage**. Women who have to suffer this kind of loss are being tested to the extreme. With this type of miscarriage, they will lose their baby vaginally, while experiencing bleeding and strong cramping.

If a doctor tells you that you suffered a **complete miscarriage** then they mean that your body has gotten rid of all pregnancy tissue, and that there is nothing left in the uterus. Often doctors send their patients for a scan though, to confirm their diagnosis, as it is the most reliable way to know for sure.

Unfortunately, women can also suffer an **incomplete miscarriage,** where part of the pregnancy tissue remains in the uterus, and an operation is necessary to remove it. This procedure is called D&C (dilation and curettage), and means the cervix is opened (dilation) and the uterine lining is scraped (curettage) to remove any remaining pregnancy tissue.

If your baby has died, but stays in the uterus, you have suffered a **missed miscarriage**; also called **missed abortion** or **silent miscarriage**. You would have signs of a miscarriage like cramping and some bleeding, but it might have not been very painful or very strong. This might have you think that the pregnancy is still going on. However, if you experienced any pregnancy symptoms such as nausea, sore breasts or cravings for certain foods and they suddenly vanish, then further investigation is needed, which means a scan.

If your baby has died, there are two medical ways open to you. You can either wait and see if your body is able to lose the pregnancy tissue by itself, or you will have to have a D&C in hospital. This needs to be discussed with a doctor though, as the waiting option will depend on your circumstances and how you have gotten to this stage. Dead tissue in our bodies can become toxic, and therefore very dangerous, so depending on how long you have been bleeding, waiting even longer is just not a possibility at all.

If a woman suffers three or more miscarriages, then they are classified as **recurrent miscarriages**. If that is the case, many doctors will suggest further testing to determine if there is an underlying cause to the losses. Unfortunately, healthcare professionals often won't get active by themselves before a woman has suffered several losses. If you have suffered one loss and wish to investigate further, you will have to be the driving force and ask for tests to be done, as doctors won't necessarily see the need to do so.

About 95 percent of miscarriages happen in the first trimester (the six to eight week mark that we mentioned before). Those that occur between week 14 and 20 are called **late miscarriages**, **second-trimester** or **mid-trimester losses** and may be investigated further by your doctor to present you with a reason as to why a loss happened so late. But again, chances are high that you may be left with no answers.

It can also be that you suffered a loss due to a **blighted ovum**. This means a fertilised egg has implanted into the uterus, but then no embryo develops. Women may have signs of pregnancy, but a scan will reveal that there is an empty gestational sac in the uterus. **Anembryonic pregnancy** and **early fetal demise** are other terms that describe this terrible event and a D&C procedure is common to remove the egg from the womb.

An **ectopic pregnancy** means the embryo has implanted inside a fallopian tube or somewhere else outside the uterus, and the baby won't be able to survive. This situation requires immediate medical attention as fatal bleeding can occur that will threaten the mother's health.

The term **interrupted pregnancy** describes pregnancies that are ended for medical reasons – meaning there are medical risks found with the baby, or the mother's health is at serious risk. **Genetic** or **medical termination** and **induced abortion** are other terms that refer to this type of loss.

Knowing the form of miscarriage you suffered is the easy part when it comes to knowing more about it all. But, it is often not really the knowledge we are after. We want to know *why* it happened. That is where we will hit a snag, as there are not many risks known that are definitely linked to miscarriage. And, risk factors are just that – a risk, but not a definitive reason or cause for the loss of a baby. In a nutshell, they are the following three: age, weight and smoking. These factors can have different impacts on a pregnancy, but they are not the bulletproof answer every time. Let's check these three out though, and see how they can potentially affect a pregnancy.

Age: A doctor or midwife might tell you that miscarriages occurring early in pregnancy are due to chromosomal abnormalities (you know, the whole 'mother nature knows best'-scenario). To really find out if that is the case, you will need to have certain tests done and await results. If there were issues with chromosomes and they were abnormal, then the maternal age could have something to do with it. Women over 35 years of age are at greater risk of losing their baby through miscarriage caused by chromosomal abnormalities than younger women. As indicated already though, it *could* be a reason; it doesn't mean it is, as plenty of women in the 'perfect' procreation age suffer the hell that is miscarriage. It is just that plenty of studies have shown that the older a woman is, the more risks there are for her when she falls pregnant or wants to fall pregnant. Why age can play such an important role in losing a baby, no one really knows for sure. Many researchers believe that a possible cause could be the woman's eggs. They are older than we are (baby girls are born with their life worth of eggs which have grown and developed during pregnancy) and it could be that their age can contribute to a pregnancy cut short. Again, no research has definitely proven the age of eggs is responsible for miscarriages, which still leaves us all with a broken heart, and no proper answer as to why we lost our precious babies.

Weight: If you plan a pregnancy, one piece of information will be thrown at you pretty early. The healthier you are, the better chances you have to have a successful pregnancy. This brings us to another known risk factor – being overweight or obese. It's a worrier, really. We as a nation tend to get bigger and bigger, with many implications on our health. One of them is the increased chance that you might not be able to carry your baby to term. That is why a healthcare professional will keep a closer eye on women that start a pregnancy being overweight, and the much-discussed BMI comes into play here. Studies have shown that having a BMI of 25 or higher can be quite the troublemaker. Not only is it a risk factor for suffering one miscarriage, but it has also been linked to multiple miscarriages. To make the news even worse, studies observed that woman with a BMI higher than 25 who suffered a miscarriage, lost babies that had no chromosomal abnormalities; the 'common' reason for early pregnancy loss.

Smoking: You've probably heard it before, as smokers are always in the public spotlight and when it comes to pregnancy, the attention is even higher. Having a history of smoking can be the third risk factor that might have caused your loss. For once, the news is not as bad though, because the number of smokers in Australia do decrease. If you have been a smoker, but decide to stop once you find out you are pregnant, you will be in good company and deserve huge praise for your effort.

While these three risk factors are probably the ones most mentioned, they are not the only ones that might have had something to do with a loss. There are other risk factors and theories out there that have been linked to a miscarriage many times. Just like the three big ones, they don't offer any definite answers but are just one of many more in the series of 'this could have been the reason, but we don't know for sure'.

One of them is **Caffeine**. It often comes up as a possible culprit for suffering a miscarriage. This is an ever-growing discussion, as you will find all sorts of facts when it comes to consuming caffeine during pregnancy. Some studies do suggest that women having caffeine during their pregnancy are at higher risk of suffering a miscarriage, even when being within the recommended doses per day, compared to women who have cut out all caffeine. A warning here: A search engine on the internet has plenty of answers when you use them to find out more. It is a fantastic tool, but also one with many dangers. It can be terribly confusing and upsetting to read different opinions, 'facts' and other information. Chances are high that you will end up feeling worse than before, and will have taken a step back in your quest, rather than forward. If potential issues like caffeine are a worry to you, talk to a trusted health professional. A good doctor or midwife will be able to provide you with much better information than the cold, dark internet can, and they will talk to you face to face, which is so much better when you are in a vulnerable position already.

A few medical conditions have been put in the mix to suggest they might cause the loss of a baby, such as **diabetes, coeliac disease** and **polycystic ovarian syndrome (PCOS)**. Diabetes - either pre-existing or gestational - can pose a threat to losing your pregnancy, but the good news is, that risk reduces significantly if the diabetes is well managed. When it comes to **coeliac disease**, only theories are available. It is suggested that the body (or the immune system, rather) rejects a foetus when it reacts to some bad foods that have been eaten, which means it could be that your body might want to lose the pregnancy just to be safe, and to make sure you are okay. There is no research though, that proves this to be the case. **PCOS** means a woman has small cysts in her ovaries and these cause a hormonal imbalance. Healthy ovaries produce the hormones oestrogen, progesterone and testosterone. If you suffer from PCOS, your ovaries produce oestrogen just fine, and in the right amounts, but overdo it excessively with testosterone. With progesterone, the one that is set free after ovulation, production is irregular, or might not happen at all. This mix has been linked to miscarriage and infertility, and will need close medical monitoring if you have been diagnosed and would like to have a baby. Unfortunately, PCOS poses many challenges for women who would love to have a baby. It often requires a strict diet, weight loss management where needed, and maybe even a journey into alternative medicine and treatments (such as herbal medicine or Chinese) to help combat PCOS. If you have been diagnosed with PCOS or suspect you might suffer from it, get yourself informed and seek medical advice. PCOS is a serious matter, but it is not always the end of the road. It can be treated and you can clear your way towards a baby. Don't give up! Reach out, connect with other sufferers, and start the fight. It will be hard, and daunting at times, but take one day at a time. You will find your way and PCOS is a challenge, and not necessarily a defeat.

PCOS hint at another potential risk factor when it comes to losing a baby – maternal health; especially serious illnesses such as heart disease, auto-immune disease, lung, liver or kidney disease, and similar conditions pose dangers to any pregnancy and need to be monitored very closely by a specialist.

If you are unsure of your health status, get yourself checked first, so the risk of loss can be minimalised as much as possible. In any case, if you had challenging health problems before, like cancer or problems with your thyroid, talk to a doctor first. Your past may have an impact on your future pregnancies, so control the risks from the start, if you can. This is not always possible, as pregnancies can be wonderful and unexpected surprises sometimes, and that is fine. Just make sure you have a good doctor that knows your medical history, and can refer you to any specialist you may need during pregnancy to monitor any issues. They will do what they can to prevent a loss, so be sure to place yourself in good hands.

As our journey into the medical world comes to an end, there is one more thing we need to have a look at. Where there is knowledge based on facts and scientific research, unfortunately, urban myths are never far. You might have come across them already, as there are always 'helpful' people that take myths for gospel and believe they know exactly why you lost your baby. They might have told you that your loss occurred because you lifted something you thought was a bit heavy, or because you were stressed about something at work, or it happened because you had a glass of wine before you knew you were pregnant. Things like that are ridiculous and not true. All they do is cause even more guilt in a woman who lost her baby, and we blame ourselves enough already, so get those myths out of your head. They are just that – a myth; totally useless, not based on any scientific research, and not worth your time. Stick to the (few) facts instead; focus on yourself, and be gentle. There are days when we have to remind ourselves more often than on others, that none of this was our fault. Guilt is very powerful and a constant companion in our lives, so fight it with knowledge, not superstition – it will help you feel a bit better.

What to expect
from your body afterwards

The emotional blow of losing a baby early in pregnancy is immense, and will be part of our 'new normal' as we rebuild our lives. We, very understandably, focus on our emotional and mental wellbeing first and foremost once we suffered our terrible loss. There is also, however, a physical side to the loss, and it will need our attention, too. In general, our bodies are expected to recover pretty well, and quickly after a miscarriage. This is often the case, but it is not necessarily smooth sailing to get to that point. You might wonder when your period will return, or when your body is ready to start trying again.

Below are a few tips and advice on what to expect as your body recovers from the ordeal it just suffered, and what to look out for. The signs that your body is healing are important to notice, and should be welcomed. They can, however trigger a lot of emotional pain when they do occur. Nothing says you are no longer pregnant like the return of your period.

The first period after a loss, is one to look out for. Many women have reported that experiencing the first period (and many after that) are hard to cope with, as the body seems to be ready to be back to normal, while their hearts and souls are far from it. It is incredibly hard to realise that your body 'moved on' and has returned to pre-pregnancy behavior. Be gentle with yourself, though – your body just does what it is supposed to do. You might think right now; how cruel it is to have a period. It is as if your body has erased all memory of the baby you just lost. Acknowledge your mixed emotions and give them room – they need to be dealt with. Write down your feelings once more, turn to someone you can trust to talk about your emotions, or pamper yourself. Do whatever feels right for you, so you can get through these days – one at a time.

Your monthly visitor can return anytime between two weeks after a loss, and several months after. Usually, women get their first period four to six weeks after. The type of your loss (e.g. early loss vs later loss) should have no impact on your period, and the same goes for any procedure you might have had (such as a D&C) after your miscarriage. It is very common though, that the very first period after a miscarriage is different than your usual periods. It can be that it is heavier than usual, longer or shorter, or even lighter than what is normal for you. If your cycle has been irregular, it might stay that way, or it can completely change. It all depends on your hormones and their effort of trying to get back into a regular cycle (one that is normal for you, of course). In any case, turn to a trusted healthcare professional if you have any worries while experiencing your first period.

As we mentioned previously, our emotional state has a huge impact on our physical wellbeing, and it is no different now. It can be that stress or emotions in turmoil delay the return of that first period. That is not necessarily anything to worry about, as we all heal at our own pace, and that is just fine. You should seek help from your GP though, if you haven't had a period six weeks after your loss. It could be that your body struggles to deal with the new situation properly. To be sure, your doctor will perform a blood test to check your hormone levels; the HCG. HCG stands for human chorionic gonadotropin, and is used to confirm a pregnancy, as the levels of it increase as the pregnancy progresses. The placenta produces HCG and the levels drop, and eventually vanish once a pregnancy has ended. If you haven't had period six weeks after, it could be that remains of HCG are still in your system, and prevent your body from returning to pre-pregnancy state. It doesn't necessarily mean that's what's going on, but it's better to be safe, than sorry. In the event that you suffered an incomplete miscarriage, and remains of your pregnancy are still found in your uterus, then they need to be removed; as difficult as this will be for you. If they stay where they are, things can turn sour and get very serious quickly, and a serious threat to your health is the last thing you want right now.

When to worry about a period is a sensitive issue, and will be different for every woman. The six-week mark might not apply to you, as you are sure you have undoubtedly lost your baby, so a blood test would only cause further pain to you. But, if you haven't had a period for three to six months after your loss, a trip to the doctor will be on the cards again, as there could be underlying issues to this. As you slowly recover from your loss, you might ask yourself if your body has returned to normal, and if it's ready to conceive again. As mentioned previously, the body does focus on getting back into pre-pregnancy standards, but it will take some time to get there. Straight after your loss, the bleeding and pain should stop within two weeks. If it goes on longer than that, see your GP or other trusted healthcare professional to find out what is going on. If your bleeding stopped in that timeframe and you had a period that is normal for you, chances are your body has healed and is back to what it was. As mentioned, the first period after your loss will most likely be an unusual one, so expect the second one to be the normal one, and the sign that your body is doing well. If you are not quite sure about it all just yet, wait for three normal consecutive periods (normal for you). If that is the case, you can be fairly sure that your body has fully healed. However, if the third or fourth periods are unusual (exceptionally strong or painful), see a doctor to ensure your body is on the right track, and you are not suffering from undetected complications.

We have covered the emotional aspect of trying again, and falling pregnant in a previous chapter. Once again, there is also a physical side to this step of your journey. It will be highly likely that your body is ready for another pregnancy before your heart and soul are. That is absolutely fine, and it will be up to you and your partner to take that step when you are ready. If you are unsure about anything, talk to a trusted healthcare professional before you take this next step, or get advice from another angel mum – anything that you need to do to, feel more comfortable and secure on your path.

Rediscover your Body

The existent knowledge of miscarriage and its causes can be deeply daunting, as we learned in a previous chapter. While it could be this, or it could be that – a definite answer will often be impossible. This alone is hard enough to deal with, but unfortunately, the lack of knowledge opens the door wide open to all sorts of confusing theories, beliefs and myths. Well-meaning people will offer you all sorts of explanations why it was that you lost your baby, and most of them are completely useless and hurtful, and will make you feel even more guilty than you already did.

So, it's high time we focus on ourselves!

Throughout your grieving process, you will have noticed the different emotions that come with it. We all experience grief differently, and choose to deal with it our own way, but there are some similarities we all encounter. For example, while there is a stage with anger and one with depression, these two don't really go away for a long time, and they tend stick with you. Grief has stalking qualities. It might jump out at you while you are in the supermarket, it can be triggered by something you read or something someone says to you, and it can be something minuscule such as a cartoon your older child watches, or a television commercial you see.

And, as soon as that has happened, anger, depression and sadness come rushing back. That is okay though, because you will learn how to handle these emotions as you go on with your journey. By now, we know that the sadness about this event will never leave us, even if we end up with children at our side. All we can do and will do, is manage the sadness, and learn to live with it. We have to welcome it into our life as a constant companion that most of the time is dormant, but can wake at any time. Losing a baby through a miscarriage leaves incredibly deep scars, and if tears will flow three or thirty years afterwards, then that is just a fact that needs to be accepted (also see chapter Acceptance – what is that? for more info).

It is important to remember that you will be fine, as long as the pain doesn't take over and you allow it to define your being, and your life. You are well within your rights to shed tears for the baby you lost. And, if that is going to happen for the rest of your life, then so be it. Losing a baby is something that goes far too deep to ever leave you entirely. The biggest challenge you will have to master is to keep your emotions in balance, because they are so powerful they can become destructive very quickly. Yes, we can and should shed tears for the little one we lost, but we should not turn it into a dark force that will swallow us up whole. When we deal with feelings such as blame or guilt, we are walking a fine line and more often than not, we become our own worst enemy.

I remember I was so angry, disappointed, sad and upset. I didn't understand why this had happened to me. I blamed myself, like so many women do. I thought there might be something wrong with my body. Why else would it have rejected the foetus? Along my journey, I met many women who harboured the same thoughts. We either felt like a failure, or felt defective, and were convinced we did something wrong. To make matters worse, many of us feel that we not only failed ourselves, but our partners. We were not able to give them a baby girl or a baby boy, and isn't that just the thing we are supposed to do? When we see them sad, we start to feel guilty, and that is a tough emotion to shake off.

Guilt follows you pretty much everywhere, and has a nasty habit of making you feel even worse. If you felt unsure about yourself to start with, after guilt kicks in, you will be filled with only negative thoughts about yourself. Guilt, shame and feelings of failure are *that* powerful. And, extremely wrong.

The thoughts and feelings we all have after our loss are very common, but they are pure poison. There is no need to feel guilty; there shouldn't be any room for such feelings at all. And don't even think you have done something wrong! *There is nothing wrong with you.* Anyone who tells you this, or thinks it, should go and take a really hard look at themselves. What a horrible thing to say! Life is a funny thing. It is not fair, and it gives different challenges to different people. For some reason, we were chosen to go through the hell that is miscarriage. There might be a reason for this, I don't know. We will probably never know why we had to experience this. The fact is, it happened. Nothing can change that. And we are left with the mess that we now have to clean up.

One of the mean things about these destructive thoughts about yourself, is that you take your energy away from yourself. Energy that you need to get back on your feet, and that will help you to start your life after your loss. As one angel mum put it: "I judged myself too harshly, and didn't allow hope to re-enter my life". Exactly! Once the negative spiral has started, it picks up pace very quickly, and thoughts like the ones above only feed it. But, oh, isn't that easily said?

What use is this, in moments when you wrack your brain and try and figure out if you did something wrong? Maybe something small, but still something. In moments like these, you have to take a step back, take a breath and calm down. The energy of negative thoughts is incredibly powerful. It is easy to succumb to it, but very hard to get rid of it. The more we hold on to things, the stronger those nasty feelings get, and the more powerful and destructive their energy is. You might wonder if there is anything you can do when you feel sad, defeated, lost or angry, and are convinced that your body is just the most horrible thing there is?

Yes, there is. It's best to start with remembering that you have done nothing wrong. Too simple? No, not really. It is, however, *the truth!* When you are caught up in taking it out on yourself, it is difficult to remember that you have done nothing wrong. I kept the thought that I had done something wrong close to my heart for a long time. It was only when another angel mum told me the following, that I was able to let go: "Remember, we all did not choose this. Therefore, the blame falls on no one". How powerful is that? You did not choose this! It hit you out of nowhere, crept up on you and took over your life. But you did *not* choose this. So, don't blame yourself or feel disappointed in yourself for something you didn't choose in the first place.

Another very powerful thought also helped me to let go of these negative feelings about myself; again, given to me by a fellow angel mum. When we are stuck in a rut and convinced we could never forgive ourselves for what has happened, remember this: We all loved our babies; all of this wasn't our fault. We loved and continue love our angel babies, and we didn't want them to go. It is so easy to forget the love we felt amongst all these dark and scary emotions. But, it was there and always will be, and in the darkest times, we need to consciously remember this love. The love for our little ones is all that matters, and negative thoughts of ourselves, our bodies, our habits, our being, will fade when we remember that there is and was love forever in our hearts for our precious babies.

Once you are in a better headspace about yourself, and have started to manage to keep the destructive and bad thoughts at bay, you can look into practical steps to take, to feel better about yourself and your situation. It is a slow process, and it is important that you take it slowly. Your physical, emotional and mental health needs to improve, and it is best to take small steps at first, so you avoid feeling disappointed or upset again. It might be best to start looking at your emotions once again, as they will have a huge impact on the whole recovery process.

Dealing with your emotions is a very unique thing to do. There are no set ways to get through what is ahead of you. The main thing is that you put yourself first. You might already know that there are a lot of people around with lots of good ideas – or what they think are good ideas. Some might tell you to just get on with it, others might tell you what they have done in a similar situation. While that is probably all said with good intentions, most of it won't be helpful to you. You have to shut your ears a bit, and do what you know and feel is right for you. If one thing helped one woman to go through the seven stages of grief and get out of it okay, then that is great. It won't necessarily mean that it will be right for you.

Every woman is different, but we do share something very common: after a miscarriage, many women lose faith in their body. They feel like their body has betrayed them. After all, it lost a baby, didn't it? So, feeling disconnected from your body, or resentful towards it is quite normal. It is also quite dangerous. While we all will go through a stage where we just hate what happened, and wonder why the hell we weren't able to keep this precious little baby, it is so destructive to linger on these thoughts. Yes, your body did not carry on the baby. But it is still your body, and it is still quite a wonderful thing. It is something to be proud of.

As we know, we live in a society that pressures women into always looking good, and young and perfect. We always have to perform, and to perform well. And then suddenly out of the blue, the body decides it won't do that anymore. You know what? Fair enough. We are not robots or high performing machines - we are human. And as humans, we sometimes struggle and fall. There is no rule, no law, and no written guidelines that say you as a woman, have to be impeccable 100% of the time. That is just in our heads; instilled into us by a patriarchic and misogynistic society, that puts unreasonable expectations on to women.

So, after a miscarriage of course, we all feel like we failed because we couldn't accomplish one simple task: having a baby. Well, first of all, it is *no* simple task to have a baby. It is a bloody miracle, and hard work – for our bodies, minds and emotions. Instead of hating your body for failing, look at it as something special that is perfect the way it is; flaws and all. While it is incredibly hard to admit that this body of yours was not able to carry this particular pregnancy, it doesn't make it any less of a gift of nature to you. Society wants you to believe that imperfections are something bad, yucky and shameful. Well, they are not! After such a traumatic loss like a miscarriage, it is the perfect time to rediscover your body and appreciate it. Allow yourself to do this. There are a few ways you can do that. See the following suggestions for starting points. If you are inspired by them, and even come up with other ideas that work for you - even better!

Pamper yourself. Always wanted to go to a day spa and get that massage or this facial, but never had the chance to go through with it? Now is the time to do it. It will not only help you feel better, but will also show you what a lovely thing your body is. It has this amazing soft skin, this lovely, thick hair, these wonderful big eyes and much, much more. Focus on these features and just get a treatment for them. Lean back, relax and enjoy.

Get stretching. If you are on your journey to rediscover your body because your loss has shaken you to your core, then what you mostly need is time. But there are a few things you can try, to help you reconnect with your body in this difficult time. Exercise is one of those things. This could be the time to try something new; something with a softer approach, such as yoga. I know yoga has been very popular, and so it should be. The ancient teachings of yoga tell us that grief affects our body profoundly. The emotions grief triggers manifest themselves in different parts of our body, like the chest or the throat. Grief affects our breathing as well, and can lead to different sorts of difficulties. Yoga teachers and followers believe that the body is an outer manifestation of our mind. So, it is only logical that you will feel pain all over your body, or in specific parts.

Yoga is a soft form of working with your body to ease tension, undo energy blockages and open our minds to peacefulness and tranquility. Unlike other physical exercise, yoga is not about pushing yourself hard; it is about working within your possibilities. So, yoga really gives you the chance to look at your body, find out what amazing things it can do, and how it builds up strength as you go along with practice. If you feel like this body of yours has let you down, then yoga might be the thing that shows you what your body can still do, despite this setback. Yoga can help you breathe easier again (quite literally) and help you feel like you're gaining back control over your body; therefore, helping you feel better slowly.

Also, yoga can be the mind quieter too, which is very important. After all, the mind is working non-stop; telling us what to do, judging everything and everyone, and in general, making a lot of annoying noise. That can be so exhausting and again, toxic in your situation, as this nagging voice in your head insists in telling you all the things that are wrong with you. So, it's high time to shut that thing up for a while. Of course, this won't necessarily be easy, as we are used to being controlled by our mind (we live in a headstrong society after all). When you decide to give yoga a try, know that this journey will also offer you the chance to change your mindset, seek relaxation, and a break from everyday thinking and worrying. It might be quite empowering to get your mind off things; especially your recent tragedy.

Be aware that even though yoga is a kind form of working with your body, it can be quite full-on when practicing it during your grieving. You are placing yourself in the here and now, which also means you are placing yourself in the midst of your grief. Yoga will allow you to experience your grief as it is right now, and embrace it. As you probably have guessed by now, that is not always a great thing to happen. Remember though, that there is no judgment. If you feel that doing yoga on such a deep level is too much for you, then that is fine. You can still go to class and focus on strengthening your muscles, joints and the body as a whole. You can stop your practice and take it up again, or you can leave it behind if it is not working out at all for you.

Do what you know. Of course, you just as well can stick with the type of exercise you already know, rather than trying something new right now. If you are a sporty woman who likes to do her exercise, you might already know that sport can be an excellent way to free yourself of your emotions, and shut your mind up for a while. For example, you had an annoying day at the office, so you go to the gym or go for a run to let your frustration out.

The same goes for anger. If you feel that taking up an exercise routine will help you deal with your emotions, and free you from the numbness you might be feeling, then go for it. It might be good to start off easy, though. Your body went through a hard time, after all (see chapter 'what to expect from your body afterwards'), so don't assume you are back to full strength straight away. Ask your doctor or another trusted health professional about when to exercise, for how long, and how intense. Of course, it is your body, and you will know what is best. When we are confronted with very strong emotions, it can be hard to feel ourselves and judge when to stop, or to realise that we are going too hard. If you are happy to have some company while exercising, the other person might act as a guardian, and tell you to take it easy if you start to go nuts.

Again, do what you know and feel is right, but know that there are boundaries to it. You want to get better, not worse, after all. If you notice that exercise is what works for you, throw some healthy eating in there, too. Nourishing your body with the right nutrients will help you to get back on track quicker. It doesn't mean that you have to go super healthy and only eat activated almonds. You will know what works best for you. If you want to introduce a new organic diet in your life, then go ahead. If you are a chocaholic and can't live without your sweet fix every now and then, don't be hard on yourself. As many of us know, chocolate has healing qualities, so let it be part of your diet if need be. It is all about you, your body and what you feel will help you improve to turn those negative thoughts about yourself into positive ones. Take this journey as an opportunity to rediscover how strong and amazing your body really is. Discover what it can do, with a little help from yummy, healthy food and exercise. Changes might be small to start with, but as you go on, you will see what an outstanding thing your body is; in combination with your mind and soul.

Get natural. If you choose to get physical to help you feel better, you might also want to think about getting some help from the pros. Quite a few of us have turned to naturopaths or acupuncturists to help them find their balance again. If you are interested in alternative ways of healing, give it a go now.

Shop around a little bit, though. You are still quite vulnerable, so you want to have a therapist that you feel comfortable with, that you can trust, and one that truly focuses on your wellbeing; guiding and supporting you on your way back up. If you are not happy with the one you choose, go and look for another. While the benefits of such treatments are well known, be careful and stay in control. You have to call the shots, and not them. If you feel you've had enough after two sessions, good for you; that will be it. Don't let yourself be pressured into coming back countless times, when you feel it is not helping you.

When it comes to rediscovering your body, you will need one important ingredient: time. Your body needs time to recover physically from the traumatic event, but the journey is even longer for our emotions that we connect to the trauma. It might be that you still feel the same after one spa treatment, or that several yoga sessions did nothing for you. The fate that was thrown upon you is very tough, and the challenges seem endless at times.

So, don't be harsh on yourself, and give yourself time. Yes, it is frustrating when we find out that there is no quick fix and that we don't feel better after one attempt at something (even though it can have instant positive effects). But, the quick fix is just not an option for us it seems, even if we wish it were. It doesn't help that our mind puts pressure on as well, and we start thinking we 'should' feel better or we 'should' do this or that. Remember the following: take a deep breath and take one day at a time. Maybe take one hour at a time, if you have one of these days. Don't think about tomorrow or what might be in a few weeks' time. It is right now you are living, and you deserve happiness and peace right now. So, if one strategy didn't work then that is fine. Accept it for what it is, and walk away from it. Rediscovering our own strength, beauty and power does take time. Don't look at it as a failed attempt, but another lesson learned. Whatever you try next is a new chance to find out how beautiful you truly are.

Ode to your Courage
The changes in your everyday life – lessons learnt

Now that you have left the worst behind you and you are on your way to a brighter future again, a few things might become apparent. And, they are not necessarily pretty either. When you were growing up, there was certainly someone who told you that only in shit times, you will find out who your true friends are, or who really cares for you. So, there is a reasonable chance that after going through your own personal shit time, that you learnt just that: who's there for you, and who is not. By now, you will probably also realise that those you expected to care, didn't really, and failed you big time. What a harsh lesson that is. It is not only that you struggle with something so huge and traumatic, but life also serves you a few more lessons; none of them light and easy.

Depending on who let you down, it might be okay to get on with life without them. But then, there are others who are not that easy to shake off, especially when we are talking family members and close friends; at least you thought they were close friends, but really, they are not. Once you have recovered and you see that your group of support people is not as big as you thought, then that is hard to stomach. There are two ways that lead out of this: either you are going to become very bitter, negative and permanently disappointed that some people have shown their true colours in a very unfortunate moment.

Or, you can see it as an opportunity for a new beginning. You can decide to start a bit of a spring clean, cross a few people out of your life, and go on without them. In fact, quite often, that will happen naturally. This might hurt to start with, but as you go on with your life, you will notice that you are better off this way, and that there are new people in your life that enrich it so much more than the ones you have left behind. It is a sad fact that sometimes after such a tragedy, we just don't match up with others anymore. It could be that they are just blissfully ignorant of life's tragedies, and therefore struggle to comprehend what you just went through. To be around such people can be very exhausting because you find yourself pretending a lot of the time. And while you are doing that, you will also notice that this costs you way too much energy. So, it really is better to let them go, isn't it? If people who deny your experience surround you, then they deny part of you. If you have people around you who are happy to be with you when you are doing well, but turn away from you when you want to talk about concerns, fears, insecurities or worries, then it is high time to give them the boot.

You might find that the cleaning out of your friends list will happen quite some time after your suffering. Perhaps once you are pregnant again and everyone doesn't understand your anxiety and fears, it will be time to turn to people who really understand you. The world only changes slowly, and most people just don't want to hear about the dark side of life, because it challenges them too much. That doesn't mean that you have to keep quiet about your experience, or stow away your feelings somewhere, so others don't feel uncomfortable. If you are not up for all the happy chit chat about pregnancy, and find it exhausting to pretend that you are just so very happy about it all, then don't do it. It is as simple as that. Of course, you will get into situations where it is a bit hard to avoid, or where it actually is easier to just play along. Most of them happen at work, for example.

Once you are pregnant and it shows, a lot of people who you don't know or just in passing, will come up to you and start a conversation about it. They obviously don't know what has happened, and only mean well. It can be easier to tell them that you are happy and excited, because that will cost you a lot less energy than telling your story from scratch. However, if your mother-in-law or your friends tell you to get over yourself when you express your fears about the new pregnancy, then it is time to change the tone a bit. You have been through a *lot*, and if people still don't get that, then what is the point of talking to them? Why would you want to spend time with someone who denies and belittles your pain? Easier said than done? Of course, that is true.

Now that you have recovered and are back into life, you would deserve a break, and maybe you are lucky enough to just get that. More often than not though, the lesson life wanted you to learn is not over yet. It wants you to use your newly gained strength straight away, and take a stand and say no. No to pretending everything is fine now, no to pretending nothing ever has happened to you, and no to people who try and force you to see things their way, so it is more comfortable for them. Instead you have to say yes to a sad phase of your life, say yes to the pain you experienced, and say yes to facing up, rather than denying. While this might sound daunting, it is also elevating.

This is also a chance to celebrate your strength, perseverance, determination and your courage to never give up; to keep on going when it was so hard to even get out of bed. Never forget how strong you are, and what you managed to deal with and accept as part of your life. A part that is important, but that doesn't dominate you. A part that made you stronger. A part that showed you what you can do, and what you are capable of achieving. Never let anyone take that away from you, no matter how close he or she are supposed to be to you.

It was you who made it through, and you can be proud of that and tackle life now with a different perspective. If life feels like throwing some shit your way, you will be prepared, you will be able to handle it, and you will be able to pull through. All you have to do for next time, is to make sure you are not dragging some old baggage around with you that holds you back. Next time around, ideally, you will have people in your life that will walk with you and won't try and stop you; people that carry you rather than let you tumble and fall. Their number might be small, but that doesn't matter. You don't need a mob of brain dead zombies that only want to talk about the sweet and fluffy stuff, when you are in the middle of fighting the forces of the dark empire.

Of course, it would be great if we could suit everyone and please them all. But it ain't happening, ladies. First and foremost, you have to suit yourself, and the ones that really mean you well, such as your partner, or the few good friends that helped you through. So, go ahead, with your head held high, and make the changes you need to make in order to move forward with energy and a positive outlook. You can do it. For too long, we have all suffered in silence because society wanted us to. Enough of that! You have fought bravely and successfully, and that needs to be recognised. Anyone who wants to push you back into silence and submission, is not worth your time, energy and love. We all have to count our losses and move on; and probably do that more than once in life.

Now is a good time to count those blessings, because you should be proud of yourself and the fact that you dealt with something so difficult, so well. Obviously, we all sometimes descend into silence, because it is just so much easier than speaking about something that not only will hurt forever, but is also often not well received or understood. You don't have to talk about it all the time, because it will cost you energy to do so. But, there is no law and no rule that says you have to be silent and suffer on your own because other people might lack the emotional maturity to deal with such a sudden, heartbreaking tragedy. Don't be silent when you feel like putting someone in their place, don't be silent when they belittle your pain, don't be silent when you are pressured into feeling happy, and don't be silent if someone thinks years and years after the tragedy, you are supposed to be your old self. If you do it, then you deny part of yourself that is now forever with you.

You decided to live on and move on, and that is a big deal. Facing something so horrible shows your strength and courage. And, for that, you deserve recognition and praise. Even if the old gossip lady down the street doesn't think that. Screw her. Grief should never be left unspoken and untreated. If it does, it will build a wall up around you that leaves you alone, and far away from happiness, joy, pleasure, and many exciting adventures you deserve. So, remember how wonderful you are, and if someone doesn't see that – point out their error and walk away.

Useful Links

There is a wide range of websites out there that cover the topic of miscarriage, as well as stillbirths and neonatal death. Below is an overview of some websites that offer great support and advice for anyone who has suffered a miscarriage. Please note: Some of them are Australian websites, some are American. Either way, they all offer great support and resources for grieving families.

www.grieveoutloud.org
This service was started by parents back in 2010 who all know the immense pain that comes with losing a baby. The site offers different resources and Grieve Out Loud is also well established on Facebook, and offers services through social media in a safe space for grieving families.

www.mymiscarriagematters.org
This great website was created for the founder's twins, who grew their wings too early. It not only offers support and resources for women who suffered a loss through miscarriage, still birth or infant death, but also for dads. Resources are available in English and some in Spanish.

www.sands.org.au
Sands (miscarriage, stillbirth and newborn death support) have provided support to parents who have lost a baby for over thirty years. Their website offers many resources for anyone who experienced a miscarriage, stillbirth or a newborn death. You can order brochures or read fact sheets, learn about stories from other parents, and find your local support group if you wish to meet others in the same situation. The website also lists a range of phone numbers you can call if you need help and support right now. Sands also hosts closed online groups, but there are tight rules to them and how you can enter them. If you'd like to connect with other bereaved mums and dads online via Sands, contact them directly and enquire what your options are.

www.stillstandingmag.com
This is an amazing website that offers a wide range of support for parents that have experienced child loss and/or infertility issues. It covers topics such as

pregnancy after loss, self-care, and dedicated support sites for fathers, siblings and grandparents. There are many contributors to the site that write about child loss, infertility and their personal journey through grief. Be sure to check out their blogs, as they offer tremendous support, advice and help for anyone that is an angel mum or dad.

www.carlymarieprojectheal.com
This outstanding website from Western Australian artist Carly Marie is a real gem. Carly Marie lost her beautiful baby boy Christian through stillbirth. During her journey, her loss has lead Carly Marie to create some very powerful, sensible and unique artworks that she shares with others in the same or a similar situation. Amongst her projects are a wonderful card line, as well as 'Christian's beach' where she writes babies and children's names in the sand and takes magnificent photographs for you. On the website are also very useful resources for healing and grieving after such a traumatic event. The website also contains helpful advice for friends and family on how to act after a loved one experiences such a horrendous loss.

www.bearsofhope.org.au
Bears of hope provides extensive support to families that have lost a baby. This Australia wide organisation helps families in hospital and beyond, connects them to others suffering the same terrible fate, and also offers support groups where bereaved families can share their story and seek support from others. Their website is a treasure box full of very helpful information for friends, family and healthcare staff and offers parents ideas on how to remember their little angel. Furthermore, bears of hope provides support via phone (1300 11 HOPE), email support (support@bearsofhope.org.au) and has private online groups where bereaved mums and dads can meet. If you are not up for online meetings, bears of hope also offers casual chats and coffees, where they put you in touch with someone in your area (if possible) that you can meet for a chat.

www.sidsandkids.org
Sids and Kids may be best known to most people for their work to prevent SIDS (sudden infant death syndrome), but this wonderful organisation also offers extensive bereavement support to families that have lost a baby. This includes parent and family support, sibling support, grandparents support groups and a 24-hour free call bereavement support line. Part of their service includes support for women who experienced a miscarriage in early pregnancy. It

depends from state to state and territory what is exactly available for support, so give them a call on 1300 308 307 to find out more.

www.facesofloss.com
This is a wonderful website on which women share their stories about their loss. You can browse through them and find comfort, knowing that you are not alone and that there are so many other women out there who have experienced something similar. It also has an excellent resources section with lots of information on how you could remember your baby, where to find support, book suggestions and a special section for dads. While the website is American and lots of services mentioned are based in the States, the site can nonetheless give you new ideas on how you would like to approach your grief and remembrance in general. Also, when it comes to sharing a story about pregnancy loss, it doesn't matter where you come from – the pain is the same all over the world. The facesofloss website also offers Face2Face friendship groups for people to come together, share their stories amongst friends and spend time together. So far there is such a group in Brisbane South.

www.pregnancyloss.info
An excellent and extensive site about miscarriage that is perfect for those who are after facts. They are provided in abundance, well researched and provide an insight into many topics such as symptoms of a miscarriage, causes and they provide you with suggestions on how to cope with your loss. The site also features stories from women who share their loss at different stages of pregnancy. Check out the topics and blog categories as they both cover a wide range of questions that many women in your situation encounter.

www.glowinthewoods.com
This thoughtful site is for parents that have experienced the loss of their baby. It offers a wide range of discussion boards where parents are welcome to have a read, comment and contribute if they wish to do so.

www.recurrentmiscarriages.com
This website offers many useful facts and advice on miscarriage and should also be visited by people who would like to support someone who experiences or experienced a miscarriage.

www.unspokengrief.com
This is a very important site that gives hope to women who have gone through a miscarriage. This site is dedicated to break the silence that surrounds miscarriage, stillbirth and neonatal loss. It offers support through stories and advice affected parents share with you. Be sure to check out 'Find support' and 'Resources – real advice' if you are looking for honest and useful tips and info.

www.babylossdirectory.blogspot.com
This blog is open to anyone who has suffered a loss of a baby, regardless of what age the baby died. You are welcome to share and submit your blog, as well as read and comment on other blogs.

Acknowledgements

I received invaluable support along the way while writing this book. The following people have helped me time and again to get back on track, believe in myself or displayed deep and selfless kindness towards me that still leaves me speechless.

A huge thank you goes to Shelley Hall, Mary Loughland and Shirley Nicholls. All of you have helped me with your beautiful psychic gifts to guide me when I hit a wall, doubted myself or just got stuck on my path. I admire you all so much and feel very grateful to have met you. A big thank you to Shelley for getting me started with writing, to Mary for guiding me to my publisher and to Shirley for her ongoing support and help ever since we met – for this book and many other challenges in life.

To Lyndell Maree Price from Sands Queensland. You are a force of nature and deeply dedicated to breaking the silence around pregnancy and baby loss. You have helped me do my research, connected me with so many other women and never stop getting the word out there about the important work Sands does. I am deeply grateful for your unwavering support you have given me ever since I started this journey to write 'How to survive a miscarriage'. I am honoured to have met you.

To Sands Australia - Queensland and Victoria especially - where I started my grieving journey, and was welcomed with open arms. A special thank you goes to the parent support program where I met women for the first time who took my pain seriously, and were there for me and listened.

To all the women I met throughout writing this book and who have kindly shared their stories with me and helped me see the depth of their pain and the beauty of their strength as they live life after losing a child.

To my brother Reto, who has been my number one fan from day one of my life. Thank you for believing in me and helping me with promoting and supporting my book. Thank you for encouraging to leaving my comfort zone and continue with this journey. It means a lot, brother heart!

To Jan Stirling and Natalie Tolley from Carers ACT who have helped me enormously in the last few months of my book coming together, may this be through practical or counseling support. Thank you!

Last but not least, to the woman who shared a hospital room with me after my D&C procedure, and who put her own pain aside and kept talking to me throughout the darkest night of my life. Thank you for your kindness, and for gently showing me that there is still much to live for after my world just ended.

About the Author

Karin Holmes is a writer, grief counsellor with her own online practice, Snowdrop, and mum to three children – two girls here on earth, and one baby in heaven. As a result of her loss, Karin has written this book, 'How to Survive a Miscarriage – a guide for women, their partners, friends and families' and she hopes to help other families who have suffered from pregnancy loss.

Karin is married and lives in Canberra, Australia, with her family. Due to her life and work experience, Karin is also a passionate advocate for mental health and works towards ending the stigma around mental illness.

www.karinholmes.com

White Light

PUBLISHING HOUSE

www.whitelightpublishing.com.au